MUSICALLY SUBLIME

MUSICALLY SUBLIME

Indeterminacy, Infinity, Irresolvability

Kiene Brillenburg Wurth

Fordham University Press

New York   2009

Library of Congress Cataloging-in-Publication Data

Brillenburg Wurth, Kiene.
   Musically sublime : indeterminacy, infinity, irresolvability / Kiene Brillenburg Wurth.—1st ed.
     p.   cm.
   Revision of thesis (Ph. D.)—Rijksuniversiteit Groningen.
   Includes bibliographical references.
   ISBN 978-0-8232-3063-1 (cloth : alk. paper)
   1. Sublime, The, in music.   I. Title.
ML3877.B75   2009
781.1′7—dc22

2008047146

Printed in the United States of America
First paperback printing 2012

Contents

Acknowledgments

This book would not have been possible without the intervention and encouragement of the following people: first of all, Frank Ankersmit, whose inspiring and dedicated supervision of the manuscript in its earlier versions has been crucial. His involvement in this project has triggered and nourished an intellectual development that I will benefit from for a long time to come. John Neubauer's critical engagement and (musical) concern was vital for the completion of the research project that preceded this book. His creative and open mind is exemplary for a very rare and special sort of scholarship. Without Arjo Vanderjagt, this book would never have existed in the first place.

Without the thorough and corrective readings of Lawrence Kramer and the anonymous reviewers, this book would definitely not have been what it is now. I am grateful for the care and interest with which they have approached the manuscript and for the numerous, careful, and often detailed suggestions they have made for improvements.

At Utrecht, I am grateful for the support of Ann Rigney and the opportunity she gave me to complete the manuscript during a research sabbatical in 2006. I also want to thank Harald Hendrix for his encouragement and the openings he has so often created for me.

Without Sander van Maas, this book would have been something completely different. I thank him for the way he has opened my eyes to a philosophy of a special kind and for the generally inimitable thoughts, intuitions, and elaborations sprouting from his mind. I feel very lucky to be close to such a mind. Finally, I want to thank Helen Tartar and the staff at Fordham: without her intervention I would have been lost. I am grateful for her encouragement, her daunting expertise, and her friendship.

Abbreviations (in Order of Appearance)

ESB Burke, Edmund. *A Philosophical Enquiry Into the Origin of Our Ideas of the Sublime and Beautiful* [1759]. Edited by Adam Phillips. Oxford: Oxford University Press, 1990.

KU Kant, Immanuel. *Kritik der Urteilskraft* [1790]. Edited by Karl Vorländer. Hamburg: Felix Meiner Verlag, 1790.

TI Lyotard, Jean-François. *The Inhuman: Reflections on Time.* Translated by Geoffrey Bennington and Rachel Bowlby. Cambridge: Polity Press, 1991.

CD James Usher, Clio, or a Discourse on Taste [1769]. Bristol: Thoemmes Press, 1998.

WW Schopenhauer, Arthur. *The World as Will and Representation.* Translated by E. F. J. Payne. New York: Dover Publications, 1958.

B Wagner, Richard. *Beethoven.* Translated by William Ashton Ellis. Available online at *The Wagner Library: Edition 1.0*, http://users.belgacom.net/wagnerlibrary/prose/wlpro133.htm (last accessed May 2007).

BT Nietzsche, Friedrich. *The Birth of Tragedy out of the Spirit of Music.* In *Friedrich Nietzsche: The Birth of Tragedy and Other Writings*, edited by Raymond Geuss and Ronald Speirs, translated by Ronald Speirs, 1–117. Cambridge: Cambridge University Press, 1999.

ME Seidl, Arthur. *Vom Musikalisch-Erhabenen. Prolegomena zur Aesthetik der Tonkunst. Inauguraldissertation der Philosophischen Fakultät der Universität Leipzig zur erlangung der Doktorwürde vorgelegt von Arthur Seidl.* Regensburg, 1887.

PK Tieck, Ludwig, and Wilhelm Wackenroder. "Phantasien über die Kunst" [1799]. In *Tieck und Wackenroder*, edited by Joseph Kürschner, 42–98. Berlin: W. Spemann Verlag, 1886.

BS Hoffmann, E. T. A. "Review of Beethoven's Fifth Symphony." In *E. T. A. Hoffmann's Musical Writings. Kreisleriana, the Poet and the Composer, Music Criticism*, 234–51.

PF   Lyotard, Jean-François. *Postmodern Fables.* Translated by Georges van den Abbeele. Minneapolis: University of Minnesota, 1997.

LA   Lyotard, Jean-François. *Lessons on the Analytic of the Sublime.* Translated by Elizabeth Rottenberg. Stanford, Calif.: Stanford University Press, 1994.

BP   Freud, Sigmund. *Beyond the Pleasure Principle.* Translated by James Strachey. New York: W. W. Norton & Company, 1961.

TG   Leys, Ruth. *Trauma: A Genealogy.* Chicago: University of Chicago Press, 2000.

MUSICALLY SUBLIME

Introduction

Exploring Sublime Varieties

Imagine the wide lawn of the Champs de Mars during the Reign of Terror in late eighteenth-century France.[1] Thousands of people are packed together to participate "universally" in one of the many festivals celebrating the cause of freedom. They sing, they shout, they merge into a massive voice. The sound of this voice alone is staggering and uncannily irresistible. It grows louder as more join in, caught by the thrill of the moment or scared to openly disengage from an agitation that seems to enforce the participation of all. This voice then takes on a life of its own. It is no longer a multifarious whole, louder here, dissonant there, but rather extracts itself from its parts, rising higher and higher until it becomes a voice hovering above the crowd—bodiless, de-composed, singular.

In the ears of the Jacobin rulers, this rising voice encapsulates the emergence of a single will—not a will of parts, but a will that rises above its sum total, no longer divisible. Its individual voices only serve the larger totality, thus constituting a body of uniform power and a body of subjection at the same time: a subjection of the many to the one, of difference to an uncompromising harmony. Consider, in this respect, the ambitious project of the composer Étienne-Nicolas Méhul: to have a crowd of thousands, divided into four sections, sing a major chord together at one of the many festivals organized during the Terror.[2] "In these times," James Johnson has remarked, "all were performers."[3]

Though typically "revolutionary" in its sacrifice of the individual to the common will, this idea(l) of unanimous participation was, perhaps, not an exclusively French invention. Ironically, before the French revolution, its future critic Edmund Burke had already pointed to the overpowering effects of the singing and "shouting of multitudes" in his *Enquiry Into the Origins of Our Ideas of the Sublime and Beautiful*.[4] "The sole strength of the sound" produced by a multitude of voices, Burke remarked, "so amazes and confounds the imagination, that in this staggering, and hurry of the mind, the best established tempers can scarcely forebear being borne down, and joining in the common cry, and common resolution of the croud." Burke identified both such sonorous overkill and the near involuntary participation in a massive unison as being productive of the feeling of the sublime: of a "great and awful sensation" that momentarily halts the mind and "fills it with terror," freezing it into a debilitating stupor (*ESB* II, sect. XVII, 76, 75). Thus, the sublime feeling boils down to a sudden transport incapacitating the mind, laying it prostrate before the tremendous force of a scene, interrupting the ability to act or reason voluntarily.

In what I would like to call its legitimate mode, the sublime feeling in Western philosophy and art criticism typically enacts a movement from the multiple and divided to the unified: from the heterogeneous to the homogeneous. It combines feelings of pleasure and pain (being referred to as a "delightful horror," "pleasing stupor," or "frightful wonder"), but this combination has been dominantly represented as a dialectic reversal. Thus, the sublime feeling often involves a negative moment of fright, frustration, or confusion—that is to say, a state of scattering, dispersal—that is relieved and finalized by a positive moment of mental relief or elevation. There is something that arrests the mind, but this arrest harbors its own release: the experience of fright or frustration screens a reversal in that it signals to the mind the possibility of its opposite. The pain becomes an occasion for pleasure; the latter is mediated by the former, so that this pain is never more than a go-between. It is this passage, as if it were a failsafe thoroughfare, that I question in this book, by rereading the sublime "musically." "Musically," I will point out in detail below, here does not only refer to the cultural practice of music in the eighteenth, nineteenth, and twentieth centuries. It rather also bears on an aesthetics of undecidability and indeterminacy that comes to be intertwined with the so-called empty sign of instrumental music in later eighteenth-, nineteenth-, and twentieth-century Great Britain, France, and Germany. The story of the empty sign is familiar enough, yet its bearing on the aesthetics of the sublime as an aesthetics of the infinite on the one hand and (suspended) shock on the other is still an open field. I here propose to traverse this field by arguing that in contemporary debates on instrumental music and the sublime, the undecidability ascribed to the former comes to destabilize the course of the "legitimate" sublime: the failsafe passage from one state (tension) into another (release) is undermined in an unresolved affective double bind.

Before elaborating on this affective double bind, it is instructive to consider the "procedure" of the legitimate sublime feeling more closely here. Kant's analytic of the sublime in the *Critique of Judgment* is most instructive in this respect.[5] Briefly put, in the third *Critique,* the experience of the sublime becomes an opportunity for the subject to show himself off with respect to nature.[6] Originally, of course, the sublime had been the domain, or rather the effect, of boundless and wild nature: deserts, oceans, mountains, volcanoes, and earthquakes, everything overwhelming that made one feel small and vulnerable but that at the same time elicited fascination and attraction. While the beautiful was brought to bear on "good" forms in art and nature, the sublime incorporated the negativity attached to formlessness (the infinite) and deformity (the terrible). Earlier on in the debate on the sublime, these types of formlessness and deformity had been framed theologically: the deserts, oceans, mountains, and volcanoes that would grow into epitomes of the sublime were seen as the hubris of the great Flood.[7]

In the third *Critique*, however, the power attributed to nature was transferred onto the subject of the Enlightenment: the subject with a capacity for reason, a capacity to think without and beyond the bounds of sensibility, which accommodated an autonomous position vis-à-vis nature, its attractions and its repulsions. What happened to this subject in the sublime was that he was confronted with an object too great for comprehension or too mighty to be resisted, experienced a painful difficulty in trying to measure itself up to or resist this object, but then overcame the pain in a delightful moment of release or self-transcendence. Somewhere in the no-man's-land between pain and pleasure, there was a pivoting point or turning leading to a newfound opening, a newly felt sense of being.

In *The End of the Line*, Neil Hertz has approached this possibility of a climactic turning in the sublime feeling as a cultural "practice" that can be traced to early modern discourses of religious conversion. These discourses compose a literature that "describes a major experiential transformation, the mind not merely challenged and thereby invigorated but thoroughly 'turned round' "—a challenge and a turning accompanied by physical or psychic pain.[8] This is an experience of "another way," which is achieved through a difficult passageway, a rite of passage leading to a radically altered perspective: a pleasure mediated by a displeasure.

A famous example is Petrarch's account of his ascent of Mont Ventoux—an ascent made after long idling and dwindling at the foot of the mountain.[9] When, after an arduous climb, he finally reaches the summit, standing there "like a dazed person," Petrarch's initial bafflement is succeeded by a double illuminating insight. This is triggered by a recollection and a reading respectively of the words of St. Augustine. First, apparently purified by the climb, he recalls his "perverse and wicked" desires and expresses the wish to "tell the truth" about them—just as Augustine had done. Contemplating a hopeful future yet also absorbed by the view from the top, Petrarch is then suddenly urged by Augustine's *Confessions* to turn his eyes away from grand nature and contemplate the life of the soul. The following words from the *Confessions* trigger a decisive turning from outside to inside: "And men go about admiring the high mountains and the mighty waves of the sea and the wide sweep of rivers and the sound of the ocean and the movement of the stars, but they themselves they abandon." Petrarch closes the book—and decides to admire nature no longer, feeling instead that "nothing is admirable but the soul beside whose greatness nothing can be as great."[10]

Significantly, it is this conversion from outside to inside, and the felt awe for an external greatness that is really a misplaced awe for a greatness within, that will resurge in the Kantian sublime: a self-experience turning the eye of the (now half-secularized) subject inward to admire the scope of reason in comparison with which even the greatest object in nature dwindles into insignificance (*KU* §26, 101). No matter how awesome nature appears to the eye and the imagination, Kant writes, it can merely simulate the unlimited extent of reason (*KU* §27, 104). As with Petrarch on the mountaintop, the experience of physical effort and difficulty overcome becomes, in Kant's analytic, an experience of groping insight and delusion (or "subreption") overcome: the soul, not nature, deserves to be the object of the respectful awe typical of the sublime feeling. Once the subject realizes this, he can switch from pain to pleasure.

Kant was, of course, not the only or—despite the commonplace historical perspective—first theorist of the sublime to argue in this manner. Before him, British theorists such as Alexander Gerard and John Baillie had already proposed that the experience of the sublime not so much amounted to an experience of nature's grandness as to the grandness of the soul *in contrast to* nature.[11] Thus, in his *Essay on the Sublime* Baillie argued that the greatness of nature and immensity of the heavens may affect the mind in such a way as to remind it of its grandeur and elevate it accordingly: "Hence comes the name of the Sublime to every thing which . . . raises the Mind to Fits of Greatness, and disposes it to soar above her Mother Earth; Hence arises that Exultation and Pride which the Mind ever feels from the Consciousness of its own Vastness—That Object can only be justly called Sublime, which in some degree disposes the Mind to this Enlargement of itself, and gives her a lofty Conception of her own Powers."[12] The sublime feeling here boils down to an "Effort of the Soul to extend its Being" and, in this way, realize its own supersensible capacities.[13] Delight and exaltation arise out of a newly felt self-consciousness: the subject looks into the mirror of nature and sees that it is not bound to the confines of (significantly enough) Mother Earth. Indeed, vast nature here only functions as an opening to awaken the subject to its "higher" faculties of mind: a "great part of the Elevation raised by vast and grand Prospects, is owing to the Mind's finding herself in the Exercise of more enlarged Powers, and hence judging higher of herself."[14] The experience of the sublime hence becomes an exercise in mental self-expansion.   /K

There is thus a challenge in the experience of the sublime, but though taxing, it can never pose an insurmountable obstacle. It will be seen in chapter 2 that this is especially vivid in Kant's analytic. Here the law of reason that whatever frightens or overwhelms the subject cannot *but* be transcended by reason functions as an affective buffer and even a guarantee for a happy ending (*KU* §27, 103). This law of reason, I will argue, functions like a narrative law in the Kantian sublime feeling. By "narrative law," I here mean the inexorable thrust forward toward an ending that directs and saturates so-called mythological plot structures.[15] These structures frame the traditional, causal sequence of beginning-middle-ending that epitomizes "narrativity" in its most familiar sense: rest, crisis, and (climactic) resolution. Because of the *causal necessity* dictating a transition from middle to ending, or from crisis to resolution, even the most harrowing, perilous crises in these plot structures are always already defined and predetermined by their "after." In this way, the transition from crisis to resolution becomes a lawful or regulative movement, inevitable and predictable: the former is always already in the service and the direction of the latter.

So it is, I will show, with the transition from pain to pleasure in the Kantian sublime experience. This experience acts out the dynamics of mythological plot structures in affective, rather than active, terms: a movement from heterogeneity to unification, from dividedness to resolution. Of course, as we will see, this is not only typical of the Kantian but also of the Burkean existential sublime.[16] Where Kant highlights a spiritual transcendence, Burke focuses on a painful feeling of a life-negating threat (terror) that is surmounted in a life-affirming sense of relief (delight): I am faced with (a fictional or imagined scene of) impending death, but when I realize that the danger is not or no longer "actual," tension is released and I am given free reign to delight in the awareness of my own safety.[17]

Kant
Burke

As in the Kantian sublime, there is thus a pivoting point—a moment of judgment regarding my own safety—that renders the feeling of displeasure a mediation of, and a preamble to, pleasure. The former is only a *passage* to the latter. Granted, the differences between Kant's critical sublime and Burke's existential sublime are there: the former revolves around the delight of having a rational mind; the latter revolves around the delight of having a physical life. This could be called the sublime as elevation and the sublime as intensification, respectively. Yet both "instances" of the sublime feeling are structured like a story with an encoded happy ending. With Kant, triumph is guaranteed due to the alleged moral and spiritual superiority of the subject; with Burke, relief is guaranteed due to the physical distance or safety of the subject.

At least since Samuel Holt Monk's *The Sublime*, this compelling narrative movement that requires a depression to effectuate transcendence has quietly cemented into a normative law of "the" sublime feeling in twentieth-century criticism.[18] In whatever ways the sublime feeling may have been rethought during the last two decades of the twentieth century, the narrative pattern of effort and difficulty overcome has firmly stood its ground. Typically, the structure of the sublime feeling is still familiarly thought of as a successive structure, with the moment of "bafflement," the pain or difficulty, functioning as an intermediary stage in a larger process of being lifted upward, or delightfully relieved and invigorated, by negative means. And just as typically, the necessity of a "turning" signaling a move from pain to pleasure has not been questioned.[19]

Indeed, even in Jean-François Lyotard's more recent and critical reconsiderations of the sublime sense this pattern and this turning persist as the legacy of a controlling past.[20] Transposing the Kantian transcendental sublime to the sphere of immanence, the sphere of sensibility rather than that of reason, Lyotard nevertheless implicitly holds fast to the narrative movement of transcendence that masterminds Kant's epic of self-realization. In *The Inhuman*, for instance, the dynamic of the sublime is rewritten as a dynamic of art and its very matter: of the experimenting with art as unpredictable and uncontrollable *occurrence*—an occurrence in the Heideggerian sense, as the wonder of the now here happening. The sense of the sublime is the sense of awe and surprise *that* there is something, *that* something has happened, rather than nothing.

Lyotard here builds on this old philosophical wonder and awe to refashion the sublime paradox of pain and pleasure within the practices of the

modern avant-gardes. The pain here revolves around a radical indeterminacy brought about by the experimental essays of abstract painting or free
tonal music: these experiments question not only the continuation of tradition but also the very conditions of possibility of the various arts. Should
painting be figurative or even be "painting," should music be organized
sound, or literature be representational and communicative? Painters such
as Kasimir Malevich, composers such as Arnold Schoenberg or, later, John
Cage, and poets such as Hugo Ball showed that such "elementary criteria"
were subject to doubt: they lacked absolute foundations (*TI* 103). Thus
these artists interrupted the certainty, the imagined given that after one
"work, another is necessary, permitted, or forbidden"—that there *will* be an
"after" in any event. There is openness, and this openness at once hides a
potential nothingness: the possibility of "words, colours, forms or sounds
not coming; of this sentence being the last"—the law dictating that after *this*
should come *that* has been wrecked (*TI* 91).

Imagine the intense pleasure, though, if this openness is interrupted: if,
in the midst of the wreckage and privation, a "work" (here not used in the
old metaphysical sense but in its progressive sense as "working," just as
wood continues to work after it has been cut and refined) shows itself after
all, new and unexpected. By "distancing the menace" of the end of art, this
"work" brings the relief that, as we have seen above, makes the terrible
sublime (*TI* 100). In a double movement, art's material experimentations
thus at once bring about the positive and negative moments of the sublime:
they can bring about the threat of privation, of a loss of continuation, and
they can alleviate the tension of suspense by making an appearance (in the
most minimal, literal sense) after all.

By focusing on artistic practices rather than moral values, Lyotard makes
the happening of the sublime a matter of imaginative resourcefulness—a
postmodern alternative to rational regulations of the Enlightenment. We
might call this the sublime as inspiration. (The Dutch philosopher Renée
van de Vall has pursued this "branch" of the sublime in her book on Barnett
Newman, re-presenting the experience of the sublime as an experience of
one's own creativity.)[21] However, though elevation is replaced with inspiration and though suspension is more pervasive, we can still recognize the
mechanism of taxation and difficulty overcome in this postmodern version
of the sublime feeling: it is the same structure with a different coating.

I believe, though, that a critical rewriting of the sublime feeling must
reconsider its narrative structure rather than the story it frames. Such a redress can, in fact, already be outlined in the history of the sublime. Thus,

some eighteenth-century British accounts of the sublime address the possibility of an unresolved simultaneity rather than an alternation of pain and pleasure. John Baillie, for one, entertained the question of a mind being subjected to two affective and mutually contradictive states at once: "it seems strange that a Being so simple, so much one as the *Mind*, shou'd at the same time feel *Joy* and *Grief*, *Pleasure* and *Pain*, in short be the Subject of *Contradictions*; or can it be true that the Mind can feel Pleasure and Pain at the same *Instant*? or rather, do they not *succeed* each other by such infinitely quick *Vicissitudes*, as to appear instantaneous; as a lighted *Globe*, moving in quick *Revolutions*, seems one continued *Circle of Fire*?" (*ES* 31).

Can the mind be divided against itself? Or is the coexistence of pain and pleasure an imaginary coexistence brought about by an infinitely quick succession of the two? Baillie seems to lean toward the latter possibility, as he cannot reconcile the paradox of simultaneity with his "common-sense" notion of the mind as inherently unified through consciousness. Some four decades later, however, Frances Reynolds—Sir Joshua Reynolds's sister— would suggest that the sublime is not to be thought of in terms of a neatly organized development from bafflement to pleasure. She proposed an interplay of apparent opposites meandering back and forth: "[The sublime is] composed of the influence of pain, of pleasure, of grace, and deformity, playing into each other, that the mind is unable to determine which to call it, pain, pleasure, or terror. . . . It seems to stand, or rather to waver, between certainty and uncertainty, between security and destruction."[22] The sublime feeling oscillates in between coexistent "states." It is not decided, but it signals contamination and irresolution—it *wavers*.

I have used this notion of interplay and hesitation as a starting point to reconsider the history and philosophy of the sublime from the mid–eighteenth century to the present. Such a reconsideration, I soon discovered, required an intermedial perspective. Wherever the sublime threatened to disband into an aporia, self-contradictory and indecisive, there was the hint of a medium that rose to prominence in the same era as the sublime: instrumental music.[23] I found that this aporetic sublime was musically informed: musically sublime.

Music and the Sublime

Resisting the persuasion that there is one consistent format of the sublime feeling, this book shows how the latter is constantly rearranged in a complex interaction with "musicality" from the mid–eighteenth century onward.

Such "musicality" is not thought as a given here, but rather it materializes as the *effect* of philosophical and fictional representations of music as an instrument of the indefinite. Insofar as the indefinite—as both the unknown and undetermined—is an attribute of the sublime, this suggests a circular relationship between the two. Yet this need not result in an empty tautology. Evidently, not all music is sublime (whether as aporia, inspiration, intensification, or elevation). Like the other arts, music needs special tricks and builds on special effects to evoke the sublime—and it will do so differently in every other instance and performance. This is, indeed, why I have not restricted myself to virtual or conceptual invocations of "music" in critical theory and philosophy but also have construed dialogues between theory and musical instances: *this, here* is where the sublime happens as *musically* sublime, this is how it *hears* here (or might hear) rather than how we can *think* it. Sometimes, such a dialogue is imminent, for instance in chapter 3, where I confront Richard Wagner's reflections on Beethoven and the sublime, as well as his directions for sublime music, with his own music—or in chapter 4, where I juxtapose Jean-François Lyotard's writings on indeterminacy and the postmodern sublime with John Cage. At other times, the dialogue has the gesture of a proposal whereby musical texts and performances are used as theoretical objects (as Mieke Bal uses the term): objects, more or less arbitrarily chosen, that not merely illustrate but also redress, invigorate, or adjust the theory they are "faced" with in a creative feedback loop.[24] To reinforce the fact that this is about *listening to* sounds rather than reading notes, I have based myself on certain specific recordings rather than scores alone. References to these recordings have been made in the form of time-indications.[25]

Yet, for all these practicalities, music is also unlike other arts in its relation to the sublime. As a philosophical concept that opens up a critical domain, "music" affects the course of the sublime sense in a rather dramatic way: it changes the track of conversion into suspension. More specifically, I argue that, in its eighteenth- and nineteenth-century interactions with "musicality," as the indefinite (endless and undecided), the sublime branches off into a feeling that defers resolution as it undermines its own progress, *or* into a feeling that always defers completion because it suspends consciousness—and hence cannot be retrieved or resolved. That is to say, in these interactions the sublime feeling often turns out unfinished or unaccomplished: it hangs suspended in between pain and pleasure, caught in a repetitive strain that obstructs a set thoroughfare, or it does not register at all, thus resisting mediation and integration. Such "unfinished" experiences register an approach to the sublime that rewrites it as a movement troubled by its own internal duality.

This immediately makes clear that this study does not aim to present a comprehensive overview of manifestations of "the" sublime in music from the eighteenth century onward. In the last decades, there have been a handful of articles on this topic that—perhaps not surprisingly—take such cultural icons as Georg Handel, Joseph Haydn, and Beethoven as their point of focus.[26] Important as these studies have been, they nevertheless tend to take "the" sublime for granted as an agitation that crushes yet then elevates the listening subject. Massiveness, force and volume, but also heroism and daringness are the encoded values and norms attached to this cult of the musical sublime. A brief exploration will illustrate my point.

The musical sublime was still a relatively unexplored terrain in the 1980s, and it only became a much-debated issue during the 1990s. In those early years, one of the few articles on the eighteenth-century musical sublime (by Claudia Johnson) suggested that representations of Georg Handel's music in terms of the new, grand, and terrible witnessed the birth of a specifically musical sublime in British musical practice and criticism in the 1750s.[27] Indeed, while eighteenth-century critics (think of James Beattie in Britain or the Abbé Dubos and François Raguenet in France) had already implicated music in the domain of the sublime through its alignment with the pathetic, from the mid–eighteenth century onward the musical register of "strong feeling" narrowed down to the two key passions of the grand style: terror and astonishment.

Burke had defined terror as an apprehension of pain or danger, and for him this passion was bound up inevitably with the idea of power, which found its supreme articulation in the all-might of the Deity (*ES* II, sect. V, 63). It was precisely such power that came to be associated with Handel in the popular imagination. Thus, in a satirical pamphlet of 1751 on the "Man-Mountain" Handel, William Hayes, professor of music at Oxford and conductor of Handel's oratorios, describes the birth of an enervating kind of music:

> [Handel], whilst at the Zenith of his Greatness, broached another Kind of Music; more full, more grand (as his Admirers are pleased to call it, because crouded with Parts) and, to make the Noise the greater, caused it to be performed, by at least double the Number of Voices and Instruments than ever we heard in the Theatre before: In this, he not only thought to rival our

Patron God, but others also; particularly Aeolus, Neptune, and Jupiter: For at one Time, I have expected the House to be blown down with his artificial Wind; at another Time, that the Sea would have overflowed its Banks and swallowed us up: But beyond every thing, his Thunder was most intolerable—I shall never get the horrid rumbling of it out of my head.[28]

Too many "Parts" and too much force—or rather, too much nature. Nature as might is everywhere in Hayes' description: there is noise rather than organized sound, and wild nature threatening to devour the vestiges of culture. Music here not just announces the threats of nature, but it embodies them in its very effects. Handel, meanwhile, becomes an author of divine power (revered accordingly even by the satirical Hayes). It is this authority that equals the Longinian stroke of sublimity, which takes an audience by surprise, transports it without mercy, and fills it with awe. This is the grand or elevated style come to life in a three-dimensional way that only music could achieve: its unique potential for "total surround" effects that endorses a more dramatic, physically engaged immersion, made possible an experiential thrill that was—in those days—beyond the reach of the other, non-performance-based arts. Music's praised immediacy is, in my view, connected to this three-dimensional reach: the fact that it can travel, occupy a space, and thus contain its listeners. In that sense, music is the most active of all media.

Sublimity, in this Handelian context, was above all *mass*. It was mass and accumulation. As such, it fostered a certain monstrosity: a transgression of form in terms of size—Charles Burney praised the Handel Commemoration concerts because "*five hundred* performers, vocal and instrumental," were "consolidated into one body"[29]—and the sonorous overkill described by Hayes. Yet the sublime also sanctioned disagreeable, dissonant effects. Charles Burney, in any case, defended Haydn's use of dissonance and fragmentary phrases in the "instable" opening of *The Creation*—for how else could one stage a scene that preceded order and form?

And what should become again (may it be asked), but *Chaos*, when chaos is to be described? Were sounds to be arranged in harmonic & symmetric order before order was born? It struck me as the most sublime Idea in Haydn's work, his describing the birth of order by dissonance & broken phrases!—a whisper here—an effort there—a groan—an agonizing cry—personifying Nature—& supposing her in labour, how admirably has he expressed her throes! not by pure harmony & graceful melody, but by appropriate murmurs. . . . When dissonance is tuned, when order arises, & chaos is no more, what pleasing, ingenious and graceful melody & harmony ensue![30]

This identity of form and content in the performance of the sublime, we will see, resurges as a central aspect of the postmodern sublime: sublime is what a work of art can *do* or *be* rather than what it is merely about. Here, however, this doing at once seeks to undo, or at least attenuate, itself. Haydn's "Representation of Chaos" performs the same dynamic of fragmentation and defragmentation that Neil Hertz has analyzed so perceptively in relation to Sappho's so-called jealousy Ode:[31] the scattered universe, the universe not yet brought into being, is reenacted in the texture of a seemingly disparate, amorphous sound world, and the subsequent tuning of this world into harmony and stability. This movement incorporates and rehearses the encoded turning from terror (tension) to relief (respite) that epitomizes the legitimate sublime feeling. Paradoxically, "The Representation of Chaos" thus rouses chaos once more to life yet at the same time transfers its inchoate, destructive might to a creative, musical activity—and becomes harmless in the process.

In the 1990s, leading scholars such as James Webster, Elaine Sisman, and Reinhold Brinkman invigorated and refocused debates on the musical sublime in critical double readings of philosophical and musical texts and performances of the later eighteenth century. It is in their hands that one starts to see the contours of a cultural poetics (in Greenblatt's sense of the term), an "energy" if you will, circulating in eighteenth-century critical theory, philosophy, music criticism, and musical practice. Thus Webster, whose prime focus has been Haydn, has stressed the difference between early nineteenth- and eighteenth-century concepts of the (musical) sublime, the latter (according to him) echoing still very much eighteenth-century concepts of "rhetoric and argumentation" that hark back to the paradigm of mimesis.[32] From here, Webster goes on to argue that it is not this rhetorical tradition but the Kantian reading of the musical sublime (performed in several articles by Carl Philip Emanuel Michaelis, a disciple of Kant) that is to be associated with the musical tradition of Haydn, Mozart, and Beethoven.

> The incommensurable—that is to say, the inability of imagination to grasp what lies beyond the reach of the senses; the infinite—plays a crucial role in this reading of the musical sublime. Indeed, Webster notes a musical advantage in Michaelis's treatment of the Kantian dynamic sublime in terms of the incommensurable: "In music . . . sublime effects depend precisely on temporal phenomena—phenomena that can arouse dynamic effects, indeed in a far more immediate manner than the other arts. In particular, the musical sublime can arise even through the effects of a single moment: such a moment

can 'reverberate' long afterwards, on different musical and hermeneutic planes. It is this multi-layered temporality that constitutes the analogy to Kant's *Bewegung* of the spirit, and therefore generates the musical sublime."[33]

In Haydn, Webster argues, the incommensurable is notably invoked by means of musical contrasts "based on common stylistic elements of the time" that are made to occur in an "unusual and exposed context" or in "unusual or 'pointed' combination."[34] Thus, in the *Creation* the sublime effect of the representation of light depends on significant dynamic contrasts and an unusual combination of different movements combined into a transition from disorder to order (the incommensurable here figuring, as I also pointed out above, in terms of the formed containing the apparently formless, the stylized containing chaos).

Yet, moving to Haydn's late vocal music in general, Webster seems to mix up the Longinian rhetorical and Kantian traditions of the sublime after all: listing "classes of sublime passage" in Haydn's work, the special effects of the incommensurable (affecting the reach of the imagination) in terms of special contrasts are entangled—almost inevitably, I would say—with a sublime "stylistic" that includes, among others, gestural shock, majesty or grand sounds and gestures (both identified in introductory movements), a making strange of verbal-musical combinations, tonal or generic disruptions (including unexpected contrasts between movements), or a carefully staged climax that (as Webster never notes explicitly) rehearses the narrative momentum and resolution of Kant's sublime feeling.[35] In listing these types of sublime passage, paradoxically, Webster distinctly echoes the prescriptive moments in the text of Longinus, likewise listing types of sublime presentation in poetry and oratory.

In her analysis of Mozart and the musical sublime, Elaine Sisman offers a more detailed focus on rhetoric, the sublime, the sublime experience, and music as well as their relation to genius and originality in the eighteenth century.[36] Sisman starts from key sections in the texts by Burke and Kant to identify instances or attributes of the musical sublime in Mozart's music and letters.[37] Thus, elaborating on Burke, Sisman refers to the terrific spectacle of the sea monster—and the panicked crowd—in *Idomeneo* (and the audience's safe removal from it) and the graveyard scene and the second-act finale of *Don Giovanni*.[38] With respect to Kant, Sisman reconsiders the "Jupiter" finale in the light of the learned style and the high degree of technical difficulty that characterizes the sublime: here, the learned style "functions as a signifier of the sublime."[39] Interestingly, Sisman also notes the plotlike structure of the Kantian sublime feeling in its progress toward crisis and then resolution.[40] Insofar as "crisis" stands for the high degree of difficulty—the effort of taxation on the part of the imagination—Sisman shows how the beginning of the "Jupiter" finale enacts a series of "aurally incomprehensible" and intensifying dissonances: "the passage is disordered and obscure, massive and repetitious."[41] Thus, this passage is presented as an instance of the mathematical sublime. Even more dramatically, the coda of the finale enacts the Kantian mathematical sublime in its triggering of a "cognitive exhaustion" that is occasioned by an overload of fragments sounding at once.[42]

Obscurity and disorder connote deviation, and this, Reinhold Brinkmann has argued, establishes a special connection between the sublime and the rise of the symphony as a purely instrumental genre in the eighteenth century.[43] Carl Dahlhaus has already noted an alliance between the aesthetics of the sublime and the symphony in an early-eighteenth-century text by Johann Adolf Scheibe. Here, the symphony is couched in a rhetoric of shock, surprise, and artistic adventurousness. A symphony, Scheibe argues, requires pathos and also an ability to move beyond conventional bounds, to startle rather than please the ear: "Unexpected flashes [*Einfälle*] must suddenly surprise all listeners. . . . One unsuspected change must follow after the other."[44] Johann Georg Sulzer would observe the same in his influential encyclopedia of the fine arts, which would even be reprinted in 1794: marking the symphony a vehicle of the sublime, he praises its "sudden modulations and digressions from one key to another that are all the more striking the more distant their relation."[45] Brinkmann maintains that these undulations of the symphony bear an elective affinity to the movements of the French Revolution. Both would feed on swift motions, violent contrasts, and sudden turns—and both were framed by the idea of the new.[46] I am not sure if, as Brinkmann claims, the aesthetics of the symphony were thus couched in the rhetoric of revolution or if, conversely, the rhetoric of revolution was here inscribed into an already available discourse of the sublime. What matters in this instance is that "the canonization of the symphony as *the* dominant musical genre went hand-in-hand with the canonization of the sublime, the new, and progressive as principal aesthetic categories."[47] This suggests in turn that the rise of instrumental music cannot be disconnected from the sublime.[48]

Yet I would like to make a reservation here: this connection only "works" for a sublime emphatically associated with ideologies of progress, new beginnings, rapid changes, and hopeful futures. In Brinkmann's words, "the events of the . . . French Revolution, which aimed at a change of reality and a radical new beginning, here come to serve as models for the assessment and representation of trends in other fields that are directed toward the new, the future—especially in the sciences and the arts."[49]

The narrative momentum typical of the legitimate sublime, the drive to go forward to realize an inherent destiny, thus significantly intersects with the transcendent-bound energy of the French Revolution. Perhaps not surprisingly, the canonization of Beethoven would take place "in the context of this new orientation in artistic production and reception," tightly associating him with the idea of the symphony as going its own, independent way.[50] Indeed, from the 1830s onward, Beethoven would embody the kind of "original genius" or freedom of artistic will that had been tied to the category of the sublime since Edward Young: "rules, like crutches, are a needful aid to the lame, although an impediment to the strong."[51]

What these interpretations of the musical sublime have in common is that they restrict the latter to the confines of the Longinian grand style (pathos, shock, surprise, timing, and daring) and/or the Kantian aesthetic of the sublime, and in doing so, they implicitly endorse the narrative law of the legitimate sublime (the epic of transcendence). The most obvious and immediate drawback of this confinement is that it restricts the possibility of the musical sublime to one, perhaps two, possibilities: shock-and-awe subjection through the massive and voluminous (with the implication of a subsequent transcendence) or the kind of rollercoaster ride that the symphony would have provided to contemporary audiences. Of course, "shock and awe" and rollercoaster rides are very real aspects of the sublime, neither of which I mean to ignore or reject here. It would be difficult to do so even if I wanted to, since the more bombastic and totalizing tendencies of the sublime as a cultural practice have become painfully evident in the last two centuries. Indeed, if the musical sublime revolves around a transportation by musical might, one could well say that the rise of the musical sublime in the later eighteenth century restructured musical experience into the kind of mass happenings of that same era: the Handel commemoration concerts in England, the festivals organized during the Terror, and the sinister echoes of such festivals in the earlier twentieth century.

However, this book aims to open up other aspects of the sublime in music than intensities of sound and mass and myths of genius alone. Indeed, it aims to show how certain aspects of "musicality" interfere with the idea of the sublime in such a way as to highlight or foreground its aporetic potential. It analyzes how "musicality" (connoted as in-definity: infinity and indeterminacy) can be seen to project a sublime as *liminality* instead of transcendence: an experience *at the limit* (in a "proper" sense of "sublime") that remains "in between"—in between two intensities, between two fields of affection—rather than breaking through to another side. In this way, I deconstruct the commonplace binary opposition of pain and pleasure by rewriting these intensities as tones in a fluctuating rhythm that are already inscribed in each other: the criss-crossing between them comes before an opposition can at all be thought.

Overview

My approach to the musically sublime is thus philosophically informed: I approach the sublime as a concept with a history, which is hence subject to change, and, as Deleuze and Guattari have put it, can be conceived as a center of vibration that resonates with other concepts without necessarily being coherent with them.[52] This center is typified by multiplicity instead of a rigid unicity, so that the concept of the sublime—as consistently as it may have been presented in much philosophical and critical writing—does not contain an unchanging essence. Indeed, starting from resonance and (mutual) vibration, I also start from the perspective that the concept of the sublime is not an isolated concept but rather one that is always already affected and contaminated by other, conjoining concepts—such as "music." This at once calls for a more imaginative, interdisciplinary approach to both textual and musical discourses: I treat these discourses as interactive, showing how they affect and illuminate each other, rather than forcing them into two separate worlds with strong disciplinary boundaries. Obviously, media (here conceived, in the McLuhanesque sense, as extensions of the senses, materializing as texts, sounds, colors, or art forms) are dynamic processes instead of rigid entities with a self-same identity. They are fluid rather than static, constantly changing, checking, and remembering each other. Never more than "interim" or provisional, media are recurring *effects* of intermedial forces.

In chapter 1, such intermedial processes come tentatively to the fore in my analyses of "musicality" in eighteenth-century British critical theories. Basically, "musicality" here comes to connote and perform indeterminacy: an indeterminate mediation that would obstruct mental seeing and specifying. According to contemporary theorists, this mode was gestured by the empty sign attributed to instrumental music. This was a sign that constantly deferred its signified, hence also constantly delaying a fixed signification.

One could say that this sign functioned as a ruin. All it presented was a trace of something that could never be entirely revealed—although precisely because of this, it allowed for a constant reinvention.

Ruins have, of course, been of great significance to the aesthetics of the sublime since the later seventeenth century. For Thomas Burnet, who traveled the Alps in the 1690s, mountains (like oceans, volcanoes, and deserts) were mighty ruins of the Deluge. As such, however, they were signs or, more precisely, indices of God's infinite power: they were the remains of an event irretrievable and unimaginable in scope and force. Thus, as hints of something that was long lost and gone, they lacked their extension.[53] There is a basic imperfection to such hints, but it is precisely this imperfection that theorists such as Edmund Burke and James Beattie promoted for artistic evocations of the sublime. In this way, the sublime occasioned a "confusion" of the arts and even a confusion of its own movement of reversal: in writings like those of James Usher, the sublime feeling is redressed as an unending desire that addresses the impossibility of a satisfying, clearly articulated sense of closure.[54] Reading this in conjunction with Usher's reflections on music and musical experience, I evoke a sublime feeling that remains dogged in its own internal duality, oscillating between conflicting intensities that are paradoxically at work in each other.

In chapter 2, I deepen and elaborate this contamination of the musical in the sublime in the context of early German romanticism and idealist philosophies. Juxtaposing a reading of Kant's third *Critique* to romantic discourses on music and the romantic affliction of *Sehnsucht*, I argue that the latter bears an elective affinity with the sublime feeling. If not related to the aesthetics of shock, *Sehnsucht* can nevertheless be firmly positioned in the realm of the aesthetics of the infinite that—in the romantic era—evolved into an aesthetics of the vague and musical. As I will argue, *Sehnsucht* performs a simultaneity of pain and pleasure insofar as it hovers in between a forward- and backward-moving tendency. Pulling back as it almost realizes itself, *Sehnsucht* constitutes a limit-experience that interlaces pleasure with pain, tension with respite, and never quite evolves beyond being on its way, beyond its own lack.

As such, *Sehnsucht* is typically projected as a "musical" feeling in the romantic era, insofar as "musicality" here enacts the inherent deficiency of a signifier never coinciding with its signified. *Sehnsucht*, however, also enacts an "older" and perhaps even more inevitable philosophical problem. Indeed, I will argue, more than a childish refusal to make choices and accept things as they are, *Sehnsucht* can be seen to perform the inherent inability of the self to coincide with itself in a continuity of past and present. *Sehnsucht* thus performs the groundlessness of the subject: the absence of a founding unity. Yet the *Sehnsüchtiger* never stops wanting to instate that unity as a past fulfillment, however illusory it may be. This is why *Sehnsucht*'s focus is not simply on a future moment in which, as with the Kantian sublime, a supersensible destiny will have been realized. Yes, *Sehnsucht* gestures a "beyond," out of this world, but this beyond is always already traversed by a lost, imaginary past that evaporates at the slightest touch. It is precisely on account of this impossible backward focus that *Sehnsucht*, as a musical feeling, can be read as an ironic commentary of the Kantian sublime as infinite. What constantly interrupts the thrust forward toward resolution of the latter is the counteractive pull of a dislocated past.

Chapter 3 continues the sublime connection of ruins, music, indeterminacy, and infinity. It considers the configuration of a specifically musically sublime in nineteenth-century German (music) philosophy and musical practice. Appropriately, this configuration bears the stamp of an accident: its origin is a more or less inadvertent dispersal of musical metaphors. Thus, I sketch a genealogy of the musically sublime that makes a casual and premature start in Arthur Schopenhauer's *The World as Will and Representation* and travels via Richard Wagner's *Beethoven* essay to Friedrich Nietzsche's *The Birth of Tragedy* and a dissertation of the nineteenth-century music theorist and philosopher Arthur Seidl.[55] As I show, the inception of a specifically musically sublime is the effect of Wagner's creative misreading of Schopenhauer's comparison between architecture and music.

In his dissertation on the musically sublime, Arthur Seidl took up Wagner's reflections on the sublime and music to pose an alternative to Hanslick's dominant notion of the musically beautiful: a sublime not just *in* but *of* music. A sublime, more specifically, that would be contained in a "specifically musical" impression—an impression, indeed, of music's "essence," instead of a sublime feeling brought about by means of association in the musical simulation of a mighty impression (the heaving of wild waters, a storm, or any wild and awesome visual impression) "external" to the musical material. Of course, this at once implicates Seidl in Hanslick's formalist discourse, which likewise seeks to establish the specifically musically beautiful. Yet Seidl is also interested in what moves *contrary* to form, what undermines form and what makes it impossible for form to materialize itself distinctly and decisively. All this is encapsulated in a concept that Seidl introduces to analyze the musically sublime: *formwidrigkeit*, or form-contrariness.

Though a typically Hegelian concept, I adopt form-contrariness (as the possibility of form undoing itself) in chapter 4 to read Jean-François Lyotard's postmodern sublime musically. Lyotard's focus is on the pictorial and musical avant-gardes, while Seidl's concept is, of course, framed by romantic musical practices. For Lyotard, there would be a crucial difference between the two: avant-garde musical experiments enact the sublime insofar as they enact a *refusal to form* in traditional, recognizable modes. Since the sublime has, since Burke, if not since the pseudo-Longinus, been engaged with the limits of representation—the limits of formation—this is why the avant-gardes can, for Lyotard, be situated in the aesthetics of the sublime. They are literally pushing the limit. Conversely, romantic enactments of the sublime would not present the sublime within the very matter of the work itself, in its very refusal to form, but rather in a beyond that is somehow external to this matter.

In my rerendering of it, however, form-contrariness rather precisely emphasizes the parallels between Seidl and Lyotard in their common attempt to establish a sublime *of* (music, painting, literature), rather than a sublime *in* (music, painting, literature). Indeed, I will use the concept of form-contrariness to argue that Lyotard's binary distinction between the romantic and postmodern sublime is finally untenable where music is at stake: both varieties foreground the matter of sound in a disruption of musical form. They may do so in very different ways, but this nevertheless renders these romantic and postmodern practices of the sublime reflexively inversed rather than diametrically opposed: no matter how disruptive, the postmodern sublime requires the notion and memory and convention of form as much as does the romantic sublime. This nevertheless also means, however, that in my analysis the more romantic phases of form-contrariness are in turn exposed to a critical urgency that redirects the latter from an "old" transcendentalism toward a "new" discourse of immanence.

Retracing the course of the sublime feeling to the sphere of sensibility alone, the postmodern sublime feeling notably lacks the transcendental resolution of the Kantian sublime. In writings such as *Lessons on the Analytic of the Sublime*, this absence of resolution is expressed in the figure of the *différend*: a conflict between two parties or positions located on either side of an abyss that cannot be solved without causing an injustice for either. I will show how the concept of the *différend* reframes the Kantian sublime and the (apparent) opposition it stages between reason and sensibility. Yet I will also show why this scenario of an unsolvable conflict never quite reconfigures the sublime feeling as an *internally* divided and *therefore* irresolvable feeling.

Irresolvability in the sublime, I will argue, is not to be traced to an un-bridgeable abyss but rather to a fatal intertwining of apparently opposed, flickering intensities.

I explore this fatal intertwining in chapter 5. This chapter offers a critical rewriting of the mathematical and dynamical sublimes—the sublime of the infinite and the sublime of terror—as specifically musical experiences. With respect to the latter, I offer the idea of a failed or unclaimed experience of an excess that cannot be overcome. Rereading the normative dynamical sublime as a traumatic interruption, I recast it as an experience that is not (yet) a mastered and therefore (as yet) unaccomplished experience. Approaching trauma as a violent shock that nonetheless feeds on the context it does violence to, I arrange trauma musically in a romantic work that at once relies on and erodes its formal setting: the Andantino of Franz Schubert's Sonata in A Minor (D. 959).

Alternatively, I recast the mathematical sublime as an internally divided experience of tension and respite that cannot be concluded as one, as unified. I here use the figure of *différance* rather than *différend* to foreground the self-defeating gesture of the sublime as an experience of the infinite. Repetition—a central figure to *Sehnsucht* and, it will be seen, to the sublime as trauma—here becomes a crucial movement to analyze this gesture. I will do so by inscribing the sublime as infinite in twentieth-century "minimal" music, Terry Riley's *In C* (1964) in particular. I will, however, not do so because "minimal" or "repetitive" music would be uniquely able to cancel out our awareness of time through a constant reiteration of the same or of similar patterns. Rather, *In C* projects the impossible possibility of two simultaneous movements pointing and pulling in different directions: forward and backward at once. In this way, it defies conventional distinctions between progress and regress, tension and relief, and, finally, pleasure and pain.

As such, my "repetitive" sublime—the sublime that will not be one—foregrounds an ancient dilemma in modern aesthetics. If we reach a limit in our imaginings of infinity, we might pretend to transcend it by literally thinking it away in a dialectic reversal. Yet what if the limit *itself* always already negates its beyond; that is to say, what if the limit constantly returns and folds back on *itself* as a delimitation in our (never more than) fictional encounters with the infinite? What if the threshold, the *limen*, contains the void that we deem beyond it? I know of no other way to express this paradox more precisely than by way of one of the finest contemporary Dutch authors, who has staged this adventure of the squirrel and the ant:

One morning, the squirrel and the ant walked through the forest.

"Where are we going?" the squirrel asked.

"To the distance," the ant said.

"Oh," said the squirrel.

It was a beautiful day and they walked out of the forest, into the distance.

. . .

They traversed an immense plane. Now and then, they passed a rock, and above their heads a small white cloud would sometimes float in the immense blue sky.

They walked for hours.

Then they suddenly halted at a wall.

It was a big, high wall. It was covered with ivy and its stones were crumbly and weather beaten.

They walked a while along the wall. There were no holes in it, or a gate, and there was no end to it.

"We can't go further," the squirrel said.

"But we can climb over it," the ant said. "Look."

He climbed on the shoulders and the head of the squirrel and mounted the wall.

"What's on the other side?" the squirrel asked.

There was a long pause. Then the ant said: "Nothing."

"But what do you see?" the squirrel asked.

"Nothing."

"But when you look down, you don't see any ground?"

"No. No sky either."

"Is it dark?"

"No," the ant said, "there is nothing."

There was a brief silence. The squirrel reflected.

"Is it very old there?" he then asked. "Or grey?"

"No," said the ant, "not old and grey either."

"Can you hear something?"

"No," said the ant, "nothing."

"Is it all silent then?"

"No."

"But if you hear nothing, then there is silence?"

"Yes," the ant said. "I would have thought so. And yet it isn't silent. It is nothing."

"But that can't be," the squirrel said.

. . .

The squirrel reflected for a while.

"If you could fly, could you fly over it?" he then asked.

"Over what?"

"Over there."

"There is no there. That's what I told you. There is nothing."

. . .

"There must be another side," [the ant] said. "There must be!"

"Why must there be another side?" the squirrel asked.

"There must be!" the ant raved. "There must be!" He stamped his feet and paced back and forth furiously. "There must be something!"

"What?" the squirrel asked.

"Something!!" The ant said with a catch in his voice that seemed to fly up.[56]

If the ant fails to conjure the beyond of the senses yet nevertheless refuses to yield to this beyond as nothingness, he also fails to recognize the wall as an inevitable part of the beyond he cannot fathom. Perhaps we had better side with the squirrel: "He looked at the sky and the plane and the forest in the distance and the ant next to him. So that is all [*alles*: also, 'everything'], he thought."[57]

1. *Empty Signs and the Burkean Sublime*

The empty sign would have to be the sign of a paradox: a sign that is not quite a sign, yet *as such* marking the process of signifying itself. It is not quite a sign (at least in the Saussurean sense), because it constantly suspends a signified. Empty signs are "pure" signifiers resisting the Saussurean logic that signifiers and signifieds invoke each other and thus cannot function without each other: wherever there is a signifier, a signified is presupposed. Yet what if the associative bond between the two is all too slippery; what if cultural conventions do not (yet) allow for a shared meaning to crystallize? What if a signifier could mean anything to anybody, and the idea of the sign is revealed as a process of endless, aimless signifying?

In his *New Method for Assisting the Drawing of Original Compositions of the Landscape*, Alexander Cozens seems to have promoted the materialization of such empty signifiers as visual indices in his elaborations on the *blot*: a crude mode of drawing that starts from a very rough, and in a sense very minimal, mode of visual configuration.[1] "An artificial blot," he explained, "is a production of chance with a small degree of design. . . . All the shapes are rude and unmeaning, as they are shaped with the swiftest hand." This is an abstract strategy of the body: not a mathematical abstraction, but quick, accidental, open dashes out of which some shape *could* be born. There are forms, "hints for composition," but no closed figures.[2]

Admittedly, Cozens may be a slippery example in this instance. His blot paintings have been familiarly appropriated in twentieth-century criticism as enigmatic imprints of times and aesthetics yet to come (romanticism, symbolism, abstractionism). Yet Cozens' blotting method is nevertheless inevitably part of a cultural poetics of the sublime circulating throughout the eighteenth- and early nineteenth centuries. One could say that this poetics manifested itself in art as a poetics of indeterminacy, with faint, unspecified shapes in painting (Cozens' blots, John Constable's clouds, J. M. W. Turner's foggy color fields), in a predilection for raw and rugged, "unfinished" landscapes, but also for vaguely suggestive modes of mediation in literature—whether for leisurely thrills (as in Gothic fictions) or to instill a sense of the infinite via the indeterminate (William Wordsworth's *Prelude*).

As I will argue in this chapter, this poetics of indeterminacy—one might even term it a "suggestive turn"—partook of a fascination with the so-called empty sign of instrumental music in critical theory. As I will stress, the aesthetics of the sublime in the eighteenth century affectively gestured an aesthetics of terror that expressed an increasing antioccularcentrism (to borrow Martin Jay's term):[3] it favored not-showing and a suspension of the known. Indeed, in Edmund Burke's *Enquiry* the existential tension of uncertainty relative to terror was translated into a visual indeterminacy where the artificial sublime was at stake. To evoke the sublime in art, one must specify and reveal as little as possible, so as to sustain terrors of uncertainty or even awed admiration. For Burke, not pictures but words could achieve this, as only words would be able to rouse *obscure ideas*: ideas that do not raise distinct images to the mind.

Yet in their turn, words reiterated another mode of mediation: they can be seen to rehearse the endless deferral of the signified ascribed to instrumental music in the eighteenth century.[4] As scarce as Burke's references to music may be, "musical" (or indeterminate) mediation nevertheless subtends his argument on words and verbal mediation in the *Enquiry*. In this way, the so-called full linguistic sign becomes implicated almost as a matter of course in the empty sign of music. This not only applies to evocations of terror but also to evocations of the idea of the infinite attached to a more "quiet" sublime feeling in the *Enquiry*. Elaborating on this urgency of indeterminacy, I finally propose a musically informed notion of the sublime that resists a decisive sense of closure or resolution. I base myself both on Burke and on James Usher, for whom the delight of indecision associated with instrumental music converged with the idea of an "alternative" sublime feeling that revolved around unending desire. By way of these two theorists, I propose a sublime as intimation that proceeds along the lines of vacillation rather than sublimation.

Obscurity and Sensationalism

In his *Enquiry*, Edmund Burke explicates the existential sublime in terms of a double privation. The first concerns a threat of the privation of certainty, corresponding to terrors of death, darkness, solitude, silence, and emptiness: I am afraid my life, my light, the people and their voices surrounding me, and even things surrounding me may be taken away from me. But then a second privation puts the terror at bay: the threat is suspended. I am becoming aware of my own safety and recognize that the threat is not, or no longer, imminent (*TI* 99). This suspension allows the tension of terror to give way to an intense and joyful sense of relief. Thus, when pains of privation melt down, as it were, in feelings of relief and reassurance, a delight can be felt, which makes the terrible sublime:

> Whatever is fitted in any sort to excite the ideas of pain, and danger, that is to say, whatever is in any sort terrible, or is conversant about terrible objects, or operates in a manner analogous to terror, is a source of the *sublime*; that is, it is productive of the strongest emotion which the mind is capable of feeling. . . . When pain or danger press too nearly, they are incapable of giving any delight, and are simply terrible; but at certain distances, and with certain modifications, they may be, and they are delightful. (*ESB* I, sect. VII, 36)

Distance, modification, implies mediation—yet how to bring about such deadly terrors second hand? The answer lies, perhaps, in the nature of the terrors described: by inducing a sense of uncertainty paralleling the disorientation of physical darkness. Only when one cannot see, oversee, or understand, when one is ignorant or insecure, does one become susceptible to apprehensions of death, danger, or pain:

> In utter darkness, it is impossible to know in what degree of safety we stand; we are ignorant of the objects that surround us; we may every moment strike against some dangerous obstruction; we may fall down a precipice the first step we take; and if an enemy approach, we know not in what quarter to defend ourselves . . . strength is no sure protection; wisdom can only act by guess; the boldest are staggered, and he who would pray for nothing else towards his defence, is forced to pray for light. (*ESB* I, sect. VII, 36–37)

For Burke, uncertainty is so particularly unbearable because it brings about an enforced passiveness: one must wait to counter a possible danger one does not yet know, has not yet seen, and accordingly cannot yet contain. Still, as Jean-François Lyotard has aptly noted, this is not simply a danger completely unknown but rather one at once "withheld and announced": there is a vague premonition of impending danger, a tentative hint (a noise in the dark, a sudden movement in the distance), but it remains to be seen if, and if so when and what, that danger will be (*TI* 92). Hostage to an as yet immaterialized threat, one is hostage to time: subjected to waiting, anticipating, and perhaps all for nothing (*TI* 92).

Thus there is this chain in Burke's *Enquiry* interweaving the idea of the sublime with indeterminacy: the latter (rather than terror) is its condition of possibility. Etymologically, "determine" has a semantic trace of "setting limits to" and "to mark the end or boundary" (even though the Latin *determinare* already suggests its opposite: *de-terminare* evokes a suspension of set limits, but appropriately *de* here connotes "completely," "thoroughly"). Indeterminacy thus signals the unsettling of such limits and boundaries: indeterminacy is what (a form, meaning, or substance) remains to be decided, to be settled.

Primarily a work of rhetoric, the *Enquiry* translates such general indeterminacy into a semantic and imaginative indeterminacy where writing (and, as we shall see later on, drawing) is at stake. Suspension is the key word in this writing: a strategic, and even necessary, deferral of resolution and disclosure. One must create an atmosphere of brooding and awful premonition in which the *effects* of some terrible thing or scene described can be felt by the audience—one must induce tensions of uncertainty, blinding one's audience so they will fear every next step or move, every turn around the corner. Do not inform, to speak with Mary Shelley, but seek "to make the reader dread to look round, to curdle the blood, and quicken the beatings of the heart."[5] Undermine, in a word, your audience's ability to predict, foresee, and place confidence in the unknown, so as to give rise to ideas of danger. Mime the absent; make them fear the worst.

While such sensationalism in art has familiarly been branded a Burkean invention, we have already seen that it is in fact part of a poetics already circulating in the times of John Dennis and Joseph Addison—if not already in the times of the pseudo-Longinus. This is a poetics of intensification that revolves around special effects: the simulation of "real" things through a staging of "as-if-real" feelings. Thus, Dennis observes in *The Grounds of Criticism*: to "bring even absent terrible Objects" before a public's eyes and ears, the speaker must become like a magician who makes us "sensible of the same Passion that we should feel from the things themselves."[6] The "same" and "things themselves": a verification of "fact" through an alleged identity of effect—I recognize the Thing vicariously; I recognize it not because I see it but because I feel my terror for it. Yet of course, in this performance the Thing is not so much reproduced as *installed* through mimicry: it is, precisely, an *effect* of the "Passion" provoked insofar as it can become present only *by way of* such mimicry. In this way, as I will show in more detail below, the happening of the sublime hinges precariously upon the mechanisms of the supplement.

Imitation and Substitution

As a special effect that somehow builds on not-(yet-)showing and not-(yet-)telling, the artistic sublime is bound to representational limits:

> [When a] grand cause of terror makes its appearance, what is it? is it not, wrapt up in the shades of its own incomprehensible darkness, more aweful, more striking, more terrible, than the . . . clearest painting could possibly represent it? When painters have attempted to give us clear representations of . . . very fanciful and terrible ideas, they have I think almost always failed; insomuch that I have been at a loss, in all pictures I have seen of hell, whether the painter did not intend something ludicrous. (*ESB* II, sect. IV, 58)

If terror builds on indeterminacy, one of the central arguments in the *Enquiry* is that any *visual* evocation of the sublime is a contradiction within the terms: pictures reveal and thus cannot keep things in the dark long enough to exploit and sustain ideas of impending danger. Yet—how do they reveal and, most interestingly, why do they reveal?

The answer is a mirror: the trope of resemblance and reflection. In Burke's text, pictures work by means of imitation and resemblance, an exact copying and showing of the "facts" of reality: "nothing is an imitation further than as it resembles some other thing." Imitation is their exclusive domain—and vice versa—for pictures would have an exact "resemblance to the ideas for which they stand" (V, sect. VI, 157).[7] This may in fact imply that due to their very "nature" (guaranteeing an exact, one-to-one relationship with the reality they represent), pictures in the *Enquiry cannot but* imitate as they *cannot but* resemble and hence *cannot but* completely and exactly show a presumed original. As such, as a clear and exact duplication, either in form, content, manner, or action, Burke argues, the business of imitation is to enlighten and inform. It is (in an overt reference to Aristotle) "by imitation far more than by precept that we learn everything; and what we learn thus we acquire not only more effectually, but more pleasantly" (*ESB* I, sect. XVI, 45). This means that pictures, as imitations, must register things as they are in a world perceived by the senses—and registering these things very clearly and reliably. Beyond this world they should not move.

In the *Enquiry*, pictures should thus be held in check—even though this is due to a *faith* in pictures and a *suspicion* of words as communicators of the real. As Angela Leighton has shown, empiricist philosophers such as John Locke and David Hume "present an epistemology based on the authenticity of sense perception. This authenticity is determined mainly by the criterion of clarity or vividness; by a language which falls back, willingly or unwillingly, on a metaphor of sight. The mind's ideas or impressions are the source of true knowledge to the extent that they are clear, distinct, simple."[8] Epistemologically, pictures have a privileged position for the empiricists. Words are already one step removed from the real thing (i.e., thinking, consciousness).[9] They would come "after" a mental process, add to this process, and thus inevitably contaminate it. Words here embody the "dangerous supplement" singled out by Jean-Jacques Rousseau (an outside infecting an inside).[10] Functioning as deceptive fabricators and even as obfuscators, they are the step "in between." This makes them a menace: words move in their move away from consciousness; they absorb and reshape the world of sense.

While the *Enquiry* implicitly embraces this empiricist distinction between ideas and words as a distinction between immediacy and mediation, it nevertheless turns the hierarchy of privileges upside down: it favors words *as* supplements. Thus, Burke argues that the relation between ideas and words is not one of sameness but one of difference: words do not visually reflect the real. In fact, in Burke's view words have little or nothing to do with the ideas they represent. Unlike pictures, they operate by means of sounds that on the basis of certain codes and conventions function as signs of a visibly perceived world that plays no part whatsoever, is indeed almost entirely lost, in a newly created, verbal reality. As a supplanting force, the latter effaces, replaces, and makes anew the former (*ESB* V, sect. II–V, 149–55). This is, indeed, what words do in the *Enquiry*: they substitute instead of imitate (though, of course, imitation never excludes the possibility of substitution, in the sense of "coming in the place of" or "using instead." The difference is evidently artificial).

In thus emphasizing the arbitrary nature of words, there is a strong tendency in the *Enquiry* to in fact challenge the Lockean assumption that words raise images in the mind.[11] Indeed, Burke remarks, "it is not only of those ideas which are commonly called abstract and of which no image at all *can* be formed, but even of particular real beings, that we converse without having any idea of them excited in the imagination" (*ESB* V, sect. V, 155). We rather steer our habitual blind course in ordinary reading and conversation, making sense of (differences between) signs, not of mental pictures: "Indeed, it is impossible, in the rapidity and quick succession of words in conversation, to have ideas both of the sound of the word, and of the thing represented; besides some words expressing real essences, are so mixed with others of a general and nominal import, that it is impracticable to jump from sense to thought, from particulars to generals, from things to words, in such a manner as to answer the purposes of life; nor is it necessary that we should" (*ESB* V, sect. IV, 153).

Rather, to speak with Ludwig Wittgenstein, it is necessary to know how to play the appropriate language game: relations between a sign and its signified are neither natural nor necessary but socially and culturally construed. What is required for reading, speaking, and listening is simply to acquire the relevant rules determining the applications of such relations within a language community.

This is, however, not to say that the *Enquiry* is a poststructuralist text *avant la lettre* that relinquishes the idea of an ultimate signified—it is just that this signified has worn off and faded away after long use. What remains is the trace of an association. This trace suffices to make communication possible, to have the signifier perform its mediating function, without even being transparent:[12]

> Words are in reality but mere sounds; but they are sounds, which being used on particular occasions . . . and being applied in such a variety of cases that we know readily by habit to what things they belong, they produce in the mind, whenever they are afterwards mentioned, effects similar to those of their occasions. The sounds being often used without reference to any particular occasion and carrying still their first impressions, they at last utterly lose their connection with the particular occasion that gave rise to them; yet the sound without any annexed notion continues to operate as before. (*ESB* V, sect. II, 150–51)

Thus the signifier bypasses the signified, acting like the Derridean supplement that absorbs the presence that it—precisely—instates or effectuates. As an *imaginary* presence, the signified slips under the signifier, opening up a virtual world only held in check by a faint, invisible recollection of the real. In this way, the *Enquiry* promotes an antipictorialist semiotics to promote the claim that words can operate like the occasions they supplement, without these occasions needing to be visually present or recalled in the mind. What words can, and pictures cannot, do is to hide *and* simulate their referent. They create an illusion of presence not by dishing up the visual "facts" of things but by supplanting and operating *as* those things.

And yet, while this functional likeness would engender some kind of affective presence or nearness, it also engenders the opposite. Words may absorb their occasion, but in their quality as supplements they nevertheless also create a strange, though inevitable, distance. To recall Derrida: the "supplement has not only the power of *procuring* an absent presence . . . procuring it for us through the proxy [*procuration*] of the sign, it holds it at a distance and masters it" (155). The supplement offers the advantages of the virtual: it is the same thing, but not quite. This "not quite" constitutes a buffer: words in the *Enquiry* produce reality-effects with a safety net. As substitutes of visible (sensible) or invisible (abstract) occasions, they at once invoke *and* mediate the effects of these occasions, so that they also moderate the effects associated with them. The result is a real that, unable to be present itself, becomes very real affectively at one remove.

Thus it is that words can realize most "naturally," so to speak, both the suspension of visual revelation that terror requires *and* the concomitant suspension of imminent pain and danger. (Or at least, they already fulfill a condition of possibility that pictures still have to acquire by negating their very *modus operandi* as imitators.) It is a package deal: words are released from the burden of the visible and bestowed with the force of the virtual, staging forces that play in between presence and absence. Their obscurity (their ability to not-raise image-ideas in the mind), one could say, imports death onto the scene of writing: death in the sense of imaginative excess and boundlessness, as we shall see later on, but also death in the sense of dismemberment. For this obscurity marks a break between words and their occasions that is unbridgeable and irreversible: words here function as prostheses that have taken on a force of their own, that have *annihilated* their signified, as feebly and indirectly as they may still be tied to old associations with the "proper." Consequently, the (passing) pains they can provoke in the service of the sublime are phantom pains: these are the pains occasioned by faint, affective threads to a lost real in a wholly artificial world of verbal replacement.

As in Music, So in Poetry?

To us, however, this distance between words and the real not only signals death—(gradual) amputation—but also foreshadows a possible birth: the birth of romantic notions of artistic autonomy. For does not this distance make possible the idea of art as a parallel world, a "world in itself" that can be experienced on its own terms and according to its own laws? Perhaps this is, to speculate still further, a byproduct of the eighteenth-century poetics of the sublime—an emphasis on blindness and affective realism that persists in the romantic dream of art's independence from the phenomenal world.

Yet insofar as Burke's world of words might foreshadow such independence, it is nevertheless a shadow with an aura of derivation in the very old sense of *derivare*: drawing off from another source. Thus, as substitutes that work the passions immediately, without the intervention of image-ideas, words in the *Enquiry* tap a mode that is other and mentioned only in passing: "so far is a clearness of imagery from being absolutely necessary to an influence upon the passions, that they may be considerably operated upon without presenting any image at all, by certain sounds adapted to that purpose; of which we have sufficient proof in the acknowledged and powerful effects of instrumental music" (*ESB* II, sect. IV, 56).

Instrumental music can do it (work the passions), and this is how and why poetry can do it: the former is put forward, however casually, to legitimate and validate the workings of the latter. In the *Enquiry*, references to instrumental music may be too scarce to grant the latter anything more than the status of an accidental subtext—yet as such, perhaps *precisely* as such, I would nevertheless dare this hypothesis: the *Enquiry* rejects the traditional, Horatian *ut pictura poesis* and instead intimates an *ut musica poesis* based on the presumption that neither music nor poetry would raise (distinct) image-ideas.

Indeed, as Kevin Barry has suggested, in this very era music "becomes, in relation to poetry, an analogy by which there can be a movement from a principle of representation to a principle of interpretation."[13] That is, in many later eighteenth-century accounts of language, ideas of instrumental music are subtextually present whenever the workings of words are evoked in terms of indeterminacy and affectivity (as they are in the *Enquiry*). Barry adds to this that since "a piece of instrumental music must appear, according to Lockean principles, to be empty of signification, its enjoyment is evidence of the necessity for an aesthetic complex enough to include the pleasures of uncertainty in interpretation."[14]

What would be the implication of this musical directive—if a directive it is—for poetic (and pictorial) mediations of the sublime? (How) do words echo musical modes in these circumstances? Or do they rather veil their own shortcomings by pretending to assume a musical "procedure" that was in fact always already their own? Does the *Enquiry* also allow for *pleasures*, rather than only terrors, of uncertainty? If so, how can these pleasures be related to the Burkean sublime? Probing these questions, I will read the *Enquiry* in juxtaposition with passages from five related texts: James Harris's *Three Treatises* (1744), James Beattie's *Essay on Poetry and Music as they affect the Mind* (1776), as well as "Of Imagination" and "Illustrations on Sublimity" from his *Dissertations Moral and Critical* (1783), and James Usher's *Clio, or a Discourse on Taste* (1769). This montage of discourses stages a context of interpretation that will call into question a binary opposition between the "full" linguistic sign and the "empty" musical sign: the two are instead closely intertwined. As such, hovering in between semantic excess and scarcity, the idea of the "empty" sign can be seen to function as the clearing or opening of the artistic sublime in eighteenth-century critical theory.

Admittedly, Harris's *Three Treatises* never so much as question the old, Aristotelian principle of imitation as the central principle of all the arts and their modes of mediation. Poetry, according to Harris, imitates just as much as painting—it is just that the *way* in which it imitates differs from *pictorial* imitative methods.[15] On the other hand, however, the *Three Treatises* do problematize the hierarchy of the fine arts as proposed by the authoritative Abbé Dubos. Dubos, as the *Enquiry* notes condescendingly, ranked painting higher than poetry "principally on account of the greater *clearness* of the ideas it represents" (*ESB* II, sect. IV, 56). In Dubos, however, clearness signals vivacity rather than dull and faithful copying. Indeed, as such it serves the realism in effect that the *Enquiry* promotes—though the latter has a different procedure and a different name in mind: the idea of functional likeness and emotive repetitions highlighted in the *Enquiry* runs parallel to the term "imitation" used in Dubos' *Réflexions critique sur la poésie et sur la peinture*. Both feed on a mimicry of circumstances that stages a scene, object, or event in such a lively way that the audience feels what it would have felt in "actuality."[16]

Oddly, apart from its Latin root *clarus* (bright, distinct), "clearness" also has a sonic connection: it is related to *clamare*, or "call out." "Clearness" thus seems to combine "illuminate" and "announce," a combination that privileges neither the visual nor the verbal sphere. What matters most in this combination is the link (in both spheres) with *pathos* or strong feeling. In the context of the *Réflexions* (i.e., as illumination or revelation), clearness refers to a sudden unveiling or apparition of the appearance: a scene, object, or event *as seen* is shown *as seen*. On the other hand, in the context of the *Enquiry* (i.e., as announcing) clearness refers to a summoning of affections without the mediation of vision. There is a sound and (by the law of habit and convention) this sound commands affections. These affections, we have seen, *suggest* a presence—and it is a very precise, exact suggestion, for it can simulate the real quite successfully.

Moving from "effect" to "cause," this annunciating mode is a reverse mode—though as such it is never diametrically opposed to the illuminating mode. (Illumination is implied in annunciation to the extent that the latter depends on *lively* effects, on *vivacity*. Likewise, annunciation is at work in illumination because the latter calls forth affections, or attempts to do so, in the mediation of appearances.) Now, as a theory of verbal mediation this reverse mode in the *Enquiry* is—to borrow a term from Richard Grusin— premediated by a theory of musical mediation presented in the second of the *Three Treatises*. That is to say, though the *Enquiry* perhaps never willfully repeats this reverse mode, it nevertheless participates in schemata of mediation already projected into the future more than a decade earlier.[17] Indeed, simply said, what Harris observes about music in the *Treatises* Burke will also observe about words and poetry in the *Enquiry*: as in music according to Harris, so in poetry according to Burke.[18]

Thus, the second *Treatise* premediates Burke's assertion that the passions can be operated upon in music "by certain sounds adapted to that purpose": by certain sounds that do not raise distinct image-ideas but that excite af-fections to which, as Harris puts it, "ideas [say, of pain or danger] may *corre-spond*."[19] Music thus does not transfer ideas but passions that may be analogous to certain ideas. (In its turn, of course, this idea of musical media-tion is premediated by the Baroque theory of the *Affektenlehre*, even though the second *Treatise* reserves a large space for the principle of [free] associa-tion.)[20] In this capacity, music can even anticipate ideas insofar as it can rouse passions to which ideas correspond that have not yet been pronounced. In-deed, music for Harris will basically serve to bring the audience in the right temper so as to be receptive to whatever a poet has to profess later on. Music thus has a preparatory function: "The ideas of poetry must . . . needs make the most sensible impression when the affections peculiar to them are al-ready excited by music."[21]

If, therefore, the power of music is not to be attributed to the ideas but to the passions it can raise, this will be the main argument of the *Enquiry* with respect to poetry: words operate by means of sounds (rather than image-ideas) that *by custom* have the effect of realities. And if, on this basis, the *Enquiry* grants words the privilege of enrapturing their audience, Harris had already described the captivating power of musical sounds in a similar vein. In the *Treatise*, instrumental music exerts a "force irresistible," pene-trating "into the deepest recesses of the soul. *Pectus inaniter angit, irritat, mul-cet, falsis terroribus implet*, as Harris quotes from Horace's *Epistolae*: He tortures his breast over nothing; he rouses it, soothes it, he fills it with imagined terrors.[22] Such a vicarious thrill will be essential to Burke's fictive experience of terror in the *Enquiry*, but by that time poetry—and language in general—seems to have entirely absorbed the qualities the second *Treatise* had reserved for music.

Typically, however, as much as the second *Treatise* premediates the mode of words in the *Enquiry* in its explication of musical mediation, it nevertheless posits a binary opposition between the two: while instrumental music raises affections to which ideas may correspond, poetry exhibits ideas to which affections may correspond. And Harris clearly puts his stakes on the latter. Privileging the verbal sign as the "decisive" sign, he contends that music merely anticipates the poetic formulation of strong affections. Instrumental music's preparatory role thus indicates that the feelings it arouses have an imperfect or, more positively put, nascent status in the second *Treatise*. It is as if they have to await further development, completion, substantiation: they have yet to be decided. Conveniently, this undecidability is thus isolated from verbal mediation. The binary opposition here prevents any instability or criss-crossing that could lead to a confusion of the two mediating modes—but as such it betrays an unspoken anxiety about the (un)reliability of words.

A similar opposition rules Beattie's *Essay on Poetry and Music*. Here, "music merely instrumental" is posited as being "imperfect" when it comes to inspiring and elevating an audience.[23] Like Harris, Beattie believes that instrumental music needs words to become wholly expressive. Though striking immediately, it can only vaguely evoke a general "sensibility" and is only useful to "prepare the mind for being affected" by beautiful images or lofty thoughts to be raised by words.[24] Instrumental music can thus be merely an overture:

> A fine instrumental symphony well performed is like an oration delivered
> with propriety but in an unknown tongue; it may affect us a little, but conveys no determinate feeling; we are alarmed, perhaps, or melted, or soothed,
> but very imperfectly because we know not why: the singer, by taking up the
> same air and applying words to it, immediately translates the oration into our
> own language; then all uncertainty vanishes, the fancy is filled with determinate ideas, and determinate emotions take possession of the heart.[25]

"Imperfect feeling": this is feeling without knowing why or what one feels precisely. One has a faint impression of being affected, but the "cause" of this affection has not yet been revealed. It is a feeling of *je ne sais quoi* that can touch the mind suddenly and inexplicably. Therefore, "the expression of the best instrumental music is ambiguous," even though this never means that it should try to be more decisive.[26] Its place is with ambiguity, and its best interpreter is poetry. In the *Essay,* imitation (used in the sense of "raising [distinct] images") in instrumental music is illicit, because there is nothing (but sounds) in nature for music to copy.[27]

Beattie then makes a striking observation. Following Charles Avison, he singles out instrumental music as an expressive art—which coincides with the reverse mode of mediation that rouses affections rather than ideas, as discussed above—because it is *not* an imitation of nature, hence not a *natural sign*:

> If we compare Imitation with Expression, the superiority of the latter will be evident. Imitation without expression is nothing; Imitation detrimental to Expression is faulty; Imitation is never tolerable, at least in serious music, except it promote and be subservient to Expression. If then the highest excellence may be attained in instrumental music, without imitation; and if, even in vocal music, imitation of nature is not essential to this art; it must follow, that the imitation of nature is not essential to this art.[28]

As Matthew Riley has pointed out, the debate on natural and arbitrary signs was an important and continuing debate in eighteenth-century critical theories—both in Great Britain and on the continent. Mostly, the natural sign was privileged, since it was thought to be God- or nature-inspired, rather than manmade, and was considered to be conveying things more directly and transparently.[29] (This coincides with the mistrust of words as obfuscators and manipulators discussed above: their mode of mediation is based on arbitrariness.) Apparently, the general tendency in eighteenth-century music theory was to associate music closely with nature so as to impose a "natural order" onto it: (instrumental) music was meaningful insofar as it reflected natural, rather than arbitrary, laws.[30]

The texts I have discussed so far deviate from this tendency by referring to instrumental music's expressive potential as ambiguous or the result of a more or less random association of ideas and affections. A natural sign, after all, would have been instantly understood by everyone. Riley describes a similar deviation in the work of Denis Diderot, who had already referred to the ambiguity and arbitrariness of musical expression in 1751.[31] Likewise, his *Leçons de clavecin et principes d'harmonie en dialogues* presents musical expression as a highly indeterminate mode of mediation, stimulating the listener's imagination and giving rise to endlessly different interpretations.[32]

For that matter, the violinist, composer, and philosopher Paul Michel-Guy de Chabanon offered a similar perspective in his *De la musique*: here, music does not copy nature but, precisely, *deviates* from and *transgresses* it by imitating "imperfectly" ("les tableaux étant toujours imparfait"). Unlike linguistic signs, musical sounds are open or "empty": they merely *suggest*.[33]

Significantly, therefore, the distinction between musical and linguistic signs is at once reinforced and undermined by critical theories that emphasize the ambiguity of musical mediation. If musical signs cannot be decided, they are open to speculation or random signification (on the part of the listener). Ironically, they thus approach the arbitrary laws that allow linguistic signs to function "decisively" through habit and convention: to individuate and communicate meanings. There is, however, also another possibility—the possibility indicated by the *Enquiry*: if the opposition between musical and linguistic signs as so-called natural and arbitrary signs is not absolute, the latter can also be implicated in the undecidability of the former, even if this merely amounts to visual indeterminacy.[34]

Interestingly, this seems to be precisely at issue in Beattie's *Dissertations Moral and Critical*. Although an avowed dogmatist in matters of moral knowledge (Beattie was a fierce, though not the most knowledgeable, opponent of David Hume), Beattie appears to take a less dogmatic view of linguistic sign systems. Like the *Enquiry*, the *Dissertations* suggest that words are not grounded in the ideas they refer to. Verbal signification rather constitutes a world of signs that we never need to depart from to make sense of the world:

> Whence comes it, that, on hearing the sounds, or seeing the characters, of a known language, the mind makes so quick a transition to the thing signified, that it seems to overlook the impression made on the eye or ear, and to attend to the meaning only? Is it not, because the articulate sound, or the written character, has long been associated with the idea signified, and had formed in the mind a habit of passing instantaneously from the one to the other?[35]

Musical signs are likewise arbitrary: "musicians express their notes . . . on paper; in the use of which, as in reading and writing, their minds instantly pass from the view of the sign to that meaning which custom has annexed to it."[36] But what is the relation between *custom* and *indeterminacy*, if *custom* might as well bring forth *determinacy*—in the customary relationship between signifier and signified? The answer is, of course, that arbitrary laws preclude absolute grounds: other signifiers might have been annexed to this or that signified. The annexation was never necessary and never the only possibility; things might have been different. The decisiveness of verbal mediation is thus never more than a random decisiveness.

In the *Dissertations*, the precariousness implied in this random decisiveness surfaces openly in poetic mediations of the sublime: foregrounding, instead of suppressing, the uncertain semantic footing of the "full" linguistic sign, such mediations are not decisive but rather leave things in the dark. Of course, this may be a luxury, a frivolity that verbal mediation can permit itself in unusual circumstances: to become momentarily what it feigns not to be—"empty," vague, incomplete. Yet in a game of mimicry, foundations and appearances are easily confused. Thus in Beattie's "Illustrations on Sublimity" the linguistic sign, *like the musical sign*, is capable of an imperfect mode of mediation that merely suggests: "In sublime description, though the circumstances that are specified be few . . . the reader's mind will complete the picture: and often . . . the image will not be less astonishing, if in its general appearance there be something indefinite."[37] After all, Beattie concedes in a lengthy note, not everything need be picturesque in poetry: "the mind is often better pleased with images of its own forming, or finishing, than with those that are set before it complete in all their colours and proportions."[38] If only to a degree, words here take on the preparatory role that the *Essays* had reserved for instrumental music: they leave something to be decided, to be pictured. As such, they are deeply implicated in a lack and it is this *lack* that makes signification possible, this *lack* that initiates an imaginative act of signification.

Could we thus say that poetic evocations of the sublime draw on musical procedures—or at least, procedures branded as "musical" in eighteenth-century critical theory—insofar as they presuppose an imaginative engagement? This may be a surprising conclusion since the effect of the sublime has been familiarly branded as baffling, overwhelming, debilitating—hence rendering *passive* an audience and precluding an active, imaginative response. Yet the idea of the sublime has, at least since Burke, also been attached to the issue of representational limits: showing less is implying more. "Imply" and "implication" connote involvement, and in texts like the *Enquiry* and the *Dissertations* the "imperfection" of verbal mediation is matched (if not conditioned) by an imaginative participation that makes the most out of bare hints. Artistic evocations of the sublime thus appear to feed on the felt presence of an absence: on an openness—semantic, visual, or both—that constantly suggests the possibility of something other, something out of bounds, which has not (yet) been presented.

Infinity and Intimation: Feelings Without End

Something other, something out of bounds: something infinite, something that refuses to materialize as concrete, finished form. In the *Enquiry*, Burke presents the idea of the infinite as an incomplete idea, an idea that (ever) requires fulfillment because it revolves around the idea of a potentially endless multiplication or expansion. Yet, as Burke rehearses Aristotle, most visible phenomena in nature *do not* multiply or extend indefinitely. Or, in reverse, the idea of the infinite cannot become an object of sense perception, since the infinite *qua* infinite transcends every measure of sense. Therefore, Burke argues, the infinite can only manifest itself in nature as an illusion. One only experiences the effect of a *suggestion* of infinity when one is confronted with apparently boundless land- or seascapes: "Infinity has a tendency to fill the mind with that sort of delightful horror, which is the most genuine effect, and truest test of the sublime. *There are scarce any things which can become objects of our senses that are really, and in their own nature infinite.* But the eye not being able to perceive the bounds of many things, they seem to be infinite, and they produce the same effects as if they were really so" (*ESB* II, sect. VIII, 67, my emphasis).

Here it is once more: a simulation; a "realism in effect" that demands a willing suspension of disbelief—an imaginative willingness to pretend as if no ends or boundaries were present. Such would-be infinite objects as appear in nature, or in architecture and art, "impress the imagination with an idea of their progress beyond their actual limits," and it is this felt possibility of an indefinite progression that "can stamp on bounded objects the character of infinity"—albeit quite emphatically an "artificial infinity" (*ESB* II, sect. IX, 68).

Such a suggestion of endless continuation is brought about by an open-ended progression of similar parts—say, a straight line of dots, which can be multiplied potentially without end. Since there is no alteration, there is no limit to successively placing one dot after another—one could go on indefinitely. This means that the artificial infinite revolves around "a *repetition* of *similar* ideas": a reiteration of the same without ever coming to a close (*ESB* IV, sect. XIII, 129).

One senses a touch of Locke in this marriage of repetition and the infinite. In the *Essay Concerning Human Understanding*, Locke had observed that the idea of infinity is based on a "power we observe in ourselves of repeating, without end, our own *ideas*." In this "endless repetition, there is continued an enlargement"—or at least, there is the open possibility of such a continuous enlargement, to which there is potentially no conclusion or resolution.[39] Thus, Locke observes (in a passage that remarkably anticipates Kant's mathematical estimation of magnitude in the *Critique of Judgment*):

> Everyone that has any *idéa* of any stated lengths of space, as a foot, finds that he can repeat that *idea*; and joining it to the former, make the *idea* of two feet; and by the addition of a third, three feet; and so on, without ever coming to an end of his additions, whether the same *idea* of a foot, or, if he pleases, of doubling it, or any other *idea* he has of any length, as a mile, or diameter of the earth, or of the *orbis magnus*: for whichsoever of these he takes, and how often soever he doubles or any otherwise multiplies it, he finds that, after he has continued his doubling in his thoughts and enlarged his *idea* as much as he pleases, he has no more reason to stop, nor is one jot nearer the end of such addition than he was at first setting out: the power of enlarging his *idea* of space by further additions remaining still the same, he hence takes *the idea of infinite space*.[40]

Typically the empiricist, Locke therefore presumes that the idea of infinity is ultimately derived from experience: the idea of infinity is "begotten" when one finds that one's mental capacity to multiply similar ideas remains equally unbounded even, if not especially, when one is not "one jot nearer the end" of such multiplication than the initial addition of one foot to one foot into two feet. One can go on *ad infinitum*, and it is this realization that makes for an idea of infinity.

Ironically, therefore, the idea of an incessant progression ultimately turns on a certain stasis or immobility: a remaining within the same place, brought about by the continuous return to one's initial position (having ultimately come not one bit further to the end of the addition than at the starting point). The idea of infinity can thus be defined as a never-coming-one-step-closer-to-an-end: it is like running after the moon, the distance between yourself and the moon remaining ever the same, though it seems to stretch ever further.

Moreover, the possibility of such a continuing without end is conditioned by an idea of *divisibility*. Only those ideas that can be divided into (infinite) parts can be multiplied into (infinite) parts: "All the *ideas* that are considered as having parts, and are capable of increase by the addition of any equal or less parts, afford us, by their repetition, the *idea* of infinity." Apart from space, these concern ideas of number and duration—only these can be extended without end, "augmented to what proportion men please, or be stretched beyond what they have received by their senses." There thus being no limit to the virtual increase of such ideas, this repeated augmentation leaves "in the mind an *idea* of endless room for more; nor can we conceive anywhere a stop to a further addition or progression, and so those *ideas* alone lead our minds towards the thought of infinity."[41] Infinity is indeterminacy—it is the absence of a fixed ending, suggesting an open space in which a "next" is ever possible.

Likewise, the *Enquiry* presents the idea of the infinite in terms of an imagination that can find "no rest" in projecting an excess of similar ideas; in continuing a repetitive rhythm of uniform parts *ad infinitum* (*ESB* IV, sect. X, 126). Now, this "effect" of the infinite can nonetheless be mimicked by finite objects that resist closure in perception. Thus, Burke explains, when confronted with some oversized object, imagination cannot take in this object all at once. Here, "a perfect unity can no more be arrived at, than . . . a compleat whole to which nothing may be added' (*ESB* II, sect. VII, 66–67). Instead, as the object cannot be bounded in perception, imagination is caught in an *open-ended, successive* reproduction of (the idea of) the parts of this object. This is what Kant will later refer to as apprehension (*Auffassung*): to represent the parts of an excessively big object successively and potentially infinitely so, *because* this object cannot be comprehended. As such, the idea of the infinite is as it were performed in imagination's inability to represent a complete whole. By its nature, the infinite is inconclusive and this—this inability to settle or decide—is what the failure to imagine a perfect unity repeats.

In the *Enquiry*, there is a peculiar pleasure annexed to such inconclusiveness, when Burke considers a special and "imperfect" form of (of all things) pictorial representation. Thus, in "unfinished sketches or drawings," Burke finds "something which please[s] [him] beyond the best finishing" because here "the imagination is entertained with the promise of something more, and does not acquiesce in the present object of the sense" (*ESB* II, sect. XI, 70). Imagination is tense, restless, and *must* not be acquiesced for the delightful expectation of "something more," as yet immaterialized, to be preserved. It keeps on searching in an apparently empty space that, precisely, sustains the promise of a fulfillment yet to come.

For the same reason, Burke takes to spring and youth, rather than summer and the fully grown. He also states that a rose is "more beautiful before it is full blown; in the bud; before this exact figure is formed" (*ESB* II, sect. XI, 70; III, sect. II, 86). In this light of the infinite—the "truest test of the sublime"—indeterminacy appears to be of more significance to the Burkean sublime than a mere breeding ground of terror alone (*ESB* II, VIII, 67). As a felt presence of absence, indeterminacy conditions not just existential but rather also imaginative uncertainties in provoking (what I would like to call) an anticipating without end. Confronted with a mere fragment before any exact figure has been formed, the power of imagination operates in a space of suspension—an "in between space"—that indefinitely postpones a full determination of a figure or form. Thus, though not quite the transcendental and transformative power it would become for the romantics, the imagination is here nevertheless already actively engaged in divining what has not (yet) been given.

In chapter 2, I will elaborate in detail on the implications that this flexible, restless imagination may have for the passage of the sublime feeling. For now, my focus remains on the parallels between ideas of instrumental music and ideas of the artificial infinite in the montage of texts presented so far. What connects both ideas is the notion of an imperfect idea: the "effects" of the instrumental music (in its eighteenth-century critical conceptions) intersect with the "effects" of the artificial infinite to the extent that both act in the manner of the empty sign. Both open up a space of unbounded imaginative activity that, however, remains inconclusive because this very same openness obstructs a *goal-directed* activity. As a faculty of image-making, the imagination fails to produce a "complete whole," a perfect picture, and is to that extent ineffective. At the same time, this ineffectiveness intimates a potentially creative excess: in the absence of a stable given, the imagination can attempt a myriad of possible forms and images, which would attest to its flexibility and inventiveness. This is, at least, how Thomas Twining (the translator of Aristotle's *Ars Poetica*) represented the effects of instrumental music—as a self-experience of imaginative freedom:

> Music . . . is not *imitative*, but if I may hazard the expression, merely *suggestive*. But, whatever we may call it, this I will venture to say,—that in the *best* instrumental Music, expressively *performed*, the very indecision itself of the expression, leaving the hearer to the free operation of his *emotion* upon his *fancy*, and, as it were, to the free *choice* of such ideas as are, *to him*, most adapted to react upon and heighten the emotion which occasioned them, produces a pleasure, which nobody, I believe, who is able to feel it, will deny to be one of the most delicious that Music is capable of affording.[42]

The pleasure of instrumental music, Barry has argued, "lies in the excess of signification over and beyond the initial and incomplete sign the music had offered. The meaning of music depends upon the enigmatic character of its signs which . . . turn the listener to his own inventive subjectivity."[43]

Likewise, the pleasure of the artificial infinite is one of excessive anticipating in the etymological sense of preparing or a "taking before": before a limit has been set, before a form has materialized, the mind can "make it ready" and freely invent its possible configurations. The suspension of the limit sustains a pleasure of indeterminacy—the Burkean promise of something more.

Usher's *Clio, or a Discourse on Taste*, makes this intersection between ideas of instrumental music and the (artificial) infinite more explicit. Infinite might and extent constitute the heart of the sublime in *Clio*, but not only as an overpowering force that leaves the mind prostrate before it. Rather, as a specifically *religious* notion, the infinite here also signals a vague potentiality that opens up a space of engagement: of active and hopeful imaginative anticipation.

This potentiality, for Usher, "is not an *idea*, it is unknown."[44] It is not so much an obscure as a *fugitive* object that the mind forever, but fruitlessly, labors to bring into view: "whence you may conceive the distress, that obliges the poet to fly from image to image, to express what he feels. No idea, however grand, answers his purpose; yet as he feels strongly he still hopes, and rushes to snatch into view another grand prospect. The variety of his efforts shows the object the mind labours with to be different from anything we know; to be beyond the power of utterance" (*CD* 120–21).

As a "mighty unknown power," this potentiality beyond words occasions "obscure fears" and "obscure hopes"—the *tremendum et fascinans*, the trembling with fear and fascination that typifies religious passion (*CD* 113, 110). In *Clio*, this religious passion makes up "the source of the sublime sensation" insofar as the latter boils down to an irresoluteness or indecisiveness in the presence of something always already missed (*CD* 110).

An irresoluteness in the presence of something always missed: this is not only an inability to *grasp* or *decide* a potentiality that is beyond the powers of (re)cognition but also an inability to *regulate* and even *direct* the "obscure" experience of this potentiality. This experience is presented as a constant digression that never reaches a goal or destination and thus could go on an on, mimicking the fugitiveness and endlessness of the idea of the infinite "itself." As such, the sublime feeling would be a *disinterested*, because not a goal-oriented, feeling that remains purposively indecisive.

Thus, in *Clio* hope carries with it "the plainest symptoms of a passion that wanders, and is astray for its object." In its "anxious search" this wandering passion is directed toward a prospect "whose completion lies in the dark"—it is without a positive destination and, for that reason, even without a name (*CD* 111). Partaking of a religious passion whose "object" remains eternally unknown, the completion of hope's prospect lies *forever* in the dark: as a nameless desire in search of its object, hope's object is, and will remain, just around the corner, just out of reach, "for ever near us and for ever [hiding] from us" (*CD* 129). It is a desire that only *seems* to go forward, never getting anywhere and always repeating its search: ends are fugitive.

This offers an interesting parallel with Locke's idea of the infinite. Usher's wandering desire likewise revolves around a stasis or immobility (however much this immobility may be obscured by the illusion of an excessive, searching movement): a continuous return to your initial position, which never takes you a step closer to an end or goal. The (search for the) infinite is a labyrinth that makes release impossible. Yet however frustrating it may be, this aimlessness also constitutes the delight of the Usherian feeling of the infinite. It leaves an open space in which—as with Burke's unfinished things and drawings—the delightful promise of an "ever next" is preserved.

Indeed, though at once the site of hindrance and anxiety, in *Clio* the annihilation of this open space would equal the "annihilation of that bright-beaming human hope, that travels on before us during life" (*CD* 133). Hope is an end in itself, sustains its own rationale—and hope can only be sustained in the continued *postponement* of the realization of some dimly felt prospect. This is why Usher also refers to the religious passion as a "mighty unknown want": it expresses the "wandering" status of a desire that has not yet found and does not yet know its object, a desire that, indeed, comes before and suspends the materialization of an object that is always wanting. Desire here approaches the status of a Lacanian itch that can never be scratched because, of course, the scratching only increases the itching.[45] Thus, the Usherian subject can hope and desire infinitely: it is focused on an "obscure enthusiastic delight which we never enjoy" but can only delay interminably (*CD* 132). As such, the delight of the sublime becomes both impossible—a moment that can never be consummated—and always already "present" in this very impossibility. Such delight can, after all, only be sustained in the absence of a consummation.

Significantly, in *Clio* this impossible experience is analogously imagined as a musical experience—or, more accurately put, according to a (metaphysical) idea of music. Anticipating Twining's account of the effects of instrumental music, Usher circumscribes such a musical experience as cognitively abortive yet sensitively rich. Kevin Barry has, in this instance, already emphasized Usher's romantic sensibility to music, leading him to insert "a concept of music into the terms of rationalism and empiricism in such a way as

to subvert their very assumptions."[46] Though on the one hand conventionally associating music with the passions, *Clio* on the other hand also premediates early German romantic theories of instrumental music by representing
it as sensuous and abstract at the same time: as being "perceivable by the
mind but too unstable to be grasped as knowledge or idea" (*CD* 62). Thus,
Ushers observes, there are few

> who have not felt the charms of music. . . . It is a language of delightful
> sensations, that is far more eloquent than words. . . . We feel plainly that
> music touches and greatly agitates the agreeable and sublime passions; that it
> wraps us in melancholy, and elevates in joy; that it dissolves and inflames;
> that it melts us in tenderness, and rouses to rage: but its strokes are so fine
> and delicate, that, like a tragedy, even the passions that are wounded
> please. . . . Particularly the most elevated sensation of music arises from a
> confused perception of idle or visionary beauty and rapture, which is suffi-
> ciently perceivable to fire the imagination, but not clear enough to become
> an object of knowledge. This shadowy beauty the mind attempts, with a
> languishing curiosity, to collect into a distinct object of view and compre-
> hension; but it sinks and escapes, like the dissolving ideas of a delightful
> dream, that are neither within the reach of memory, nor yet totally fled. The
> noblest charm of music, then, though real and affecting, seems too confused
> to be collected into a distinct idea. (*CD* 152–56)

A sublime connection here first of all appears in music's "strokes" being
so gentle that even painful passions please and, of course, in its association
with tragedy. Second, and more important, in eluding appropriation instrumental music becomes the very equivalent of the vacant or open, fugitive
object of the Usherian sublime. Like this fugitive object, music in *Clio* kindles and challenges imagination, but its "visionary rapture" cannot be cap-
tured and individuated as "an object of knowledge." At once very close and
distant, at once intimate and obscure, music contradicts an exact and complete appropriation.

Usher's analogy of "musical effects" with the at once lingering and dissolving ideas of a "delightful dream" are, for that matter, illuminating here.
It points to the impossibility of exactly recalling and retrieving an unconscious state within the (verbal) representations of consciousness: on waking,
the dream is irretrievably, if not totally, lost; it has become inaccessible *as
such*. Even when immediately recalled, there is always something missing,
something escaping in one's very recounting or remembering of it. And one

cannot say precisely *what* is escaping—all one knows is that one's recon-
struction does not quite cover the strange, little details or the precise atmosphere of the dream dreamed while asleep. So it is with music for Usher.
Like the fugitive object of the sublime, it leaves a trace of something other,
something different that could not be held or kept: something of which one
cannot say if it was ever really present at all.

I would like to call this vague hint of unstable presences an *intimation* and
connect it to the sublime for the following two reasons. First, intimation
connotes something intimate, inmost even, and distant at once, something
that is privately and intensely felt (like a dream) yet at the same time dodges
the full grasp of imagination, memory, and cognition. Second, and as such,
intimation is a radical form of suggestion that leaves not so much an open
space to be filled in as an emptiness that, one feels, *cannot* be satisfactorily
and completely filled. An intimation is a barely perceptible hint or trace of
something indefinable that cannot be entirely recovered, which is lost or
"beyond" yet in a strange way also part of oneself. It fades as an unknown
but it also lingers inside as an indeterminate feeling. In intimation, all one
has is a remainder or residue of something persisting systematically as lack—
and this is precisely how one feels the infinite.

This concept of intimation recollects the texts discussed in this chapter.
As I have tried to show, ideas of the sublime and instrumental music intersect as imperfect ideas, the latter triggering affectively the metaphysical "attributes" of the former through a hesitating, imperfect feeling. Thus, we
have seen how in the *Enquiry* the sublime can only be occasioned through
lack and indetermination, since it is these that evoke—or at least quicken—
the affect of terror. As clear and unmistakable an affect terror may be, it is
nonetheless typically troubled by a lack of overview, of sensing a possible
danger without being able to see. In these situations it is the organ of hearing that, as Barthes has remarked, is "poised like an animal on the *alert*"—
the ear is the organ of fear, as Nietzsche once noted, the organ of the night:
in the dark, alone at home, I am sitting downstairs while upstairs I suddenly
hear a door slam shut.[47] I am caught by the impending that I cannot yet
determine. It may be nothing, it may be just the wind . . . or yet. This
undecidability of the ear is, perhaps, only rivaled in the uncertain reading of
barely visible shadows, faint outlines in the distance, or (as Burke suggested)
unfinished forms. In these instances, the eye bends to the ear; the visual
becomes like an aural field in that one sees not in overview but in
indetermination.

While in Beattie's texts such indetermination still appears solvable, Usher cultivates it into an affective intimation: an affect that counterpoints, as it were, the musical and sublime. Over the course of the nineteenth century, as I will argue in the next chapter, this affective movement of intimation will come to dominate especially German romantic aesthetics of instrumental music and the sublime. Echoing Usher's wandering desire, the romantic sublime feeling becomes a feeling of endless desire that not only thrives on empty landscapes and long distances but also on the empty sign and the material evanescence of music: musical sounds embody a movement of loss insofar as their appearance marks their instant departure, their drifting and dispersing away into space. Conceived as such, instrumental music comes to perform the sublime "as such": as a movement of loss.

2.   Sehnsucht, *Music, and the Sublime*

In his *Allgemeine theorie der schönen Künste*, Johann Georg Sulzer does not confine the experience of the sublime to feelings of wonder, terror, respect, or elevation. The sublime is "the highest in art, and must be employed when the mind is to be attacked with powerful strokes, when admiration, awe, powerful longing, high courage, or also fear or terror are to be aroused."[1] Powerful longing, excessive and aimless—this recalls James Usher's mighty unknown want as a modality of the sublime feeling. Filtered by our readings of the pseudo-Longinus, Burke, and Kant, today's outlook has obstructed this modality from view, but there it is, tucked away among passions such as awe, courage, fear, and terror, which we have familiarly associated with the sublime: *sehnen*.

Sehnen—*Sehnsucht*: the romantic, catastrophic longing for the infinite that can repeat itself infinitely. Bent on preventing its own realization, *Sehnsucht* overturns conventional distinctions between pain and pleasure, end and endlessness, want and fulfillment, stasis and infinite movement. Pain becomes a pleasure, endlessness an end, want a fulfilment—all these distinctions collapse into each other when *Sehnsucht*'s peculiar logic reigns. Yet it is not an altogether unreasonable logic. We have encountered the same logic in Locke's theory of the infinite and in Burke's adaptation of it: endless movement that is at the same time stasis, stillness, immobility.

In this chapter, I will argue that *Sehnsucht*, instrumental music, and the sublime can be seen as intersecting concepts that partake of a poetics and an aesthetics of indeterminacy in later eighteenth-century German criticism. I use the term "concept" to emphasize the status of instrumental music as a philosophical tool rather than a concrete phenomenon in this context. As Mark Evan Bonds has suggested, early romantic views of instrumental music "reflected fundamental transformations in contemporary philosophy and . . . aesthetics that were unrelated to the music of the time." Notwithstanding the "new-found prestige of instrumental music in the later eighteenth century," the new aesthetics of music in Germany and central Europe were

47

"not primarily driven by changes in the musical repertory."[2] Thus, when writers such as Wilhelm Wackenroder and Ludwig Tieck were engaged with instrumental music, they were engaged in thinking and debating issues relevant to (a then resurging) idealist philosophy, rather than only with "real" issues and developments in contemporary instrumental music.

Seen in this light, "instrumental music" in early romantic German criticism and aesthetics signifies less a heterogeneous cultural practice than a conceptual vehicle to think and fantasize the infinite. This, of course, does not deny the presence of such a heterogeneous practice (indeed, the appropriation of instrumental music as a conceptual vehicle signals a cultural practice in itself). But it does locate the "musical" in a more ideational, metaphysical space. Hence the early romantic tendency to refer to instrumental music in the general instead of the singular: *this* or *that* music hardly matters. This is not so say—as Daniel Chua has suggested—that instrumental music (as a "real practice") is invested with metaphysical significance, but that metaphysical issues such as the absolute, the infinite, or the eternal are thought musically.[3] The difference is subtle but real, and it should prevent us from viewing later eighteenth-century instrumental music solely as a practice "out of step" with contemporary musical imaginings (such as Tieck's and Wackenroder's) that allegedly foreshadowed the nineteenth-century practice of absolute music.

Likewise, I approach *Sehnsucht* in early German romantic literature and idealist philosophy as a vehicle to intimate the infinite in terms of radical indeterminacy. As real a feeling as it may be in the fictional world of Goethe's *Werther* or Jean Paul's *Hesperus*, *Sehnsucht* is much more than "just a feeling": it is, rather, a particular *configuration* of lack and endless movement that can figure in many different settings. Thus, *Sehnsucht* is not restricted to literary genres as "theme" but also features prominently in philosophical discourses of German idealism as a *rhythm* and *figure* of thought.[4] Indeed, I will argue, far from being a mere childish refusal of the given, *Sehnsucht* premediates a strand of German idealist philosophy that tries to think through the impossible unity of subject and object: the impossibility of the I (as a thinking, reflecting I) to coincide with itself as not-I.

In romantic music criticism, I will show, this impossibility of coincidence is foregrounded in the representation of the semantically "empty" ways of instrumental music: the suspension of a coincidence between signifier and signified. The dynamic between them has the nature of an infinite regress— which is why the idea of the infinite is thought "musically" so easily, so "naturally," in the romantic period. I will thus argue that, as a vehicle of the infinite, instrumental music invokes *Sehnsucht* as a movement that differs and defers at once.

Analyzing these intersections between instrumental music and *Sehnsucht* in the light of the infinite, I show how they rehearse *and* transform the standard, eighteenth-century German conception of the sublime. I trace this standard conception to the discourse of elevation typifying Immanuel Kant's analytic of the mathematical sublime in the *Critique of Judgment*. To show how this standard conception can be countered from within the romantic tradition, I use E. T. A. Hoffmann's criticism of Beethoven's Fifth Symphony as my starting point.[5] Both are well-worn texts in the literature of the sublime and music, but in their juxtaposition they also reinvent each other. Thus, presenting a famous "case" of musical *Sehnsucht*, Hoffmann's account of Beethoven's Fifth can be at once posited as an alternative to the logic of transgression that marks the Kantian sublime. While Kant's analytic casts the experience of the sublime in a plotlike structure that allows pain to be succeeded and removed by pleasure, musical *Sehnsucht* resists such a dialectical moment. As an "instance" of the infinite, it rather allows pain and pleasure to be thought as fatally intertwined, as two aspects of a movement that cannot be concluded.

Sehnsucht *and the Divided I*

Suspense—which is of crucial significance to Burke's *Enquiry*—relates to suspension (from Latin *suspendere*: "to hang, stop"): a word that connotes delay or deferral with a specific echo of "hanging" (loosely) or "dangling" due to the Latin relation to *pendere* (to cause to hang, weigh). Thus, to suspend not only has the dimension of postponing, but also—and at once—of an uncertainty of footing and direction: of dawdling, one might say, and dangling in mid-air.

As a romantic condition, *Sehnsucht* revolves around this space of suspension. It denotes the suffering of a desire that constantly eludes its goal or destination: *Sehnsucht* is typified by—to borrow an aspect of the Kantian aesthetic judgment—a purposeful purposelessness.[6] Its *movens* is a deferral of finality, a paradoxical drive to render the provisional permanent. Thus, Goethe's Werther exclaims:

> Oh, it is with the distant as with the future! A vast, dim All [*ein großes dämmern-des Ganzes*] rests before our soul, our feeling [*Empfindung*] melts in it like our eyes, and we yearn [*sehnen uns*], ah!, to completely surrender ourselves to it,

to be filled with all the delight of a single, great, delicious feeling—And oh! when we run towards it, when the yonder now becomes here [*wenn das Dort nun Hier wird*], everything is as it was before, and we stand in our poverty, in our limitedness, and our soul craves for comforts slipped away [*entschlüpftem Labsale*].[7]

Typically, Werther can only intimate a harmonious "All" and the unitary fulfilment it would instill in his soul. He has a dim awareness of it, but of course it dissolves precisely when it comes near. The magic is gone when the anticipation, the distance, is gone, precisely because his desire *projects* that wonderful "All." The latter does not "exist" on its own—it is but a symptom, a side effect that cannot be reached outside the movement of desire. And so Werther speaks of a mental world full of premonitions and vague desires that he prefers to a world of presentation or *Darstellung*.[8]

In this respect, *Sehnsucht* could be said to rehearse affectively the movements of a free imagination that in the Kantian aesthetic judgment "produces traces of forms without aiming at particular forms": that suspend a definite presentation.[9] In Kant's analytic, this suspension is intimately tied to the most defining quality of the feeling of the beautiful: this is a pleasure that has the nature of a disinterested feeling. It is in no way concerned with the "actual" existence of an object but bears purely on the reflective engagements of the power of imagination with the formal qualities of that object.

To connect (however provisionally) such disinterestedness to *Sehnsucht* might nonetheless be hazardous: in a "proper" aesthetic judgment, after all, I do not "want" the object of contemplation. I have no interest in it; I do not desire it. And still. There is desire and desire. There is, indeed, a *movens* of desire that undoes any "interest" in actual objects. This *movens* is lack— and the need and absence this lack wants to feed itself. It wants no objects; it wants repetition. And this is what *Sehnsucht* embodies: the very disinterestedness of desire *qua* desire. It does not want its objects as *real* objects—not only because they are not "real" but projected objects anyway, never existing outside the rhythm of desire, but because as "real" fulfillments they would obstruct desire's condition of possibility. Such objects are therefore strictly experienced in their suspended potentiality rather than in their possible actuality. Their existence remains indifferent.

Seen in this light, *Sehnsucht* needs the possibility of expansion, of a future in a most general sense: an empty space ahead that opens up prospects of becoming. It bypasses objects (hence its disinterestedness) and thrives on outlooks that remain distant ever more (hence its purposeful purposelessness). Anthropologically it is, perhaps, just this possibility of expansion that the *Sehnsüchtiger* wants to (re)instate—a possibility symbolized in fictional worlds of youth and spring, of dawn and early hours where things have not yet been definitely configured. Give me back the times, as the poet in Goethe's *Faust* exclaims, "When I was still becoming, / . . . When mists [*nebel*] shrouded my world, / The buds still promised wonders, / . . . Give me back my youth!"[10] It could well be that *in* the unfulfilled yearning for a dim "yonder" such a desired state of youthful incompleteness is enacted: as an indeterminate feeling that instates the promise of an "about to be," of hope, it also preserves the promise of a future in which things may yet come to be. *Sehnsucht* thus performs again and again a "great outlook of becoming" that cannot well be sustained in a life-track of choices and decisions. It is a desire that defies limitation.

Seen in this light, the paradoxical delight of indeterminacy central to *Sehnsucht* consists in the fact that this wandering desire *itself* seems to amend for a future irretrievably lost. However painful, *Sehnsucht's* unrealized longing repeats experientially the desired incompleteness associated with youth, dawn, or spring. Therefore, the place where the *Sehnsüchtiger* would like to linger (always repeating the openness ascribed to a magic "once" where something may yet be occurring, and all one has to do is wait for it to happen) is at a point right before a moment of fulfilment or revelation—just a glimpse of these, and never more. Despite all the restlessness involved, what the *Sehnsüchtiger* wants to do is to postpone the course of time, change, and movement. He wants to remain in a vacuum where things have not occurred or evolved just yet. In this way, the ungraspable infinite for which he yearns is already felt in the openness of an impossible, permanent not-yet. As with Locke, infinity is felt in never coming one step closer to an end, so that there remains endless, empty room for more (repetition). If this emptiness hurts, it also helps against hurting: it makes for tension but for respite at the same time.

Disinterested, purposefully purposeless, repetitive, paradoxical, or at least internally conflicting: this is how we could conceptualize *Sehnsucht*. Its aesthetic frame, but most of all its impossible mixture of contradictory "states" and "affects," brings the experience of the sublime irresistibly into view: the experience of a pain that is a pleasure at the same time. However, at this point I will ward off this imminent approach. There are many threads leading from *Sehnsucht* to the sublime and vice versa, but there is a critical aspect to the former that must be elucidated before putting it in juxtaposition with the latter—and it will make this juxtaposition all the more pressing.

An Unattainable I: Différance in German Idealism

We have seen that *Sehnsucht* (re)enacts a desire "forward" that is really an impossible desire "backward." It never coincides with its object. This impossibility of coincidence could be symptomatic of a self that is internally divided: a self that fails to coincide with itself because it can only define itself negatively *through lack*: a craving for the craving to be One (Werther's "vast, dim All"). This raises the question if *Sehnsucht* is not so much about an I longing for an All outside of itself, out of bounds, as about an I longing for an All it can only possess as loss, as "once-own," however imaginary this "own" may be. Seen in this perspective, I would like to propose that *Sehnsucht*'s fugitive rhythm or movement—and the concomitant suspension of the I—premediates a strand of German idealist philosophy that tries to think through the impossible unity of subject and object.

One of the key figures in this respect is Friedrich Hölderlin, who critically attempted the issue of self-consciousness addressed by Kant and Fichte.[11] Both had claimed that the subject constitutes itself by contrasting itself to an object. Both, however, had failed to explain the nature of the object as well as the ways in which the subject as a configuration in the abstract and the actual experience of a conscious self could be connected. How can I be I, how do I know objectively that "I" is "I," and how do I know what is not-I? The answer to this question is evidently beyond the bounds of this chapter, yet its ramifications are relevant to the ways in which *Sehnsucht* can be said to be absorbed in a speculative play on the preconditions of the self. This would render *Sehnsucht* less an existential theme that foregrounds the pains connected with choices and decisions than a pattern of infinite approximation rehearsed in the ontological dilemma that the self as subject cannot coincide with the self as object: the unity between them is a unity that remains necessarily beyond reach.

Fichte, Andrew Bowie has stressed, already recognized this dilemma when stating that self-consciousness cannot ensure self-sameness, since to recognize myself *as* myself always already presupposes a splitting of self: *in* the very act of thinking, some part of the *Ich* already differentiates itself as subject *and* object, looking at itself looking.[12] The result is an infinite series of reflections that never really touches ground. I can go on thinking myself *as* myself but never actually reach myself in perfect unity, since I constantly try to approach myself by separating myself as other.

Fichte tried to resolve this pattern of infinite approximation by grounding self-consciousness in the very act of *becoming* conscious: the act of recognizing myself in opposition to material objects that are not-self (*Nicht-Ich*). I am I when I see what is not-I; I depends on not-I in a process of differentiation. Hölderlin problematized this approach: such an act would have to be preceded by a judgment that allows the self to recognize *at all* what is self and not-self—how else would I know which acts belong to which self? Judgment or *Urtheil* in Hölderlin's notes on Fichte's lectures thus becomes *Ur-theil* or arche-partition, of which subject and object (self and not-self) are *the effect*.[13] They are *instated* by a movement of separation inherent in reflection (when the self ponders on itself and dissociates itself as an object *to be* pondered on): "*Judgment*—is in the highest and most strict sense the original [*ursprünglich*] separation of the most tight unity of object and subject in intellectual intuition, that separation which makes object and subject first possible."[14]

The absolute I, the prereflective unity of subject and object, is therefore an unknowable entity: a point that will never be reached. Since lack is originary, the I has no recoverable basis. It cannot point and say: this is where I originate, since "this" is no positive place but always already a process of differentiation, dispersion, and disappearance. As Jean-François Lyotard would say, there is a veritable *différend* or irresolvable conflict between the I as unity and the I as identity, since the absoluteness of the absolute I as unity lacks the consciousness of identity, and vice versa:

> [Fichte's] absolute I (= Spinoza's substance) contains all reality; it is everything and has nothing outside it; there is thus no object for this absolute I, for otherwise all reality would be in it; but a consciousness without object is unthinkable, and if I am myself this object, then I am as such necessarily limited, even if it is only in time, and thus not absolute; therefore it is not possible to think consciousness in this absolute I; as absolute I, I have no consciousness, to that extent I am (for myself) nothing, which means that the absolute I is (for me) nothing.[15]

This absolute loss of absoluteness in the I as self-identification—and the absolute loss of consciousness in the absolute I—stages an aporia of the limitless and the limited. This aporia sets in motion a process of infinite reflection (whereby the I keeps on breaking itself up in attempting to unite itself with itself) that recalls the structure of infinite approximation characteristic of *Sehnsucht*. Like the "yonder" that *should* remain "yonder" if it is not to disappear in the here and now, the absolute I as unity evaporates *just when* the I identifies itself—and inevitably divides itself. This reciprocal process of striving and dividing parallels (if not performs) the logic of *Sehnsucht*, and it sets in motion a thought process that has the nature of an eternal discord—the strife for something lost that is tied to us *as* lack. Or, as Hölderlin puts it in the *Fragment of Hyperion*, there is something "defective that thinks and lives in me, wants to extend itself, and encompass the infinite."[16] I have, so to speak, a defective drive to un-become myself.

In his *Fichte Studies*, Novalis addressed the same issue, though his account of the (im)possibility of self-presentation focuses prominently on the problem of the I as signifier.[17] For Novalis, the I can only present itself through an endless series of mediations. Consciousness can only "look at" itself by *representing*—and thus once more dividing—itself. To coincide with itself, the I would have to *feel* itself instantaneously *as* itself, but then, Novalis asks, what "is a feeling? It can only be observed in reflection—the spirit of feeling is then gone."[18] The I as absolute unity is therefore unknowable and an imaginary site of endless striving: the I never reaches rest (oneness, undividedness) so long as it is an I.[19] This endless striving has the nature of an infinite shifting or deferring. Following Fichte, Novalis postulates that "I is only thinkable through a not-I" and *is* "only an I insofar as it is a not-I"—that is to say, is posited *differentially*; the I is what it is in the difference with not-I, the other of itself. This indeed makes the absolute I inaccessible, for as an "origin" it is only instated afterward, as an effect of the act of opposition between I and not-I.

Central to the impossible unity of subject and object, of I and not-I, is thus the idea of an interminable postponement. In this way, I would like to suggest, Novalis's idea of constant delay remediates (reworks and transforms) the rhythm of infinite approximation typical of Goethean *Sehnsucht* into a *conceptual pattern*: literally a mode of thinking. Insofar as (idealist) philosophy revolves around the uncovering of the ground of the absolute I, this makes the "drive to philosophize"—the drive to hit ground and know it—into an "unending activity": this drive can always only be satisfied "relatively," because this ground can only be posited differentially. As such, this ground can only be known "negatively": "All searching for a *single principle* would be like the attempt to square the circle."[20] That principle is always already beyond reach and conception, since it postulates a beginning that is older than the moment of reflection. Philosophy, as Bowie has put it, should therefore learn to live with "its own inherent failure to be complete."[21]

How do these idealist discourses deepen and enlighten *Sehnsucht* as an interminably suspended experience of the infinite? Read in juxtaposition with these discourses, *Sehnsucht* emerges as a feeling that foregrounds the (epistemological) groundlessness of the subject. The subject, we have seen in Hölderlin's and Novalis's speculations, has no basis or beginning that is recoverable. Indeed, its basis is an "after" since this basis is the effect of a differentiation. It is this idea of origin as lack and diffusion, I would like to propose, that critically informs *Sehnsucht* as a romantic affliction: it accounts for the fact that *Sehnsucht* is *inherently destined* to *un*realize its (apparent) goal—the fulfilment or unification of the I. It is not simply boredom, disappointment, or a childish refusal to accept the given but rather the fateful process of an I that makes its originary moment—its blissful "once"—disappear again and again as it tries to recover itself that motivates *Sehnsucht* as a rhythm of constant, aimless return.

Musical Sehnsucht *and the Romantic Sublime*

In romantic literature, *Sehnsucht*'s dependability on lack and absence opens up a special connection with instrumental music. For writers such as Jean Paul, a felt sense of lack precisely becomes a *condition* for musical response-ability: what music purely instrumental "wants" or "requires" from its listeners is a penetrating self-insight, a recognition of their "own nameless longing." It wants involvement, submission, and even faith, so that these listeners sigh and exclaim: "Truly all that [music] you name I lack."[22] These words from Jean Paul's *Hesperus* are in fact Horion's, who is reflecting on *Sehnsucht* while hearing a garden concert from the distance. Echoing Usher's wandering desire, Horion describes *Sehnsucht* as a "great wish that will never be fulfilled": "it does not have a name, it is in search of its object [*er sucht seinen Gegenstand*]."[23] It comes when, "on a summer night, you look to the north, or to the far mountains, or when moonlight shines the earth or the heavens are full of stars, or when you are very unhappy. This great, awesome [*ungeheuer*] wish moves our spirit upward [*hebt unsern Geist empor*] but with pains: ah! lying down, we are tossed into the sky like epileptics [*Fallsüchtigen*]."[24]

Comparable to the sublime-as-elevation, upward movement is attended by pain, yet this pain does not signal the success but the very failure of transcendence. Instead of rising above ourselves, we are "tossed into the sky like epileptics," prone to falling, which no doubt symbolizes the disillusionment of wish fulfillment already described in Goethe's *Werther*. Insofar, however,

as the tones of music here nevertheless name the incurable lack that cannot
be expressed *as* name in words, they become a vessel of truth, mirroring the
rising and (inevitably) falling movements of the spirit. They name not *what*
I lack; they name my *lack*, my endless, unresolved yearning.

Wilhelm Wackenroder describes the articulation of a likeminded, restless
desire in relation to music in the *Phantasien über die Kunst für Freunde der
Kunst* (*Fantasies on Art for Friends of Art*), published after Wackenroder's un-
timely death in 1798, by Ludwig Tieck in 1799. In these rhapsodic reflections Wackenroder positions instrumental music as a vehicle of unresolved
longing. Reducing music to abstract patterns that seem to be derived from
the recurrent increase and decrease of tension in tonal music, Wackenroder
recognizes in these patterns "the ever-oscillating swelling and subsiding of
Sehnsucht."[25] These patterns mimic *and* trigger a continuous up-and-down
movement of tension and respite. With "lascivious rancor [*wollüstigen
Unmut*]," the soul twists from one "unsatisfied striving" to another, fruitlessly struggling for resolution (*PK* 73). Even when it comes, this moment
of resolution is not so much relieving as sad and undesirable: the tension
of *Sehnsucht* is a tension that "in the end resolves itself only with tears"
(*PK* 73).

The cyclical tensions of tonal music thus enact for Wackenroder the
movements of tireless *Sehnsucht*, but the lack that it names is also the lack of
its ambiguous, open sign.[26] If the romantic craving for yearning revolves
around a continued deferral of presentation, Wackenroder represents instrumental music as being most suited to the purpose: as a holy mystery, allowing the listener to the limit of revelation and then withdrawing itself again.
As Wackenroder cryptically describes the indeterminacy of musical meaning: "Music wraps itself around people [*sie spielt um den Menschen*], it wants
nothing and everything. It is a medium finer than language, perhaps softer
than its thoughts. The spirit can no longer use it as a means, as an instrument. Rather, music is substance itself [*sie ist Sache selbst*], which is why it
lives and moves in its own magic circle [*Zauberkreis*]" (*PK* 45–46).

Music wants, means "nothing and everything," and, like the impossible
feeling of *Sehnsucht* it arouses, cannot be used as a means for an end: it is an
end in itself. Musical sounds do not individualize specifiable objects, they
are engaged in their own self-enclosed game—a prison-house of music—
which touches the romantic listener profoundly yet at the same time eludes
him (or her) completely. The "*spielt um*," after all, suggests *Umspielen*: an
almost physical nearness on the one hand, an encircling or entwining, but

on the other hand a teasing distance, a skirting around or past the listener's conceptual grasp.

Ludwig Tieck is likewise fascinated by music's alleged autonomy and its semantic indeterminacy. Thus, in "Die Töne" ("Tones") he states that music operates beyond the confines of any mimetic principle. Sculpture, drawing, and painting, according to Tieck, derive their images, their "subject matter," from a living and identifiable nature—from an "other" that is not themselves, however much transformed and beautified—and to that extent depend on it. Music, on the other hand, operates in the absence of a signified, engaging the listener not in a play of make-believe and illusory recognition but in an infinite play of signifiers that "speak nothing." Its tones "do not imitate, do not beautify, they are a separate world onto themselves" (*PK* 88).

This is why these tones do not make any immediate, definite sense to their listeners. Musical tones refer to and differ from each other, rather than beyond themselves to a world in waiting. Accordingly, Tieck describes the constitutive elements of music as "fluid," like

> a transparent, crystal-clear stream. In the shimmering tones, the eye in fact often believes to see delightful, ethereal, and elevated figures trying to merge as one, working themselves up from the deep, growing clearer and clearer in the flowing tones. The true pleasure of music, however, is that it allows nothing to become a true reality [*daß sie nichts zu wahren Wirklichkeit gelangen läßt*], for with a glaring sound everything bursts [like a bubble] again, and new creations are in preparation. (*PK* 89)

Here, musical tones are condemned to what Paul de Man has described as a "persistently frustrated intent toward meaning."[27] As "signs," the sounds of music are open, transparent like a water surface. Yet as such they do not allow the listener to "see through" the looking glass and find a fixed reality on the other side. Rather—and hence the association of musical tones with a continuous flux—though possible "signifieds" shimmer through the stream, they burst apart just before they reach the surface, just before they materialize as one, as concrete meaning. Then the whole process starts anew, with "new creations" in the making that likewise will never be finalized. As open signs, transparent and opaque at once, musical sounds thus not totally exclude a signified but continuously defer the realization of a *determinate* signified. They raise, so to speak, a promise of meaning that is never made good, which evaporates in the very act of listening. The ear, here represented metaphorically as an eye that cannot "see through" and cannot contain or retain a signified, is caught in an infinite, circular play of signifiers.

Jean Paul would couple this semantic diffuseness to a material diffuseness in his *Preparatory School for Aesthetics*. Romantic sounds, he writes, such as the "wavelike ringing of a string or bell," materialize the idea of indefinite "*expanse*" as they ever-fade into the distance.[28] Growing "faint in endless space," these sounds allow imagination to linger without end in what he calls "a twilight realm of holy anticipation": imaginative freedom.[29] A similar claim had, in fact, already been made by Carl Grosse, a practitioner of the Gothic and a theorist of the sublime in the Burkean tradition. Critically elaborating on the notion of obscurity (and its centrality to the sublime as expounded by Burke and Beattie), Grosse states that unclear or difficult ideas, unfinished things, silence, and emptiness overwhelm yet also activate the power of imagination, allowing it to fantasize without limits. For that same reason, "a soft music heard from afar is much more stirring than if heard in the concert hall; and the wavering tones of the distant [*Entfernung*, connoting separation] set off the power of imagination [*Einbildungskraft*] into a realm of scattering images; a few brushstrokes [*Züge*] suffice to inspire their course, just as they bring the passions to a greater intensity than full clarity and thoroughly painted [*ausgepinselte*] sketches."[30]

For Grosse, the sublime of sounds manifests itself in broken or faint tones signaling an indefinite expanse: an undersaturated presence that works its effects by concealing its full extent. In fact, it is the organ of the ear that is, according to Grosse, *already* most suited to an indefinite *Schwärmerei* (literally, a swarming out or about, but also connoting a rapture or enthusiasm) of imagination.[31] Given the obscurity that conditions the possibility of sublime evocation, Grosse remarks, "the ear is more suitable than the eye to create images and agitate the passions." Seen in this light, obscurity presents the difficulty, the incitement to imaginative "labor," without which the delight of the sublime can, for Grosse, not be felt.

This labor is, so to speak, indefinite in music's endless shimmering of signifiers: it becomes an approximation without end, an ongoing activity and productivity—the mind is here excited indeterminately, aimlessly. Scholars such as Andrew Bowie and James Hodkinson have pointed out that precisely because of this indeterminacy instrumental music brings "a feeling of wholeness to the listener": as an art without words, Novalis suggested, instrumental music dodges the reflexivity of language and would thus temporarily relieve the self's constant awareness of its own, inherent need.[32] (And this is very generally speaking.) The self, as Bowie epitomizes Novalis, forgets this need for a while when addressed by the "language" of instrumental music, which is more dominantly self-referential than verbal language.[33] Music would thus be intoxication, blissful interruption. Yet at the same time music's self-referentiality problematizes such interruptions. Self-referentiality in this context bears on the notion of the empty sign that "guarantees" the autonomy of music celebrated by Wackenroder, Tieck, and Novalis. As we have seen, there is nothing in nature for music to copy, nothing already there that it represents: its signs lack a stable signified and rather release a free play of signifiers referring to each other instead of a world beyond. Thus, music constitutes a universe on its own that has no imitative bearing on "external" reality.

Now in my view, this earmark of the empty sign in the early romantic conception of instrumental music precisely *foregrounds* the impossible recovery of a lost unity "lived" by the reflecting self. That is to say: the (romantic) "fate" of musical signifiers never coinciding with a stable signified but always hesitating on the brink of signification reflects the "fate" of the subject (I) that never overlaps with its object (not-I). As an open sign, the musical sign is subjected to a lack that perpetuates the play of signifiers, constantly deferring a shortcut to the signified, and, as such, it motivates its privileged position as a vehicle of the infinite and of infinite longing in early romantic writing.

In the following paragraphs, I will show how this identification of music with the infinite can be transmitted to the Kantian sublime by way of (musical) *Sehnsucht*. I will do so by juxtaposing Hoffmann's reviews of Beethoven's Fifth Symphony as facilitating a sense of endless yearning with Kant's representation of imagination's fruitless attempts to present the infinite as a coherent whole. In both texts, the frustration of a comprehensive overview (however differently conceived) plays a central role. Yet it is only in Hoffmann's text that this frustration is connected to the productive lack of instrumental music as a medium of semantic undecidability.

Hoffmann's Beethoven

In 1798, Václav Jan Tomášek attended a Beethoven concert in Prague. In the annual *Libussa* for 1845, he recalls how the music gripped him instantly: "Because of Beethoven's grand performance [*großartiges Spiel*] and most of all because of the daring expression of his fantasy my mind was astounded in a very strange way." During a subsequent concert, however, Tomášek decided not to let himself be carried away that easily and to listen with a rather more distanced and critical ear. This time, he recognized many mistakes in Beethoven's work as it jumped from one motif to another, concluding disapprovingly that the "unusual" and "original" was here an end in itself. Thus, he concluded, Mozart is like "a sun which shines and warms, without departing from its lawful course; Beethoven I call a comet marking bold orbits without subjecting itself to a system, its appearance giving rise to all sorts of superstitious interpretations."[34]

Insofar as this metaphor of a comet embodies the supernatural, eccentric, and terrible, it is not only expressive of Tomášek's personal ambivalence toward Beethoven but also epitomizes the "Beethoven controversy" at large in the later eighteenth and early nineteenth century. The idea of Beethoven as comet suggests the idea of an unguided missile suspected of all sorts of frivolous, unexpected, and dangerous turns, yet also points to a Longinian striker of the sublime moving beyond the limits of fixed and established formal systems: a composer-genius who creates his own daring course, and in aiming this high his audiences will have to take his abrupt and startling turns for granted. These two positions, opposed yet related, typify the ambivalent stance toward Beethoven until the first decade of the nineteenth century: on the one hand, Beethoven's music was reviewed as merely strange, oppressive, and difficult in musical reviews; on the other hand, it was praised precisely because of the challenges it posed to contemporary performers and listeners.[35] In both cases, however, Beethoven's music—especially with reference to the symphonies—was positioned willingly or unwillingly in the discursive context of the sublime: the bold and agonizing, or the grand and captivating, the ugly and difficult, or the out of the ordinary and awesome, the lawless, or the "brave" and "high" style.

Sulzer had, for that matter, already aligned the difficult with the sublime in his aesthetic encyclopedia. He had argued that the feeling of awe or admiration typical of the sublime comes from a hampering of imaginative grasp, such as grand things or extraordinary representations that resist easy assimilation: "we admire those objects of representation [*Gegenstände der Vorstellungskraft*] which, because of the multitude and richness of things, instantly appear to us, and which we cannot grasp [*die wir zu fassen nicht vermögend sind*]," which we, as it were, cannot keep up with (*die sehr viel weiter gehen als wir folgen können*).[36] Apparent disorder here signals a "higher" imperceptible order that one literally cannot follow.

Familiar with Robert Lowth's *Lectures on the Sacred Poetry of the Hebrews* (to which he refers in his text, on 107), Sulzer may for that matter have also been familiar with Lowth's idea of the sublime feeling as an experience of something beyond reach that exhausts imagination in frustrating its attempts for a comprehensive overview. The feeling of admiration for unassimilable objects to which Sulzer refers recalls Lowth's idea that the sublimity of an object is attested to in the frustrated attempts of imagination to comprehend it:

> Here the human mind is absorbed, overwhelmed as it were in a boundless vortex, and studies in vain for an expedient to extricate itself. But the greatness of the subject [i.e., the topic] may be justly estimated by its difficulty; and while the imagination labours to comprehend what is beyond its powers, this very labour itself, and these ineffectual endeavours, sufficiently demonstrate the immensity and sublimity of the object. . . . Here the mind seems to exert its utmost faculties in vain to grasp an object, whose unparalleled magnitude mocks its feeble endeavours . . . [37]

In articles published in the *Allgemeine musikalische Zeitung* and the *Berlinische musikalische Zeitung* between 1805 and 1807, Carl Friedrich Michaelis presented such an exertion of the imagination in (instrumental) music as a sign of the sublime. Loud, sudden, and capricious turns, according to Michaelis, offer an intense challenge to the imagination: in its vain attempts to comprehend a sonorous mass or a multitude of eccentric movements, imagination becomes aware of its limits—and the possibility of transcending these limits. As Michaelis puts it, in being overwhelmed the musical imagination is triggered to "exert itself and expand beyond its normal bounds." Beethoven's work is, for him, an example of such music that has "no immediately pleasant effect on the . . . imagination," inciting it to hard labor rather than granting it the ease of familiar forms.[38] The pleasure it gives comes through frustration and (painful) effort.

In his 1810 review of Beethoven's Fifth, E. T. A. Hoffmann reworks this notion of difficulty within the parameters of *Sehnsucht*: the pains of imagination to achieve a comprehensive overview are translated into the pains of a constantly frustrated desire for wholeness. As for Wackenroder, instrumental rather than vocal music for Hoffmann constitutes an ideal vehicle for such endless, "indefinite yearning"—though it must be noted that Hoffmann is just as enthusiastic a supporter of church and vocal music in his essays on ancient church music (Palestrina) and opera (Spontini) respectively, so that his defense of Beethoven's instrumental music is less exclusive than it may seem at first sight (*BS* 238).[39]

With this precaution in mind, let us consider Hoffmann's remark that instrumental music is the most romantic—expansive in Jean Paul's terms—

art because it has no business with "feelings circumscribed by intellect" (*BS* 236). Its mode of mediation is (to recall James Beattie and James Usher) imperfect, *inti*mative instead of *imi*tative, and this deficiency is what the other arts sadly lack. Indeed, Hoffmann adds in a reworking of the 1810 review, the "sole subject [of music] is the infinite" [*nur das Unendliche ist ihr Vorwurf*], which is to say that music should have no determinable subject—determinable in words, in concepts, or in figures—but must leave listeners to an endless process of signifying that mimics the aimless, constant movement of rehearsal and expansion associated with the infinite. Such music is for Hoffmann only "purely" instrumental music and it is only as such that music can be an "independent" art.[40]

In musical-analytical terms, the infinite in Hoffmann's Beethoven reviews is epitomized by repetition and (apparent) irresolution. In his 1812 review of Beethoven's *Coriolan* Overture, Hoffmann would show how the sense of a speedy and seemingly unstoppable thrust forward is excited by "perpetual modulations" rushing forward. These modulations, however, in fact offer a steady *return* of the same phrase—albeit ever new and different. Restless and relentless [*rastlos*], Hoffmann remarks, the same phrase hurries from one key to an other, and arguably it may be this impression of a modulation without end (which would be an illusory impression in tonal music) that makes for an anxiety, a waiting without end.[41]

In the 1810 review, Hoffmann likewise alludes to a persistent tactic of delay in the Fifth Symphony. This tactic, as I read Hoffmann, creates precisely the tense experiential effect that Locke and Burke had attributed to the idea of the infinite: the feeling of never coming one jot closer to an end. For return is what, according to Hoffmann, Beethoven's Fifth revolves around and what accounts for its powerful effects: it suggests an unending movement by constantly returning to (and reworking) the same phrases. Daniel Chua has accounted for the "intensifying effect" Hoffmann attributes to the symphony's third movement in particular by pointing to the phrase extensions repeatedly postponing resolution: as anticipatory structures, he observes, they are "anacrustic in content and form, delaying and deferring the downbeats both within the phrase and as part of the structure." These structures are, moreover, "repeated end on end, piling up anticipation after anticipation, with each repetition extended to intensify the force of expectation."[42] As a listener, Hoffmann constantly has the sense of being positioned "on the verge of"—never beyond it, but at best working toward, preparing for that beyond.

This tension of anticipation increases, firstly, after the climax to the development of the fourth movement's opening theme and, secondly, during the coda of the finale. Here Hoffmann hears an ending ever postponed. The chord that seemed to be the final chord is sounded three times over, with full-measure silences in between, and again over three measures in quarter notes, then silence, then once more the same chord, and finally once more silence, followed by the last *tutti*-chord on C (*BS* 249–50). As the music cannot seem to get it over with, the mind is stirred anew through these chords, which for Hoffmann recall the earlier Allegro strokes: "they act like a fire that is thought to have been put out but repeatedly bursts forth again in bright tongues of flame" (*BS* 250). Hoffmann's ears are redirected to a previous stage, so that the "beyond" is once again held in suspense and the suggestion of endless continuation is once again reinforced. There is for Hoffmann no ending to Beethoven's Fifth. Apparently, instrumental music has here outwitted itself, as it performs what Hoffmann perceives of as its romantic "essence": infinitude.

There is, however, something extremely doubtful about the reality of this performance. For, after all, conceived within the traditional framework of the sonata form, the C-minor symphony gravitates around a tonal center to which the music inevitably returns at the close: a triumph over uncertainty and ambiguity, one might say, hammered out over and over again during the finale in the home key. Seen in this light, the finale embodies an ultimate mastery over tension incessantly worked up, a heroic gesture that wipes out all the conflicts encountered along the way. It is, as such, far from sustaining any tension of indeterminacy until after its own sounding. Indeed, harmonically speaking, tension (harmonic ambiguity) is required and introduced here only insofar as it constitutes a necessary occasion to reinstate rest and resolution, to allow for an eventual delight of relief and confirmation.

Nevertheless, there is one issue in Hoffmann's review that might explain the sense of irresolution to which he constantly alludes. This is the issue of an absolute whole that Hoffmann recognizes in Beethoven's Fifth: a whole without parts that cannot be grasped imaginatively *as such*, yet constantly suggests its presence negatively, in fragments. Thus Hoffmann states with respect to the symphony's first movement: "all secondary ideas and episodes" rhythmically relate to the simple *short-short-short-long* theme and only serve to gradually unfold the nature of the *Ganze* or whole that this theme "can only hint at" (*BS* 244).[43] In themselves, he continues, the "ingredients" of the symphony hardly make any sense. They merely create the impression of something "disjointed," hard to grasp, and only having their function and significance within the "pattern" [*Einrichtung*] of the whole that "maintains the mind in an ineffable yearning" (*BS* 244).[44] This whole, however, cannot make itself apparent [*dartun kan*] on the level of sensibility. It can only be alluded to even by the central theme, as if it were hovering beyond the music heard.

To fully assess the significance of this absolute whole, and its significance to Hoffmann's sense of *Sehnsucht*, I now turn to Kant's analytic of the sublime in the *Critique of Judgment*. Here, the notion of an absolute unity is presented as an unreachable goal for the imagination: the impossible presentation of the unconditioned (that which transcends the bounds of sense). Though this goal can never be realized, it is precisely *in* the realization of a mental limit that the Kantian subject also gains a sense of de-limitation. Can this sense of de-limitation be related to Hoffmann's sense of musical *Sehnsucht*?

Kant's Mathematical Sublime

Kant's analytic of the mathematical sublime revolves around the impossibility to fulfill ideas of reason on the level of sensibility. On the face of it, the subject here experiences a paradoxical combination of pain and pleasure as the senses and imagination are confronted with apparently immeasurable objects in nature: nature that appears boundless and that cannot be grasped. To explain the pain, the third *Critique* contrasts two mental "modes" of estimation: mathematical and aesthetic. The first is an estimation by means of numbers and the second an estimation in (a blink of) the eye: an immediate intuitive grasp of things as one coherent whole (*KU* §26, 94–95).

The mathematical estimation of magnitude is always relative, since "the power of numbers extends to infinity" and a greater number is therefore always possible ($1 + 1 + 1 + 1 + 1$) (*KU* §26, 95). Yet in the aesthetic estimation of magnitude, one's physical scope encounters a limit beyond which apparently no "ever greater scope" is possible. Only in such an aesthetic estimation of greatness one is therefore apt to call something "not alone great, but, without qualification, absolutely, and in every respect (beyond comparison) great, that is to say, sublime." This "is a greatness comparable to itself alone" for which no "appropriate standard outside of itself" can be found (*KU* §25, 93). And only in such an aesthetic estimation does one experience a high degree of difficulty: in counting one can go on indefinitely without much effort, yet in intuition one fruitlessly pains oneself to achieve an impossible, greatest, all-inclusive scope. Kant henceforth associates this endless, successive counting with imaginative *apprehension*, and the aesthetic estimation of magnitude with *comprehension*.

Typically the armchair traveler–theorist of the sublime, Kant uses a secondhand example to illustrate the case: Savary's account of the pyramids of Cheops in Egypt (*KU* §26, 96). From afar, when they look very small, the sight of them presents no problem. One can easily "place" them visually in their totality. Closer, however, the matter is altogether different. As I look up and down the Great Pyramid, I do not succeed in representing its various parts as one whole in one blink of the eye, at one glance. For as I focus on one part, try to retain it, and combine it with other sighted parts (i.e., use my imaginative power), I already lose my visual grip on what I have focused on before—it literally escapes my view and visual memory, as there is too much to be assimilated. Thus, all the time there is an excess that is left behind and left out, a remainder or residue that sensibility as a whole cannot contain and retain. The Kantian subject experiences this failure of sensibility as painful. It wants totality and it cannot get it. It wants not just to apprehend (*auffassen*), to represent successively, endlessly, aimlessly; it wants to *comprehend* (*zusammenfassen*): to have it all at once, in a single representation unifying these successive representations as coexisting (*KU* §26, 95).

Why would this subject want this impossible picture? As it transpires, the imagination's strive for comprehension is not self-motivated but inspired by the faculty of reason. Or, in Kant's more dramatic terms, the mind here listens to the voice of reason, and this voice says: comprehend this or that phenomenon as an absolute totality, make the single intuition holding the many in one as great as possible (*KU* §26, 98–99). This means that the desire to form such a complete picture is due to an *illegitimate interference of reason* in the realm of sensibility. Reason wants the latter to do something that it is, as witness its abortive efforts, not equipped to accomplish.

It should be noted here that comprehension, in Kant's critical system, is an idea of absolute totality, and absolute totality is an idea of reason. Now, if in looking at the Great Pyramid from the right angle I feel a compulsion to comprehend the entire pyramid, with all its minute details, at a glance, this compulsion to comprehend is really a claim of reason forced on my sensibility: "the idea of the comprehension of any phenomenon whatsoever that may be given us in a whole of intuition, is an idea imposed on us by a law of reason"—whereby the latter "recognizes no definite, universally valid and unchangeable measure except the absolute whole" (*KU* §27, 102).

In apprehension, imagination would have encountered no difficulties or obstacles, would have happily (if not also rather frantically) continued its successive representations *ad infinitum* (*KU* §26, 95). Only the imposition of an idea of comprehension, the urge to grasp an absolute whole, will painfully stretch and frustrate the imagination here.

It could well be argued that this imposition is acted out in Hoffmann's account of Beethoven's Fifth. The singular unity that cannot be presented *as such* on the level of sensibility could, in this instance, be read as an idea of reason: a supersensible idea that tries to force itself onto the shapes of the sensible. In this perspective, the imagination would be a victim of reason gone astray and ultimately would have to admit to its own failure by passing on, as it were, the intrusive idea to this higher mental faculty it cannot compete with.

However, though Hoffmann's singular unity clearly rehearses the idea of an absolute whole analyzed in the *Critique of Judgment*, his account hardly attests to a failure of imagination that is only painful—or to a triumph of the faculty of reason that "makes good" this failure. Indeed, what follows in Kant's analytic only reinforces the impression that Hoffmann's review of Beethoven can be seen as rewriting and in a sense decapitating the Kantian sublime for its own purposes.

A crucial passage in this context is Kant's (rather sudden) introduction of the idea of infinity. If reason requires totality, Kant argues, it wants a *presentation* answering "to all members of a progressively increasing . . . series of [apprehension]." From this requirement, Kant continues as a matter of course, reason "does not even exempt the infinite . . . but rather renders it inevitable for us to regard this infinite . . . as *completely given* (i.e., given in its totality)" (*KU* §26, 98–99). Now, as we have already seen in the *Enquiry*, nothing in nature can ever *be* infinite, just as for Kant the infinite can never become an object of perception, since the infinite transcends every standard of sense (and obviously no object of sense can transcend all standards of sense). Kant had, for that matter, already stated in the first *Critique* that the "true" transcendental concept of the infinite boils down to an incomplete synthesis: "the successive synthesis of unity in the measurement of a quantum can never be completed [*vollendet*, also connoting accomplished]."[45] Infinity is an *Unvollendete*, an ongoing work in progress—it can therefore not possibly be *determined*.

Given this unconditional nature of the idea of the infinite, the analytic attributes the failure of imagination to comprehend entirely to the fact that infinity is one of those extravagant ideas of reason without an object.

Infinity, as Kant had already argued in the first *Critique*, is "just an idea": an empty idea. For such an idea, no instance can be offered or presented (*dargestellt*) in sensibility. Within this context, imagination's unfinished synthesis serves to underline the Kantian dictum that ideas of reason—such as the infinite—*cannot be used constitutively.* That is to say, the fact that the synthesis of unity remains incomplete or undetermined (*unbedingt*) in this instance exemplifies, as it were, experientially the Kantian rule that an idea of reason "is and must remain undetermined," that is, can never become an object of cognition.[46] Now, if only the truly infinite is sublime and if this infinite is strictly an idea of reason that cannot be positively realized on the level of sensibility, this means that "the sublime is not to be looked for in the things of nature, but only in our own ideas" (*KU* §25, 93–94). It means, in effect, that the pain of the sublime is not to be traced to a would-be infinite, oversized object in nature, nor even to the compulsion to comprehend such an object in a whole of intuition, but to an intrusive reason commanding imagination: *give me an instance of infinity as absolute totality.* And imagination sets to work. And it does not stand a chance—it fails as a rule.

If this failure is appropriate within the larger scheme of Kant's transcendental critique, it is also not without result.[47] For the crux of the matter is that *in* this failure, *in* the pain experienced on the level of imagination, the Kantian subject is awakened to the superior capacities of its supersensible faculty of reason. In the analytic, pain is not felt for nothing; it is felt to disclose an inner truth to me: it not merely points to the limits of sensuous presentation but also to the limitless extent of my reason. If, after all, the pain of the sublime is caused by an idea of reason that exceeds even the greatest greatness in nature and also the greatest power of sensibility (i.e., infinity as absolute totality), that very pain also attests to a side of my being that is able to *think* such an idea. It attests to a suprasensuous side of my being that is capable of forming ideas in comparison with which sensibility *and even nature dwindles into insignificance* (*KU* §26, 101). As soon as I become aware that it is my very own reason that is giving my imagination so much pain and trouble, my initial feeling of being frustrated on the level of sensibility is turned into the opposite realization of being happily unbounded on the level of reason. This realization, earned through pain, is what ultimately composes the soul-stirring delight of the Kantian sublime.

Resolved and Unresolved Feeling: Decapitating the Kantian Sublime

As such, the mathematical sublime seems governed by a dialectical law. In the analytic, pain or frustration presupposes its opposite: the frustration of being limited on the level of sensibility is not the end of it but in fact "awakens the consciousness of an unlimited faculty of the same subject" (*KU* §27, 104). *Through* the inadequacy of imagination the superiority and infinite scope of reason is disclosed. Or, as Bowie explains this dialectical mechanism, because "we feel our limits we must *also* feel what is not limited in ourselves, otherwise we would have no way of being aware of a limit": we can only interpret sensibility as inadequate by virtue of a higher inner vantage point.[48] Thus, a felt limit yields its own beyond: frustration is resolved into a subject-validating experience of self-transgression. The Kantian sublime may be a feeling with a high degree of difficulty, but it is also a highly rewarding feeling. I would even say it is a *tonal* feeling, since, just as in tonal music, tension is here only introduced to reinforce stability with a vengeance. Or, differently said, an initial displeasure here mediates and facilitates a final pleasure.

What I would like to propose is that Hoffmann's Beethoven review turns this movement of mediation (connoting an intervention to achieve a settlement or reconciliation between two parties) into the stasis of a deadlock. The sense of reward that pervades Kant's analytic—the subject recognizing *itself* as sublime, which is delightful for the entire province of mind—is here replaced by a more complex pleasure lodged *within* (rather than evolving out of) a pain of frustration. This is to say that, in my view, Hoffmann's account of musical *Sehnsucht* problematizes the reward of subjective finality and is able to do so because it relocates the infinite at a distance.

Thus, in Kant's analytic absolute unity can be realized after all, if only one is prepared and able to move to the perspective of reason rather than lingering in the province of imagination. (And this movement, I have shown, signals the realization that the subject *itself* "contains" the sublime.) Hoffmann's review, by contrast, offers no such easy way out. Thus, Hoffmann reports being steeped in one and the same "persistent" feeling of *Sehnsucht* oscillating between pain and pleasure rather than progressing to a higher self-realization. Closure is, apparently, not an option: as a listener, he keeps dangling at the limit of the ungraspable instead of transgressing into a higher mental sphere. In contrast to Kant, the infinite remains ungraspable as a singular unity to the *entire* province of mind and cannot, according to Peter Schnaus, "be thought . . . as a reachable goal."[49]

As such, it is only fitting that Hoffmann's experience of the infinite remains undetermined: it performatively repeats what Kant had appropriately called the unaccomplishedness of the infinite. Such unaccomplishedness is, of course, inherent to the irony at work in *Sehnsucht*: it is a desire that constantly undoes itself to keep going without end. As a desire that develops itself only insofar as it reverses that development again, *Sehnsucht* embodies a pattern of repetition rather than the transformative dialectic of the Kantian sublime. It knows no apotheoses or breakthroughs; it does not evolve out one state into another. It rather resumes its own lack.

Seen in this light, *Sehnsucht* decapitates the Kantian experience of the mathematical sublime as a *narrative* experience of a pleasure mediated through a displeasure. By "narrative" I here mean a canonic narrative structure of beginning-middle-ending that (as Theresa de Lauretis has put it in a different context) is pervaded by the "sense of an ending": by a purposefulness progressing to a moment when the Kantian subject can close itself off from nature, turn inward, and exorcise its frustrations in marveling at the infinite extent of its own mind.[50] Thus, evolving along the lines of an Aristotelian plot, the Kantian sublime experience features a (sudden) initial confrontation (beginning) leading to a predicament (middle: pain in the form of frustration or helplessness), which in turn leads to an overcoming of this predicament (ending: delight in the form of pride or joy). The decisive moment or turning point in all of this is when the subject, so to speak, changes perspectives. This is a moment of judgment that intervenes or mediates between the spheres of the sensible and the supersensible: once the pain of imagination is judged as being subjectively purposeful (i.e., in accord with reason), then pain gives way to delight. In other words, as Paul Guyer has rightfully stated, the feeling of pleasure in the Kantian sublime is only possible "once this judgment has been made"—only on the "cessation" of uneasiness due to this judgment does there arise "a feeling of joy."[51] Pain and pleasure are here not interlocked but arise sequentially.

Acting out a typical drama of self-transformation that revolves around this passage from the sensible to the supersensible, the Kantian sublime even features the familiar hero, the "mobile character" of myth and romance plots. This is a hero who actively submits himself to a trial to fulfill his personal destiny: honor gained through peril. Nature, in all of this, is the immobile character. It is the obstacle to be overcome, "fixed at a certain point of the plot-space and representing, standing for . . . a boundary which the hero alone can cross."[52] As a mere occasion for frustration or fear, nature is but a necessary impediment to be confronted and defeated by the Kantian subject (hero) on its way to manhood as an autonomous being. Thus, motivated by a "movement forward toward resolution," the Kantian sublime experience is defined by an ultimate reconciliation I would like to define as a closure-in-transcendence: an achieved move "up" that signals a conclusion to pain and discord.[53]

If Hoffmann's musical *Sehnsucht* lacks this sequential movement from pain to pleasure and constantly postpones closure—which is not to say that it is completely absent—another reading of the sublime might prove more fruitful to contextualize its logic of infinite movement. A more likely candidate for comparison, in this instance, is Burke's version of the experience of the artificial infinite already encountered in chapter 1. As I read Burke's account of the feeling of the infinite, it does not provide a dramatic transition from pain to pleasure—and in that sense appears monotonous—but nevertheless harbors a constant tension of oscillation between two "inclinations" of the power of imagination. Thus in being faced with objects that appear without bounds, or in projecting an excess of similar ideas, the imagination is here said to find "no rest" (*ESB* IV, sect. X, 126). Restlessness connoting agitation, impatience, and eagerness, this suggests the possibility of an imagination *desiring* an ending to an open-ended succession. This can be called the pain, the labor, of Burke's experience of infinity. Like the romantic fragment, Burke's fragmentary rehearsals presuppose a larger whole and this is, I believe, what the Burkean imagination seeks to, but cannot, arrive at.

At the very same time, however, the absence of an encompassing form tricks imagination into a delightful illusion: it "meets no check which may hinder its extending" any given number of parts to infinity (*ESB* II, sect. VIII, 67). Imagination *itself* takes on the apparent boundlessness it encounters. It feels no limits in reiterating the same over and over again. What is more, this reiteration is not experienced as such, that is, as an insistent repetition but as a *progression* or *extension*. As with Locke, stasis, a consistently remaining within or returning to the same place, here allows for the idea of an indefinite expansion. Just as in Burke's passage on unfinished drawings a space must be kept open in which the promise of "something more" can be preserved, so in the artificial infinite the absence of any boundaries preserves the illusion of an "ever next." This open horizon occasions the pleasure of the Burkean experience of artificial infinity: it makes for an agreeable and even joyful suspension in which, first, imagination is deemed to expand itself without effort, and, second, the tension or labor required for change or development is happily postponed. Instead, the subject can painlessly and tirelessly revel in a continuous return that is felt as a progression without end.

Seen in this double light, the Burkean experience of artificial infinity can be described as an experience pointing in two different directions at the same time: it moves forward and backward at once. On the one hand, Burke's impatient imagination looks forward toward an ending, toward fulfillment, overactivating itself without becoming productive in a conclusive sense. At the same time, it looks backward toward a return, suspending any tension of change or renewal in a reiteration of the same in the face of an always open space. In this way, a lack of fulfillment allows for pain and pleasure at once, and on one and the same level: while Kant proposes two different faculties of mind, imagination and reason, whose respective limits and limitlessness make for the mediation of a pleasure through a displeasure, it is in Burke's experience of artificial infinity that the same power of mind— imagination—gets caught in an internal and irresolvable double movement: it wants to progress and regress at once, hesitating in between pain and pleasure.

This irresolvable double bind illuminates the aporetic logic of *Sehnsucht* as an endlessly differentiating desire for wholeness and its manifestation as a musical feeling in Hoffmann's review of Beethoven's Fifth. I would like to posit this unresolved feeling of the infinite as a romantic alternative to the Kantian way of experiencing the infinite. This is not a heroic but an ironic mode of the sublime, one that does not presuppose an overcoming of limits and difficulties but rather explores the experience of a limit *and nothing more than that.* As such, this ironic mode of the sublime feeling could well qualify as an instance of what Thomas Weiskell has called the liminal sublime. This is not a sublime of transcendence but of hesitation: it revolves around an indecisive imagination dawdling in an open space in which nothing has yet been definitely or concretely configured.[54] Feeding on a suspension of revelation, the liminal sublime no longer starts from an integral, autonomous self that posits itself as an elevated *Herrschaft* over nature,[55] but from a divided self that sees the impossibility of coinciding with itself reflected in the endless dispersal of the absolute. It is this liminal sublime, I suggest, with which the idea of the "musical" in early romantic criticism is to be aligned.

3. Ruins and (Un)forgetfulness: A Genealogy of the Musically Sublime

In "Nietzsche, Genealogy, History," Michel Foucault (re)introduced a concept in philosophy and the writing of history that he had derived from Friedrich Nietzsche: genealogy.[1] Foucault presented this concept as a history-writing against the grain insofar as it no longer starts from timeless values and realities lying in wait behind the stories of the past. Genealogy, for Foucault, was no longer naïve, in that it no longer searched for the pure origin of things but rather showed how such origins were constituted out of incoherent fragments, accidents, errors, and failings. Insofar as genealogy had to do with *descent*, this was a descent in terms of dissemination: "to follow the complex course of descent is to maintain passing events in their proper dispersion . . . it is to discover that truth or being does not lie at the root of what we know and what we are, but the exteriority of accidents."[2]

Foucault's envisioned practice of genealogy was, of course, very much aimed at uncovering power structures, power struggles, and other instances of "petty malices" at work in the values and morals we so easily tend to take for granted as pure and eternal.[3] Though this chapter will not be explicitly concerned with Foucauldian analyses of domination and subjugation, Foucault's concept of genealogy—with its stress on accidents and failings—is nevertheless a suitable concept to frame the chance descent of the musically sublime in nineteenth-century German (music) philosophy.

This descent will start here (not as a hard beginning but as a moment of intersection) with a casual and playful gesture in Arthur Schopenhauer's *The World as Will and Representation*, which suggests the possibility of a musical ruin—the equivalent of a building without symmetry (*WW* II, 39, 454). Little more than an accidental aside, this gesture nonetheless found its way into the aesthetic writings of Friedrich Nietzsche and Richard Wagner. Mutated, the musical ruin would even inform the idea of a specifically musically sublime. A product of chance and creative misreadings, this idea represented perhaps little more than a Foucauldian "unstable assemblage of faults, fis-sures, and heterogeneous layers."[4] It was, in any case, far from being a solid, unequivocal model for a sublime that could only make its appearance by musical means. Even so, this assemblage would co-facilitate the rise of Wagnerian absolute music and indeed become its legitimization. As I will show, such music was to be a music disconnected from the sensible world, without "plastic" forms and without rhythmic regularity: a music that would have come to "itself" in the formlessness and rulelessness of the sublime.

A Frozen Cadenza: Music as Will and Ruin

In *Towards a Newer Laocoön*, Gotthold Ephraim Lessing—through an inter-textual dialogue with Burke's *Enquiry*—elaborated on a binary opposition between the spatial (painting, sculpture, architecture) and the temporal (lit-erature and music) arts.[5] The opposition, it must be stressed, is not so much absolute as regulative: *Towards a Newer Laocoön* explores the limits of the different art forms by exploring the degrees in which they can (in the sense of being able *and* being allowed to) become terrible without actually be-coming revolting. Can art represent terrible things and events without dis-torting itself so that it is no longer pleasing to behold—can it be painful in a pleasurable way? In *Towards a Newer Laocoön*, this is a privilege reserved for the temporal arts. While sculpture and painting (in conformity to classi-cal laws) must never leave the bounds of the beautiful, the temporal arts can, according to Lessing, evoke the terrible without becoming formally revolting.

In Arthur Schopenhauer's art-philosophy, this distinction between the spatial and temporal is still commonplace, even though the ghost of inter-mediality is here already an intrusive presence. This ghost violates both me-dial boundaries and articulations of meaning dependent on these boundaries. Indeed, in the second part of *The World as Will and Representa-tion* the problem of medial confusion is in effect a tropological fusion of medial functions in the commonplace cliché "architecture is frozen music" (*WW* II, 39, 453–54). As Schopenhauer contends, this is a dysfunctional cliché, a *Wortwitz* at best, since the temporalization (music) of the spatial (architecture), and vice versa, is a contradiction within the terms. Indeed, insofar as *The World as Will and Representation* follows Lessing's formal dis-tinction between the arts, it remediates the latter and turns it into a meta-physical distinction: the distinction between architecture and music embodies a "deeper" distinction between different spheres of reality and being.

In *The World as Will and Representation*, these are the quasi-Platonic spheres of the phenomenal and noumenal respectively. The latter is not simply an unreachable outside but rather an all-pervading force at once inside and outside. As such, the noumenon is both familiar and strange: at the same time part of the subject and beyond its modes of cognition. Thus, while the noumenon can only enter "consciousness . . . immediately," without intervention, it cannot be cognized objectively. Any such cognition, Schopenhauer argues in imitation of Kant, would be a contradiction within the terms, as "everything objective is representation, therefore appearance"— and the noumenon is, precisely, not appearance but the thing-in-itself (*WW* II, 18, 195).

Within the confines of *The World as Will and Representation*, this thing-in-itself is the Will: an irrational, blind, uncontrollable, and omnipresent force that grounds the world of appearances. Paradoxically, this is a groundless grounding: as a ceaseless and unconscious force, the Will is an aimless and invisible drive pushing forth different life forms (that do battle among each other and themselves) and finally annihilating them just as blindly and vigorously. One is born and then one dies, without any plan or purpose. In the end, it was all for nothing: life is but a detour to death—and beyond death there is no salvation.

Likewise, the world of appearances is a detour (at once a deviation and diversion) from the world-as-Will. All that we perceive in the phenomenal world is always already invested by the Will; it is a manifestation or the becoming-as-object of that Will. Sometimes beautiful and alluring, such manifestations can make us forget the harsh ugliness of the Will and even briefly liberate us from its grasp. Within the confines of *The World as Will and Representation* we can, however, never completely escape the Will, because it constitutes human nature: every act of the body is an act of the Will made perceivable, just as the body itself is nothing but the Will made physical within the conditions of time and space (*WW* I, bk. 2, §20, 106–7). Thus I am nothing without being always already the Will inscribed: as a subject of willing, I am primarily an individualized, embodied, objectified drive.

In *The World as Will and Representation*, this distinction between the world as Will and the world as appearance or representation works, among others, to make the distinction between music as a temporal art form and architecture as a spatial art form unbridgeable. Schopenhauer's "system" situates painting, sculpture, and architecture exclusively in the world as representation—they can at best represent Ideas (in the Platonic sense of the term), attempting "a domain between the Will and its empirical [objectification]."⁶ Indeed, because the different art forms embody, according to Schopenhauer, different stages and aspects of the Will, they can be placed in a hierarchical order that moves from the "baser" ideas of gravity and cohesion (architecture) to the "higher" movements of actions and thoughts in (wo)man (literature) (*WW* II, 39, 453–54). The art of music is absent from this hierarchy because it has a status apart. Unlike all the other arts, including its temporal sister poetry, music *stands apart* from the world of appearances: just as the world is an objectification of the Will, so is instrumental music. Consequently, it does not copy or imitate (individual) things within that world but rather runs parallel to it, like an analogy with its own independent status. It is closer to the Will than the other arts and, indeed, provides a direct access to that noumenal sphere: there is no detour, no repetition of a phenomenal layer in between. Music thus (in)famously "never expresses the phenomenon, but only the inner nature, the in-itself of all phenomena, the Will itself" (*WW* II, 39, 453).

As with the romantics, music thus becomes a vehicle of the infinite, a tool to think and perhaps even figure the unimaginable through abstract movements and allegedly empty signs. This becomes especially significant when Schopenhauer points to what I would like to call music's emotionally de-realizing potential. Music may move us and may even echo "the affects [*Regungen*] of our inmost nature," but it does so "entirely without reality and remote from its [i.e., the Will's] pain" (*WW* I, bk. 3, §52, 264). Like tragedy, music affects its listeners powerfully, but these affects are somehow not their own, too general to be appropriated as such. Such affects are thus not affects in reality but in Platonic ideality: they precede and precondition specific affects. Seen in this light, music does not resonate with *individual* affects but with their so-called essence, with what Schopenhauer likes to call fear or joy or pity *as such*:

> [music] expresses not this or that particular and definite pleasure, this or that affliction, pain, sorrow, horror, gaiety, merriment, or peace of mind; but it expresses affliction, pain, sorrow, horror, gaiety, merriment, peace of mind *themselves*, to a certain extent in the abstract, their essential nature, without any accessories, and so also without the motives for these emotions. Yet we understand them perfectly in this extracted quintessence. (*WW* I, bk. 3, §52, 264)

Thus, if eighteenth-century critics thought of music as being merely able to *prepare* for "fixed" or determinate affects, Schopenhauer turns this impairment into its opposite: affects resonating in music may be empirically indeterminate—and to that extent imperfect—yet this attests precisely to music's metaphysical connection. It presents the "kernel" of things, not the particularities related to the visible world. Because of this, Schopenhauer rejects the metaphor of "frozen music" with respect to architecture: music and architecture are worlds apart.

But still. The tropological contamination cannot quite be contained, even if it is a contamination that remains on the "outside": what symmetry is to architecture, rhythm is to music (*WW* II, 39, 453). Both are ordering principles, building blocks (which Schopenhauer compares to measures in music), and parameters of a greater whole. Structure can be thought spatially and temporally, in terms of spatial and temporal balance. This, of course, also invokes its reverse, and Schopenhauer pushes the correspondence a bit further. Casually, almost for the sake of the game, he states that music without the ruling principle of rhythm is like buildings without symmetry. It is this passage about the metaphorical possibility of a musical ruin that will be central to the rest of my argument: "when music, in a sudden urge for independence, so to speak, seizes the occasion of a pause, in order to free itself from the control [*Zwang*, also: force] of rhythm, to launch out into the free fancy of an ornate cadenza; such a piece of music, divested of rhythm, [is] like a ruin devoid of symmetry, and can consequently be called . . . a frozen cadenza" (*WW* II, 39, 454).

Clearly, the "frozen cadenza" is an inverted extension of the metaphor of "frozen music": a frozen movement in music, a musical "snapshot" or "still," so to speak, without contours and beginning or ending. This would be a music, if only a *rubato*, that has released itself from its conditions of possibility: the steady, directed progression of time. Or at least, a music that makes its listeners forget the course of time and that oscillates in a free movement without prominent rhythmical pressure. Would this be an endless music, a music embodying the stillness of the infinite? In *The World as Will and Representation*, the game of comparison ends here—but it would be picked up and transmuted by Wagner and Nietzsche in their music-philosophical writings. Indeed, for Wagner the idea of a frozen cadenza would, so to speak, be the entry of a music no longer dictated by recognizable rhythmic patterns. This, I will show, was to be an "unsurveyable" music, opening up a world of unending melody.

Architectonic Music: Wagner on Rhythm

In *Opera and Drama*, Wagner presented the thesis that the "true" music drama would have to conform to the (multimedial) spirit of Greek tragedy.[7]

For him, the "error in the art-genre of Opera" since the seventeenth century had consisted in a downplaying of the drama in relation to the music: "a Means of expression (Music) has been made the end, while the End of expression (the Drama) has been made a means" (17). The binary opposition thus presented between music and drama is, of course, highly problematic—even Wagner downplayed the dichotomy in his claim that in contemporary opera the poet (the writer of the libretto) is all too dependent on the musician (the composer) in the construction of the action (the drama):

> This holds as good to-day as 150 years ago: that the Poet shall take his inspiration from the Musician, that he shall listen for the whims of music, accommodate himself to the musician's bent, choose his stuff by the latter's taste, mould his characters by the timbres expedient for the purely musical combinations, provide dramatic bases for certain forms of vocal numbers in which the musician may wander at his ease,—in short, that, in his subordination to the musician, he shall construct his drama with a single eye to the specifically musical intentions of the Composer . . . (15)

As a result, Wagner maintained, modern opera such as Rossini's was an empty spectacle without proper plots, situations, or characters: drama was here a mere occasion to stage a music-spectacle serving petty, lighthearted, bourgeois needs of easy and commercial entertainment. Only a revival of the standards of the old, Greek music-drama (itself a development of the lyric-drama, which evolved out of the multimedial practice of thanksgiving to the Gods) could reverse things and render music a "proper" dramatic supplement.

By the 1870s, however, Wagner's conception of the music-drama had changed considerably. Instead of music surrendering, so to speak, to the contents and restraints of the drama, in music dramas such as *Tristan and Isolde* and *Parsifal* it was the other way around. Likewise, in his *Beethoven* essay and (as Carl Dahlhaus has pointed out) in texts including "Über die Benennung 'Musik-Drama' [On the Name Music-Drama]," Wagner reconceived the music-drama as being primarily motivated or propelled by music—the latter, always female connoted, had the "dignity" of being the "womb" of drama.[8]

What intervened, what came in between these two positions, was of course the experience of reading Schopenhauer's *The World as Will and Representation* in 1854: the notion of music as a privileged embodiment of the Will informed Wagner's idea of music as an art of unconscious forces, of drives unfit for the sphere of representation. Indeed, not merely reconsidering the relation between words and music in favor of the latter, Wagner now abandoned the possibility of any wedding between them. As Magee emphasizes, Wagner now claimed that there was "no quality, and therefore no real reciprocity, between the two."[9] His *Music of the Future* (1861) aside, it was in his *Beethoven* essay that Wagner would spell out his theory of music as the Will made audible. As I will show, this essay projects the possibility that music belongs "in essence" to the category of the sublime, since it is uniquely able to break through the forms of time and space.

1870: Wagner's eulogy of Beethoven, commemorating the latter's hundredth birthday and celebrating him as a genius who gave birth to new artistic deeds, coincided with the Prussian victory over France. For Wagner, this was potentially at once a victory of "German" tastes:

> So let the German Folk be brave in peace as well; let it cherish its native worth, and cast the false show [*Schein*] from it: let it never seek to pass for what it is not, but recognize the quality in which it is unique! To it the art of pleasing is denied; in lieu thereof its veritable deeds and thoughts are heartfelt and sublime. And beside its valor's victories in this wondrous 1870 no loftier trophy can be set, than the memory of our great *Beethoven*, who was born to the German Folk one hundred years ago. (*B* 126)

"False show" or "appearance" and "the art of pleasing": two attributes of the beautiful, which revolves around the appearance of forms, the quiet, disinterested perception of these forms, and the harmonious play of imagination and understanding that grounds the aesthetic judgment of these forms. In Western art philosophy, this has always been a visual process, or at least a process modeled on the scope and possibilities of visual perception: traditional aesthetic theory is in essence visual theory. Associating the visual with "false show" (as a verb as well as a noun), Wagner tries to extend its opposite to a "German" spirit. This is not a spirit of pretence but of sublime activity—intense, "heartfelt," boundless. The link between the sublime and nationalism intimated here is uncanny yet undeniable: we will keep this link in mind to recall that the sublime is never without interest.

Wagner's interest is chauvinistic (which is of course a very ironic term in this context) in more than one direction: toward Germany as a new nation, toward its trophy Beethoven as an incarnation of a new artistic activity, and toward music as a force, I would almost say, that needs to be liberated from the oppressive norms of the visual and the plastic in the field of aesthetics. In this last direction, the *Beethoven* essay creatively and extensively misreads the casual reference to frozen music in *The World as Will and Representation* as a historical reality rather than as a play with metaphors. The "illegitimate" tropological analogy between architecture and music is here rewritten as an illegitimate *dominance* of the architectural over the musical in actual, contemporary musical practice. If Schopenhauer toyed with a pun, Wagner reworks the pun into a teleology.[10]

Thus the *Beethoven* essay diagnoses a disownment of the musical in a subjection to the plastic, visual, and spatial imperatives of (what is presented as) the architectonic paradigm. "Architectonic" in this context is synonymous with symmetry—the kind of symmetry that Wagner's opponent Hanslick deemed essential to music:

> The primordial stuff of music is regular and pleasing sound. Its animating
> principle is rhythm: rhythm in the large scale as the co-proportionality of a
> symmetric structure; rhythm in the smaller scale as regular alternating
> motion of individual units within the metric period. The material out of
> which the composer creates, of which the abundance can never be exaggerated, is the entire system of tones, with their latent possibilities for melodic,
> harmonic, and rhythmic variety.[11]

"Rhythm" is an ambiguous term, etymologically hovering in between flow and containment, movement and moderation.[12] In Hanslick's text, however, rhythm is stripped of its excessive potential and in the "form" of moderation makes up at once music's ground structure, its base material, and (together with melody and harmony) one of its specific, syntactic parameters. In this view, music always presupposes an essential proportionality—it cannot *but* be symmetric. It is this essence the *Beethoven* essay contests: insofar as music has been subjected to rhythmic regularity, it has been degraded into taking up an "architectonic," which is to say, plastic-symmetrical, aspect (*B* 78, 80). This aspect would have directed music into the cobweb of appearances, where it does not belong (*B* 76–79):

> We are conscious of the existence of a second world, perceptible only
> through the ear, manifesting itself through sound; literally a *sound-world*
> beside the *light-world*, a world of which we may say that it bears the same
> relation to the visible world as dreaming to waking: for it is quite as plain to
> us as is the other, though we must recognize it as being entirely different. As
> the world of dreams can only come to vision through a special operation of
> the brain, so Music enters our consciousness through a kindred operation
> . . . (*B* 68)

Music is another word for the Will—it comes from the inside and directs, propels, motivates the outside. It is a force that comes before the phenomenal and even before the subject, operating in a force field that has neither subject nor object but always already instates both. Pursuing this logic to its rightful end, one would have to say that the distinction between inner and outer, between not-seeing and seeing, no longer holds, as the force associated with "inside," with music and the Will, is the very force that instates the (phenomenal) difference between inside and outside to begin with. Yet for Wagner, dreaming somehow comes before waking, and is in any case independent from it, as a secret and autonomous inner mechanism: "Everywhere we see the inner law, only conceivable as sprung from the spirit of Music, prescribe the outer law that regulates the world of sight" (*B* 71).

Wagner cannot resist the visual appeal of metaphor here, as he pictures the mechanism of music as a dream mechanism that allows the mind to reverse its direction, as it were, and turn off the seeing mode. Indeed, Wagner contends, the true effect of music on its listeners is that it disrupts sight in such a way that "with eyes wide open we no longer intensively see" (*B* 74). This implies a demand, as Lydia Goehr suggests, "that we turn our *out-sight*, if I may so speak, into an *in-sight*, our eye of seeing into an ear of seeing; our eye of seeing into an eye of listening."[13] And what we would thus hear, or see, is "the oneness of our inner essence with that of the outer world": the unconscious productivity of the Will (*B* 71). Listening to music is thus experiencing the possibility of losing one's borders or limitations as an individual and extending into an infinite life-force.

As a representative of the visual, however, the architectonic reinstates what Wagner calls "the floodgates of Appearance," facilitating out-sight through a rhythmic figuring of movements that would echo physical, bodily movements (*B* 73). It is "through the *rhythmic* sequence of his tones in points of time [that] the musician reaches forth a plastic hand, so to speak, to strike a compact with the waking world of semblances" (*B* 75). For Wagner this is particularly evident in dance music, which would facilitate a "plastic" perception in such a way that it obstructs a transition to the noumenal. This explains, perhaps, why Wagner rereads and extends Schopenhauer's contention that the only possible relationship between architecture and music is an *external* relationship between symmetry and rhythm. The *Beethoven* essay presents the architectonic as being cast over the musical, mutating its "external form," and draining, ruling music so severely, almost parasitically, that the latter is no longer recognizable as an art of the Will: it is, for Wagner, an art disowned. Thus, though merely an "external" imposition, it is an imposition that has—in Wagner's uncomfortable terms—corrupted music to its core. And it is an imposition that constantly reinforces itself, for *due* to this incursion, music is judged according to the norms of the plastic arts: it is required to excite "a pleasure in beautiful forms" (*B* 77).

In Wagner's self-concocted teleology of music, the architectonic dominance in music thus works on different levels: it contaminates formal musical procedures, musical "effects," and listening conventions. The *Beethoven* essay urges these conventions to be rethought along absolutely musical lines. First, music should give up the lure of beautiful forms: this it can safely relegate to the plastic arts, which have always been the point of reference of the aesthetic category of the beautiful. Thus, second, music should relinquish the "measuredness" and surveyability of rhythmic regularity to wander off into an oceanic formlessness that cannot be pictured or overseen. It is this formlessness that is associated with the sublime, ideally occasioning "a temporary reduction in the waking power of sight" that (through this reduction) facilitates in-sight (*B* 110). Music, for Wagner, can indeed only be judged according to the category of the sublime (*B* 77). Since Wagner in turn derives this category from Schopenhauer, I return to *The World as Will and Representation* before elaborating on Wagner's idea of the musically sublime: the absolutely musical.

The Schopenhauerian Sublime

Within the confines of *The World as Will and Representation*, the subject is a mere provisional and passing symptom of the Will—the Will that is everywhere as need: "the basis of all willing is need, deficiency—in short, pain" (*WW* I, bk. 4, §57, 312).[14] "Symptom" carries the etymology of "to befall," and the subject in Schopenhauer's need-driven world literally happens *as* want: hands, teeth, throat, intestines are all stages, phases, forms of want made flesh (*WW* I, bk. 2, §20, 108; bk. 4, §57, 312). Given this primacy of need, pain in *The World as Will and Representation* signals not the absence of pleasure; the latter is a mere momentary deliverance from a constant pain: "satisfaction . . . is really and essentially *negative* only, and never positive" (*WW* I, bk. 4, §58, 319). Life is suffering without end or purpose. Even when all want is gratified, "when everything is finally overcome and attained, nothing can ever be gained but deliverance from some suffering or desire; consequently we are only in the same position as we were before this suffering or desire appeared" (319). The impossibility of pleasure to remove pain conclusively offers an interesting starting point in the nineteenth-century debate on the sublime. Whereas Kant's third *Critique* still allowed for a dialectic reversal of want (frustration) into fulfillment (transcendence), *The World as Will and Representation* already precludes such a reversal on the premise that want is primary. This preclusion is, however, not immediately evident in Schopenhauer's account of the sublime. Echoing Kant's narrative of transcendence, he claims that the experience of the sublime involves a subjective transition from the subject of willing (the subject tied to the determinations of the Will, which can be roughly interpreted as Kant's being of nature) to the subject of knowledge (the subject freed from the determinations of the Will, which can be roughly interpreted as Kant's transcendental subject as rational being): from a desiring, irrational, animal creature to a spirit that dwells in pure, disinterested perception. If the subject encounters objects so mighty and dreadful that they oppose the Will objectified, that is, the human body,

> they may threaten it by their might that eliminates all resistance, or their immeasurable greatness may reduce it to naught. Nevertheless, the beholder may not direct his attention to this relation to his Will which is so pressing and hostile, but, although he perceives and acknowledges it, he may consciously turn away from it, forcibly tear himself from his Will and its relations, and, giving himself up entirely to knowledge, may quietly contemplate, as pure, will-less subject of knowing, those very objects so terrible to the Will. He may comprehend only their Idea that is foreign to all relation, gladly linger over its contemplation, and consequently be elevated precisely in this way above himself, his person, his willing, and all willing. In that case, he is then filled with the feeling of the *sublime* . . . (*WW* I, bk. 3, §39, 201)

Here is, once again, a subject superseding and denouncing its physical being, floating freely in the air above itself as it severs all relations with the Will. Detached, indifferent, and even with a sense of pleasure, the subject considers grand nature, transcending its sense-bound humility, inadequacies, and invalidities. It does so, however, with an effort of will: this subject "forcibly" detaches itself from its Will. The sublime is an experience with a high degree of difficulty; it requires labor and effort, and this is what distinguishes it from the experience of the beautiful. Indeed, in the experience of the beautiful such a severing of the Will appears to be achieved without any pain or trouble, one's memory of the Will being, in fact, for a brief moment entirely erased in an aesthetic safe haven detached from the world of striving

(202). More than this *momentary* liberation of the Will is not an option: at some point, the body, as Will incarnate, is bound to reassert itself and invade the vacuum of disinterested contemplation.

Interestingly, however, just because the experience of the sublime involves not a harmonious but a forceful, conscious break with the Will, it never involves the *complete* forgetting of the Will that typifies the Schopenhauerian experience of the beautiful. As Schopenhauer puts it, the exaltation of the sublime "must not only be won consciously, but also be maintained [consciously] retained, and is therefore *accompanied by a constant recollection of the Will*, yet not of a single, individual willing, such as fear or desire, but of human willing in general, insofar as it is universally expressed in its objectivity, the human body" (202, my emphasis).

The sublime feeling may take one "up high," but it nonetheless never grants a complete erasing of the "down there." If in Schopenhauer's experience of the sublime the subject moves up, briefly liberating itself from its individual status as Will incarnate, this move up is all the same constantly subtended by the constant awareness of also being *tied* to the Will as a general, unconscious force. Or, as Paul Deusen remarked in 1877, in elevating oneself to a knowing subject, the *factum* of one's physical, Will-bound being is never completely exorcised but rather remains floating "in the background of our consciousness" without immediately troubling "our own I."[15] That is to say, the recollection of the Will is here not a recollection to *this or that* desire or fear but to the state of the subject as an objectification of the Will *per se*. I may momentarily transcend my needs and inabilities, but I do so through an act of de-realization that, precisely, awakens the memory to my inevitable subjection to the Will. I feel myself with and without body, with and without willing, at once.

As an exaltation of transcendence, the exaltation of the sublime is therefore always already undermining itself: it is won through the recollection that such exaltation is impossible. Or at least, that this exaltation *can only be felt and is in fact sustained* in the juxtaposition with its apparent opposite—the painful reminder of the subject being a symptom of desire. In contrast to Kant's analytic of the sublime, there is no conclusive transition from the sensible to the supersensible here, but rather an impossible hovering in between the two. In this way, *The World as Will and Representation* highlights an irresolvable conflict at work in the sublime experience by representing it as a simultaneous experience of liberation (i.e., being momentarily lifted above one's individual fears) and frustration (i.e., being nevertheless rooted in the ultimate source of all suffering) at the same time. It is a feeling of oscillation instead of transgression, and this oscillation is perhaps already an-nounced in the very brevity of Schopenhauer's sublime moment: it is an untenable and ungraspable moment that at once discloses (the knowing sub-ject disconnecting itself from individual willing) and forecloses (in the pro-cess of disconnecting, the subject is constantly reminded of its own "state" as a symptom of the Will) the possibility of transcendence. The sublime opens up, in a fragment, what it will not yield; it nags, it baits: now you see it, now you don't.

Timelessness and Endless Time: Wagner and the Sublime

The dynamics of the "inner organism in profound sleep," the dynamics of unseeing, unknowing dreaming: in the *Beethoven* essay, these are at once the dynamics of the experience of the sublime and the absolutely musical (*B* 109). This is the musical in its Wagnerian "proper" sense; music without a perceivable link to the world of objects moving in space, music that no longer makes one desire to *see* "something" (*B* 80). It is a music of forgetful-ness, recasting the eye along uncertain, aural "lines" of perception. The eye will need to learn what it means to hear and to listen: to see aurally. This, in a Wagnerian setting, would not be a matter of instant identification but of a suspension of the shapely and the known.

It may be hard to imagine such a music in a Wagnerian operatic setting: Wagner the arch-entertainer, whose ingenious musical motifs facilitate rather than obstruct a vivid imagining of characters and events, even if events have been reduced to a bare minimum—this Wagner is hard to asso-ciate with blind seeing and vague divining. And yet it remains his dominant claim that his (post-Schopenhauer) music-dramas no longer conform to out-sight, imaginative or factual, in releasing themselves from the architectonic.

In a more general sense, this release would signal a release from the aes-thetics of the beautiful that, as we have seen, has been familiarly modeled on the visual modes of perception. *Beethoven* lays claim to the possibility of a music that bypasses the stage of disinterested contemplation, during which one is no longer focused on an object as an object of use (practically or ethically), producing rather a state of visual indifference that no longer even recognizes the object as form. If only for a brief instant, one loses touch with the world, and it is this brief loss that for Wagner constitutes the moment of the sublime.

There is, however, a considerable difference with Schopenhauer in this respect. The *Beethoven* essay associates the experience of the sublime with such an easy and imperceptible gliding into oblivion that it precludes the *conscious* enforcing of forgetfulness typifying the Schopenhauerian sublime. Indeed, insofar as beauty in *The World as Will and Representation* is precisely related to effortless forgetfulness, the *Beethoven* essay puts the categories of the beautiful and the sublime in a continuous spectrum, positing the latter as the ultimate realization of the former (and, conversely, the former as an initiation into the latter). What, Wagner argues, the experience of the beautiful achieves in relation to the plastic arts—what the plastic arts yield as a net result, so to speak, through disinterested contemplation (the tranquilizing of pleasure)—this is what music would effectuate *immediately*, as a matter of course, "inasmuch as she withdraws us at once from any concern with the relation of things outside us" (*B* 78). Seen in this light, music, "proper" music, is in principle always ahead of the other arts, and this is why it cannot be judged according to the same aesthetic principles.

No doubt there is too much of the automatic here: the listener reduced to a will-less automaton mimicking the dumb waking of the somnambulist, the music mechanically mesmerizing the listener into that between-state. The problem here would be the intertwining of the essential and the artificial that circulates as an accidental subtext in the *Beethoven* essay. Wagner presents the "spiritual" as the essential, the ultimate vision of life, but insofar as the "essential" is here an inner, self-evident truth, it is nevertheless always already imbued with the traits of the automaton that apparently has no inner self but acts helplessly and unthinkingly on external stimuli. Typically, the automaton is posited as an extension, in contrast to the intensity of the soul, but it is precisely in its status as an annexation that the automaton informs the alleged autonomy of the soul: *in* its subjection it is *self*-moving, touched from the outside but persisting on its own, going on and on, without end.

Likewise, the automatic transitions from the conscious to the unconscious sphere that "proper" music would be able to effectuate are questionable as inherent, necessary transitions. If we were to take Wagner seriously, and music just as much, music would be a looming hypnotic power that could cast us at any time, at any place, into a state of complete self-forgetfulness, without any effort on either part. It would just *happen* (and perhaps, to a certain extent it *has* happened in the twentieth century through the strategic uses of subliminal music). Wagner's promotion of music's noumenal potential almost reads like a Barthean mythology: "music" no longer merely denotes a sound world but becomes a secondary sign that connotes the promise of a spiritual experience of self-loss and self-fulfillment at the same time: an experience in which an individual objectification of the Will (the subject) merges with the larger life-Will. "Music" is thus constructed as a mystic passage, a promise of return to the One.

A first requirement for such a regressive experience would nevertheless be an impossible transcending of the forms of space and time. Insofar as music is traditionally conceived as an art existing in, grounded by, and giving shape to (the passing of) time, this poses an irresolvable paradox. Here Schopenhauer's concept of the frozen cadenza offers an easy way out: if music can never quite kill time in the sense of doing without it, the *awareness* of temporal progression may be interrupted all the same in a musical fragment released from the constraints of an all too strict and obvious symmetric rhythmic emphasis. Starting from this, the *Beethoven* essay radicalizes Schopenhauer's suggestion and posits that music can *already* make for a temporal forgetfulness when it turns away from the architectonic. Or, to put this in reverse, if music only has to release itself from the grip of architectonic symmetry to redirect itself to the sublime, *then the despatialization thus achieved at once makes for (the possibility of) an atemporalization*: for a sense of timelessness that is, according to Wagner, typical of the sublime. After all, if rhythmic regularity derives from an uncouth analogy between music and architecture—that is to say, if this regularity is an architectonic instead of musical aspect—then this *regularity* is music's *spatial* aspect. Breaking this aspect momentarily is potentially also breaking the consciousness of time extended in space, of movement in space. This break, in the *Beethoven* essay, constitutes the sublime moment, the moment when the visible world disappears, when sight is disrupted and the subject momentarily walks with eyes wide shut.

Theoretically at least, Wagner thus presents music ("music" as mythology) as an implicitly sublime art. If the architectonic conditions an even, temporal progression in music, if this is not and never was a properly "musical" procedure, and if the sublime requires an undoing of such a progression, then it is really only in the sublime that music can come to "itself" and reveal its "proper" nature. In the Wagnerian mythology, the two require each other. The sublime requires the possibility of an idea of boundlessness, while music must, precisely, be (re)made to perform a break in the temporal context suggesting a timeless, endless leap. If this amounts to a tautology, then this is probably precisely what the Wagnerian musical mythology purports: music repeats the gesture of the sublime, and vice versa.

Requirements, however, still involve demands and imperatives—they involve regulations. In the *Beethoven* essay, these are concrete regulations that point to the suppression of a strict and rigid pulse. Music as mythology (as a sign of the sublime) here starts to dictate the specificity of music as a cultural practice—its modes of presentation. The church music of Palestrina qualifies as an example:

> [here] rhythm is still only perceivable through the change in harmonic chord-sequences . . . here, therefore, the temporal sequence is still so immediately tied to the harmony, which is in itself without time and space, that the form of time cannot yet at all be deployed as an aid to understand such music. The only temporal succession in such a musical piece manifests itself in the faintest transformations of a primary color, whose myriad transitions . . . are brought before us. . . . Because, however, this color does not appear in space, we receive both a space- and timeless image, a thoroughly spiritual revelation . . . (*B* 79)

There is, perhaps, something very naïve about the presumption that the "nature" of harmony is neither temporally nor spatially determined. Likewise, the idea that the dependence of rhythm on harmony would by implication undo the "architectonic" element in music is questionable. For one thing, the dominance of harmony in much eighteenth- and nineteenth-century music hardly ensures a move away from rhythmic regularity. Within the dominant structure of tonality, harmony is the formative principle, making for a movement of tension and resolution, whereby rhythmic symmetry is made *dependent* on the oscillation of consonance and dissonance. Significantly, classical as well as much romantic music presents a hegemony of harmony and it is precisely in its service that rhythm performs its "architectonic" function—that it is made to provide for the sense of oversight or "surveyability" Wagner seeks to undo.

However, for all its apparent preposterousness, Wagner's claim that music can adopt a temporal stillness, an unprogressive quality, by withdrawing into a play with colors not yet spatially determined, nevertheless has an intriguing plausibility to it. "Color" in this instance would be timbre or tone-color rather than any visually explicit coloring: the foregrounding of harmonics (instead of harmony: i.e., the overtone series) and resonances determining the aural characteristics of a tone that "backgrounds" a strict rhythm. One would only have to think of Claude Debussy, Federico Mompou, or Olivier Messiaen to imagine a musical ruin as a (pure) play with coloristic nuances that—however briefly—arrest or withhold clear and insistent pulsations *within* the confines of an ongoing (inner) temporal stream. That is to say, the impression of timelessness can only "take place" *set against* a framework of temporal organization (however damped, however minimal): the former requires this juxtaposition with the latter to delineate, to unfold itself. Timelessness in this matter is therefore not to be regarded in the essentialist mode (can there be timeless music?) but in the theatrical mode (how can timelessness be staged or simulated within an inevitable [perceptual] flow of inner time?). Within these parameters, musical ruins could be embodied as fragments floating in a-tactical harmonic sequences that are no longer (completely) determined by predictable tonal dynamics but that cut short the sense of time progressing in a rigidly balanced environment. Thus, these sequences could be imagined as a series of chromatic inflections materializing in moments without an apparent before or after—they would be, precisely, frozen points of "now."

To say "chromatic" is perhaps at once to invoke Wagner's *Tristan* Prelude and its irresolute opening measures, which perform precisely the kind of timbral foregrounding discussed above. Can this music, in listening to it, freeze time within the unfolding of time? And could this be related to the chromatic "twist" that Wagner raised to a style in the Prelude as a whole, rather than in the *Tristan*-chord alone?[16] Though not quite removing tonal harmony, *Tristan* nevertheless seriously undermines it, and it is this undermining that renders the Prelude its typical indeterminacy. My analysis of the first eighteen measures of the Prelude is based upon James Levine's performance with the Metropolitan Orchestra , which acts out emphatically the dynamic hesitation between stillness and movement that marks out the Wagnerian sublime.[17]

From a twenty-first-century perspective—after the serialists and the minimalists—these sounds may hardly invoke (however briefly) a sense of time interrupted. Even though Wagner explores the edges of traditional harmony in his tonally undecidable chord "progressions," the Prelude is still very much metrically balanced, with a conventional emphasis on first beats (as at $0'13''$, $0'21''$, $0'42''$, $0'49''$, $1'10''$, $1'17''$, $1'25''$, $1'32''$; corresponding to mm. 3, 4, 7, 8, 11, 12, 13, 14). Such emphases facilitate an orientation in time through the anticipation of a more or less steady pulse: the dynamic is up and down, up and down, the opening beat of each measure coinciding precisely with the advent of each new chromatic chord. Rhythmic regularity and harmonic developments are thus still very much intertwined here.

However, in between these conventional dynamics, the Prelude to *Tristan* defers and interrupts metric continuation ($0'25''$–$0'31''$, corresponding to mm. 4–5, and $0'53''$–$0'40''$, corresponding to mm. 8–9), stretches rests and pauses that postpone the unfolding of new cadenzas ($1'22''-1'25''$, corresponding to m. 12, $1'37''-1'40''$, corresponding to m. 14—although these cadenzas are emphatically anticipated), and even hesitates in between the chromatic steps of each ascending cluster (cf. f–e at $0'05''-0'12''$, corresponding to m. 2). If not a real transcendence of pulse, this nevertheless suggests a slippage *within* emphatic time: *within* an accented unfolding and returning of temporal patterns, these deferrals and interruptions are indices of an impossible fluidity that can only announce itself as provisional, intervallic. As such, aurally mimicking the sudden slippages of daydreaming, these timed intervals point to a different experiential possibility that can be called fugitive—untenable, immemorial (for timeless), and elusive.

Contemporary critics of *Tristan and Isolde* were quick to label these experiments in fugal time and chromatic borderlining "formless." Hanslick, for one, dismissed Wagner's "doctrine of endless melody" as a doctrine of nothing but chaos, "formlessness raised to the level of a principle."[18] Likewise, H. F. Frost claimed that "the composer has thrown aside definitely and unflinchingly the laws of form which were once carefully observed in opera as in other species of composition."[19] For Frost, the Prelude was "rhapsodical," probably due to the peculiar, chromatic tonal relations that create a sense of groundlessness, of a melodic fragment without a place or origin.[20] This, of course, is related to Wagner's practice of unending melody that Hanslick refused to acknowledge as a proper musical procedure, since it issued from a more or less a-functional harmony. Here, it is well known, the "regular" relationship between dominant and tonic is subverted: instead of letting the latter (granting resolution) succeed the former (requiring resolution) in a decisive way, Wagner made the tonic, or what listeners attuned to classical harmony expect to be tonic, into a *dominant*—and so on, and so on. As we know, this is a potentially endless mechanism of suspension, since "one chord always becomes the dominant of the next," an imminent resolution dissolving into a renewed indeterminacy, which in turn wants resolution, et cetera.[21]

In the discourse of romantic *Sehnsucht*, one could of course also say that endless melody opens up an infinite prospect of deferral that is sustained by the process of one chord becoming never more than an anticipation of the next, which in turn is nothing but a renewed anticipation. The process exemplifies, perhaps, Schopenhauer's claim that "the object of desire had only *seemed* to be that; possession takes away its fascination; the wish, the need, reintroduces itself in a new form; when it does not, then follow desolation, emptiness, boredom, against which the struggle is just as painful as against want" (*WW* I, §57, 430). And of course, as is well-known, in his letter to Mathilde von Wesendonck (which has been exhaustively discussed in *Tristan* criticism) Wagner already projects such a scenario of infinite longing for *Tristan*.

The combination of temporal "gapping" and chromatic anticipation may be described metaphorically as a disruption of what Wagner calls *Überschaulichkeit*: deprived of harmonic "signposts" (a clearly established tonic) and metric rigidity, the listener is also deprived of a sense of orientation, a sense of overview. In this case, this would literally translate into a disability to see "past" the next tone toward an ending or opening: as yet another anticipation that next tone functions like a blind wall blocking a narrative-progressive listening toward a beyond which will resolve the ambiguities encountered. Thus, ironically, the play with anticipation here precisely obstructs the kind of structural anticipation, the controlling foresight the listener is granted in mainstream classical and romantic music to project a consistent, comprehensive whole.

Reverting to metaphor once more, one could visualize this decentered listening as ascending a downward-moving escalator, whereby every step forward is at once a step backward, every progression at once a regression. Recalling Burke's Lockean-based experience of infinity, in which one remains standing in one place while only seeming to move ahead (see chapters 1 and 2, above), the beginning of the *Tristan* Prelude invokes a sense of stasis, of a movement that becomes itself immobile—an apparently eternal present. As such, paradoxically, the opening of the Prelude effectively simulates an idea of timelessness, of a timeless moment, through an anticipation without end issued by a chromatic transition without end. Listening, one does not progress from a before to a present to an after. One remains, instead, suspended in an immobile instant that is, precisely, brought about by a movement repeatedly returning to its starting position.

Thus, significantly enough, the idea of timelessness is here occasioned by *a simulation of endless time*. It is triggered by a potentially endless succession or chromatic color switching, which, always already retracting as it proceeds, constantly undermines its own development and accomplishment. It is this movement without movement, if you will, that arrests the listener in a moment *as if* without temporal progression, whereby an "after" is not absent *per se* but rather constantly postponed. In this way, while never actually transcending time, the Prelude's opening measures create an experiential illusion of timelessness that draws from a repeated deferral of temporal progression as a progression of *narrative* time with a clearly marked before, present, and after.

Knowing this, it remains very much to be seen if the Prelude's opening evokes a sense of complete forgetfulness: the forgetfulness that Wagner considers a sublime intensification of the not-so-complete forgetfulness excited by the beautiful. Listening to these tones, do I somehow forget my individuality, do I forget the world of appearances, do I forget time in an undivided joy of eternity? Hardly. Forgetfulness here implying tensionlessness, and tensionlessness in turn implying an ultimate, definite pleasure, the music allows for neither an absence of tension nor for an absence of pain. Rather, insofar as forgetfulness is a forgetting of time, and insofar as the forgetting of time is here precisely made dependent on, or embedded within, an anticipating without end, the ostensible forgetfulness triggered by a timeless moment is subtended by a painful awareness of not being able to transcend time as constant flux. It is a tense awareness of an endless sequence (a chord constantly turning into the dominant of the next, a sequence constantly returning to its starting point) that can neither be comprehended nor overcome: of not being able to move along or ahead, being stuck before an "ever-next" obstructing a cathartic release. Seen from this perspective, the Prelude to *Tristan* approaches more Schopenhauer's idea of the sublime as an internally divided feeling of forgetfulness and an inability to forget at once than Wagner's idea of the sublime as the superbeautiful. It performs, as it were, the Schopenhauerian dictum that a brief and ultimately untenable moment of ecstatic release is already undermined as it is "lived" in a frustrating, counteractive memory to the Will relentlessly pulling from the other side.

Nietzsche: The Sublime, the Musical, and the Dionysian

This invokes the specter of a divided subject that represents not so much a unity as a contradiction: an interplay, as Nietzsche would call it, between the Apollonian (the phenomenal) and the Dionysian (the noumenal) spheres. Elaborating on Schopenhauer and Wagner, Nietzsche presents these spheres as interdependent in *The Birth of Tragedy*: insofar as the world is determined by unconscious drives (formlessness), these drives *sustain* themselves by way of "show" (beautiful forms, here emphatically including artistic forms). Conversely, *Schein*, the world as representation, is the *product* of that terrible, primary force that Nietzsche, too, alludes to as the life-Will.

As with Schopenhauer, *Schein* is a buffer or beautiful illusion fending off the aimlessness of a Will-driven existence. As a *life*-Will, the Will requires this illusion; it feeds on the lure of the Apollonian that makes life bearable and worthwhile. If we could see through the forms that enchant and stimulate, *The Birth of Tragedy* postulates, we would see right into the destructive, aimless rhythm of life and reject it: we would no longer want to be. But the Will *demands* individual life forms to sustain themselves, and *needs* to redeem itself through the Apollonian illusion. By means of "an illusion spread over things," Nietzsche remarks, "the greedy Will finds some way of detaining its creatures in life and forcing them to carry on living" (*BT* chap. 18, 85). Or, as he states it earlier: "the eternally suffering and contradictory, primordial unity, simultaneously needs, for its constant release and redemption, the ecstatic vision, intensely pleasurable semblance (*BT* chap. 4, 26). Thus the subject (as an individual manifestation of the Will) is cunningly attached to life—and thus the Will, as the presumed other of transfiguring *Schein*, has a deep interest in it.

Given the fact that Nietzsche associates the Apollonian *Schein* with the pleasure taken in radiant appearances and the Dionysian *Rausch* with the self-loss of an overwhelming intoxication, it is hardly surprising that he should connect the former to the category of the beautiful and the latter to the category of the sublime in their mutual exchange. Christian Lipperheide has, to this effect, retrieved the following fragment from Nietzsche's *Nachlaß* of 1869–1874: "If the beautiful is rooted in a dream . . . then the sublime is rooted in an intoxication [*Rausch*]. . . . The storm at sea, the wild, the Pyramid is the sublime in nature. . . . The excess of Will occasions sublime impressions, overwhelming drives. The terrifying experience of the boundlessness of the Will. The curbing of the Will [*Das Maaß des Willens*] gives rise to the beautiful. The beautiful and the light, the sublime and the dark."[22]

Comparable to Burke's notion of an astonishment tinged with horror in his sensualist aesthetics of the sublime, Lipperheide observes that Nietzsche's idea of Dionysian *Rausch* involves a sudden experience of attraction and repugnance, of ecstasy and terror, at the same time.[23] This moment is, however, as brief as it is uncontrollable. It is, after all, somehow experienced beyond the bounds of consciousness in a moment of radical forgetfulness that redirects the individual to the Primal One. As Nietzsche describes this moment:

> For brief moments we are truly the primordial being itself and we feel its
> unbounded greed and lust for being; the struggle, the agony, the destruction

of appearances, all this now seems to us necessary, given the uncountable excess of forms of existence thrusting and pushing themselves into life, given the exuberant fertility of the world-Will; we are pierced by the furious sting of these torments at the very moment when, as it were, we become one with the immeasurable, primordial delight in existence, and receive an intimation, in Dionysiac ecstasy, that this delight is indestructible and eternal. Despite fear and pity we are happily alive, not as individuals, but as the *one* living being, with whose procreative lust we have become one. (*BT* chap. 17, 81)

This epiphany holds pain and pleasure in one. Just as one is "pierced" by the indestructibly destructive power of the Will, one also partakes of—in becoming—the immeasurable and eternal delight in existence that, ultimately, accounts for the destruction witnessed. An excess of life forms, driven by an insatiable lust for life, pushes its way in and, thus, pushes others out: the greed for life inevitably involves a destruction of life, the one form feeding on the other, constantly evolving, constantly devouring, constantly becoming. This is looking at Will-full destruction from a different perspective—not with fear and horror and repulsion alone but also with a delight taken in a primal and imperturbable life-Will that infuses and sustains all. It is a momentary (self-)recognition that Nietzsche calls a *metaphysical consolation*: not a seeing away but a seeing "through" (81).

This unwarranted seeing-through marks the difference between artistic and tragic culture: it draws consolation not from a bright-beaming illusion but from the affirmative recognition that "eternal life flows on indestructibly beneath the turmoil of appearances"—that the death of the individual only signifies death to the extent that, precisely, one ceases to be as an individual but continues to live on in the single living force that is the Will (*BT* chap. 18, 85). The delight occasioned by the Dionysian *Rausch* thus not so much amounts to a Burkean delight of one's vitality within the limits of individuation but as part of the life-generating (if also individual life–consuming) power of the Will. It is a delight in *partaking of* the Will and no longer fearing it, in seeing the horror but also, and at the very same time, sensing the delight of an ongoing, life-sustaining desire. A mystical experience, one could well say, without a traditional Western God.

Thus, the Nietzschean sublime seems to repeat the closure of the Kantian sublime, with a difference: the closure of a consoling insight not that nature cannot touch the individual, that one is morally independent, but rather that one is part of nature as a creative if also terrifyingly destructive force. That one is, if you like, indestructible precisely in joyfully partaking of the Will that also threatens one as an individual. Expanding into eternity in a momentary loss of ego boundaries, one here hears not the voice of reason but the voice of nature saying, in Nietzsche's words: "Be as I am!—the primal mother, eternally creative beneath the surface of incessantly changing appearances, eternally forcing life into existence, forever satisfying myself with these changing appearances!" (*BT* chap. 16, 80).

Within the confines of *The Birth of Tragedy* there is, however, something inconclusive about this "sublime turning" from terror to joy. For one thing, Nietzsche insists that the joy of sensing an infinite existence is felt *just as* one is pervaded by the destructive torments of the Will—this is, then, not a joy that concludes but a joy that accompanies pain. For another, metaphysical consolation is only had during a consciousness-suspending instant. Now, in the experience of *Rausch* this forgetfulness radically separates the Dionysian reality from the world of "everyday life": the two are separated by a "gulf of oblivion" that cannot be mediated (*BT* chap. 7, 40). This carries with it the implication that the metaphysical consolation cannot fully pervade the waking subject *as* subject, that the delight it issues cannot be fully felt or retained. That is, differently said, the delight is instantly forgotten in the immediate loss of the instant; it does not stick and cannot be retrieved. Once more: now you see it, now you don't.

At the same time, this delight of a complete self-loss is *incompatible* with the desire for self-preservation, which, to all appearances, governs the individual in the phenomenal world. The joy of sensing an infinite, self-less existence in the eternal life-Will requires a (heroic) transcending or letting go of the terror of losing one's individual limits. This, however, in turn conflicts with the (necessary) desire brought about by the Apollonian *Schein* to cling to one's individual life. For the conscious subject, moving in the waking world of appearances, such joy seems almost too much to bear and is in fact too dangerous to be fully consumed: just as dangerous, in fact, as the insight into the nullity of existence gained from the painful recognition of an aimless, usurping Will.

Music as Rausch—*with a Safety Net*

In *The Birth of Tragedy*, this danger is foregrounded in an elaboration on Wagner's *Tristan*: somehow, it would provide the listener with an immediate, almost insupportable experience of the Will's raging force. As an embodiment of the Will, music embodies the Dionysian sphere and the

boundlessness and formlessness that sphere entails: it does not specify, individuate, or represent, but rather it brings that "blissful ecstasy which arises
from the innermost ground of man, indeed of nature itself, [at the] breaking
down of the *principum individuationis*" (*BT* chap. 1, 17). Semantic hesitation
thus connects to ontological revelations in *The Birth of Tragedy*, since it is the
indeterminacy of musical signification that here connects it with the general
"in itself" of the Will and dissociates it from the specific, recognizable
shapes of the Apollonian domain. As such, as Nietzsche repeats Wagner,
music

> is to be assessed by quite different aesthetic criteria from those which apply
> to all image-making arts, and not at all by the category of beauty . . . despite
> the fact that an erroneous aesthetics, following the example of misguided and
> degenerate art and basing itself on a concept of beauty which is valid in the
> world of image-making, has been in the habit of demanding from music the
> same effect [*Wirkung*] as is demanded of the arts of image-making, namely
> that it should arouse *pleasure in beautiful forms*. (*BT* chap. 16, 77)

Nietzsche here persists and extends Wagner's creative misreading of
Schopenhauer's game of thought: music has degenerated into an Apollonian
art in an "improper" analogy between the sonorous and the plastic. Such
impropriety is here doubly connected to duplicity, insofar as Apollonian (or
"architectonic") music would oblige a game of mirroring or recognition: it
seeks to "excite our pleasure merely by compelling us to seek out external
analogies between events in life or nature and certain rhythmical figures and
characteristic musical sounds" (*BT* chap. 17, 83). It is such music, Nietzsche
ventures, which had been long familiar to the post-Hellenic Greeks: a music
with "a wave-like [i.e., regular] rhythm with an image-making power. . . .
The music of Apollo was Doric architectonics in sound, but only in the
kind of hinted-at tones characteristic of the *cithara*" (*BT* chap. 2, 21). All
that is characteristic of Dionysian music and "music in general" (which by
definition makes Dionysian music into "true" music) was kept at bay in this
Schein-oriented music. It effaced "the power of its sound to shake us to our
very foundations, the unified stream of melody [cf. Wagner's unending mel-
ody], and the quite incomparable world of harmony" (*BT* chap. 2, 21).
Thus, familiarly sublime (and indeed Wagnerian) musical effects—
disconcerting, overpowering tone, the simulation of the infinite in unending melody, the disruption of the visual—are its Dionysian and, to that
extent, its "proper" effects.

There is, however, a limit to what the listening subject can bear as a product of individuation—and to what the Dionysian can achieve on its own. The abyss of life-greed requires the transfigurative veil of the Apollonian to prevent the individual from a complete regress into that abyss and fall apart. Taking Wagner's *Tristan* as an example, Nietzsche claims that—just as the Dionysian and Apollonian are interdependent in their very opposition—the overwhelming and excessive effect of the music (the sublime) heard is here nevertheless necessarily absorbed in the image-world (the beautiful) of the drama enacted. Thus, he asks:

> [can a genuine musician] conceive of any person capable of perceiving the third act of *Tristan and Isolde* purely as a vast symphonic movement, with no assistance from words or images, and who would not then suffocate as their soul attempted, convulsively, to spread its wings. How could anyone fail to be shattered immediately, having once put their ear to the heart of the universal Will, so to speak, and felt the raging desire for existence pour forth into all arteries of the world as a thundering torrent or as the finest spray of a stream? Is such a person, trapped within the miserable glass vessel of human individuality supposed to be able to bear listening to countless calls of lust and woe re-echoing from the "wide space of the world's night," without feeling, unstoppably, with the strains of his shepherd's dance of metaphysics in his ear, towards his first and original home? (*BT* chap. 21, 100–101)

How could one bear the separation? The answer could be the following: "Tragedy absorbs the supreme, orgiastic qualities of music" that, as Dionysian qualities, tend toward a denial of self, a dissolving of self in the eternal existence of the primordial life-current (*BT* chap. 21, 99). Evidently, insofar as music is thus able to "break" the mind, the joy of sensing an eternal, selfless existence is just as lethal to individual life as the sudden recognition of the cruelty inherent to that eternal existence. It kindles a regressive desire that denounces individual existence. What, however, the drama would here achieve to counter this self-dissolving tendency is a move away from the "general" world of music to the world of individuals and individual actions. Tragedy is, for Nietzsche, already the symbolic expression of the unconscious "Dionysian wisdom" allegedly immediately embodied in music (*BT* chap. 21, 104). Here, this symbolic transfiguration serves to take away the immediately disarming effect of the world-Will (the disarming effect, one could say, of a death wish that is ultimately an infinite [self-less] life-wish) through a process of *imaginative identification*. Aristotelian catharsis provides the safety net:

This is where the power of the *Apolline*, bent on restoring the almost shattered individual, bursts forth, bringing the healing balm of a blissful deception; suddenly we believe we are hearing only Tristan as he asks himself, motionless and dumbed, "the old melody; why does it wake me?" . . . And where we had imagined we were expiring, breathless, in the convulsive reaching-out of all feelings, and that there was little which still tied us to this existence, now we hear and see only the hero. . . . Powerfully though compassion may reach into us and seize hold of our feelings, in a sense compassion saves us from the primal suffering of the world . . . just as thoughts and words save us from the unchecked outpouring of the unconscious Will. (*BT* chap. 21, 101)

Compassion, immersion, identification saves us from ourselves. Whence the duplicity (in the form of identification) after all? If the listener must somehow be protected from music, then why not use music as an art that redirects the listener to the phenomenal world? Why reject the "plastic rhythm" and "Doric architecture" of Apollonian music, when the Apollonian force is needed to remove the immediately overwhelming effects of Dionysian music, that is, music *per se*? The answer could be twofold. First, insofar as music is made to assume an Apollonian veil, it can for Nietzsche do so only insufficiently. Even if it suggests the movements, outlines of a scene, it can do no more than suggest rather than fully specify it. Second, in *The Birth of Tragedy* music is not supposed to assume such a veil. What it is supposed to do is to operate like an ominous but also powerfully attractive undercurrent in cooperation or dialogue with a represented, Apollonian world of myth "that tears us away from Dionysiac generality and causes us to take delight in individuals (*BT* chap. 21, 102). This suggests that an Apollonian music effaces the Dionysian element altogether, while Wagner's music-dramas—resembling for Nietzsche the Attic tragedies—sustain the Dionysian element though at the same time putting it at a distance in combination with the Apollonian illusion of the drama witnessed. The two must work together, instead of the latter absorbing the former completely.[24]

The effects of myth thus accompanying music are, we have seen, not to be underestimated. They provide, if you will, the necessary fictional context not just to make bearable the Dionysian "truth" sensed through the music but (in Jos de Mul's words) to allow it to "become capable of being experienced" without the subject instantly crashing apart.[25] What is at stake here is that a real threat is transformed into an imaginary threat through the interposition of the characters on stage: the myth must project a virtual space for the sounds not to become lethal. The spectator-listener, in the case of *Tristan*, indeed hears the innermost abyss of things (through the music heard), but the tragic myth—interposed like some concrete barrier—deludes this spectator-listener into thinking that it is through the *myth*, and the imaginary identification with the tragic hero/heroine, that he or she witnesses an *imaginary* abyss.

In this way, one could say, the Wagnerian music drama in Nietzsche's perception effectuates not an effacing of the Dionysian through art but a facing of the Dionysian abyss in the presence—and through the protective filter—of an Apollonian safety net. It is pain and pleasure, danger and safety, in one, the music constantly resounding with the greedy life-Will, the myth containing and transfiguring it in such a way that the tragic hero (or heroine) takes on the entire Dionysian burden, relieving the spectator-listener from it (*BT* chap. 21, 99). However, insofar as the Apollonian safety net prevents the spectator-listener from drowning into the Dionysian current, the former never conclusively covers or removes the power emanating from the latter. "In the total effect of the tragedy," it is not the Apollonian but the Dionysian that "gains the upper hand" (*BT* chap. 21, 103). This inconclusiveness is already preordained by the fact that the Nietzschean sublime does not revolve around an external threat but around an inescapable, internal conflict at the heart of life itself: the threat of the life-Will. Embedded within a tragic worldview, the self-conflicting experience of the sublime here takes on a more profound and irresolvable aspect in its relation to the irremovable conflict that defines, and in a way sustains, existence.

Thus, just as Schopenhauer's aesthetics of the sublime revolves around a duplicity within subjectivity, so Nietzsche's approach to the sublime as associated with the Dionysian brings home, in Andrew Bowie's words, "the inherent transience and incompleteness of individual subjective existence," while at the same time "suggesting . . . a striving for the infinite," a joyous "affirming of eternal life."[26] It presents a subject that is at once a subject of representation and a subject of the Will, at once suffering from and delighting in the (regressive) loss of the *principium individuationis*, the loss of its own limits that finally constitute it *as* a subject. Together, music and myth embody the possibility to experience this impossible duplicity.

Seidl: Musically Sublime

In the writings of Wagner and Nietzsche, Schopenhauer's notion of a frozen cadenza at once points to a musical device and a general musical "trait":

how music "is" or should be as severed from the architectonic. This indicates a regulative movement from music as a concept, as myth, to music as practice: the one suggests and informs the gestures of the other. In a now relatively little-known dissertation on the musically sublime, the philosopher-musicologist Arthur Seidl rehearsed and recast this duplicity more systematically.[27] Inspired by Schopenhauer and Wagner, Seidl both sought to determine how the sublime can be invoked *in* or *by way of* music and asked what specifically makes for the sublime *of* music. Can one conceive of a specifically musically sublime experience, relative to musical aspects and events *as such* (such as sounds, sound colors, or tonal inflexions), rather than an imaginary experience of, say, a violent sea or raging storm conducive to the idea of the sublime as suggested or simulated by musical sounds and movements?

The question is typically formalist, and even though Seidl positions himself in opposition to Hanslick's notion of the musically beautiful, he cannot relinquish the formalist discourse—indeed, this discourse is always already present in Seidl's defense of the musically sublime. He is in search of that "something" that distinguishes music from the other arts and, indeed, from the reality that we daily live.

Within these parameters, one could consider Seidl's essay as an attempt to launch a new aesthetics for a new music. According to him, Hanslick's theory of the musically beautiful only applies to the Mozartian school (*ME* 1). Here, everything would stand "as fixed and concluded in itself," the music ruled by proportional metric symmetry and "plastic surveyability" (*ME* 128). Seidl in this instance alludes to the Hanslickian notion of "tonal arabesques" [*Tonarabesken*] that "always mutually correspond with each other in their windings, connect with each other in ranks [*Gliedern*] and groups and . . . together always make up a specific tonal drawing, an accomplished, self-enclosed, finished musical painting: Limitation!—everything rests harmonically, firmly rooted in and on itself (as Hanslick has also described this . . . in a similar way)" (*ME* 129).

Ironically, when Hanslick comes to speak of the arabesque, he emphasizes its *sublime* effect, as its lines "expand and contract and forever astonish the eye with their ingenious alternation of tension and repose."[28] It is not difficult to connect boundlessness to such an intricate weaving of forms evolving in and out of each other in a pattern potentially without end. No doubt, such shapely designs are all too neatly proportioned and visually oriented in Seidl's perspective, yet they nevertheless intimate what his new musical aesthetics would be after: to accommodate a music that defies limitation, and that does not conform to the idea of neatly bounded forms. What if music strives toward the unbounded and, to this end, defies the easily graspable proportions of the beautiful? What if, as Seidl observes with respect to the Adagio of Beethoven's Ninth, music feeds on metric freedom and displays such an "extraordinary connection of . . . melodic phrases, the one already starting where the other stops," without any kind of "satisfying ending" setting in, so that the whole cannot be easily overseen (*ME* 128)? Hanslick's theory of the musically beautiful would be "totally inadequate" to account for such music (*ME* 130).

In Seidl's alternative, the first—and rather awkward—step is a short-circuiting of the imagination. If Kant had already pointed to such a short-circuiting in the third *Critique* as an interruption of the formative power, Seidl radicalizes this interval into a general law where the musically sublime is at stake: to evoke the specifically musically sublime on the basis of "purely" musical impressions, the creative and associative faculty of the imagination must be cancelled out. Seidl thus assumes a direct (and somewhat naïve) causal relation between a short-circuiting of the force of visualizing and the "arising" of the musically sublime. In the setting of this short-circuiting, listeners might begin to feel the sublime *of* music.

This route to the musically sublime is once more derived from Wagner's appropriation of Schopenhauer's frozen cadenza: the possibility of an unarchitectonic music that blocks out-sight and obstructs a recall of the movements and figurations of the phenomenal world (*ME* 113). Building on Wagner's Schopenhauerian notion of music as an immediate objectification of the Will, Seidl suggests that such an "intrinsic" musically sublime is conditioned by a rupture of music's (inordinately) plastic element: its rhythmic regularity. Thus, he states,

> A music will answer to the specific character of its nature all the more, will, in this sense, fulfill its sublime calling all the sooner, the more . . . the absolutely rhythmical recedes behind its lively expression, and the less the tonally embodied (infinite) realm of the Will . . . is ensnared in the "guilt of appearances" by the medium of rhythm. . . . It can, further, be all the more sublime the more it renounces, within the rhythm set, the even, the symmetric-over-seeable. . . . As concerns melody, a . . . "bel canto" will ever more recall a [plastic] line . . . while by contrast the "unending melody"—more correctly put, the free-floating, fluctuating melody of a Richard Wagner—will generally touch [listeners] with the character of that truly musical "sublimity."
> (*ME* 117)

Music is here subjected to the kind of transcendental calling encountered in Kant's third *Critique*: it has a "sublime" destiny· or *Bestimmung* it is obliged—"calling" in the sense of obligation—to fulfill. It is to turn inward, like the Kantian subject is to turn inward and realize its own sublime potential. (And of course, the reference to the Kantian subject is ironic here since Kant decisively denied music the status of a fine or even "civilized"—let alone sublime—art). Music must be converted, insofar as conversions involve a moment of insight and a moment of change, and relinquish the memory of the sensible. Hence, the directions for irregular rhythms (Seidl suggests 5/4 or 7/4) that frustrate the kind of easy oversight relative to perfect symmetry: such irregularities would filter away, so to speak (inadvertent), recollections to bodies moving in space as they preclude the possibility of recurrent, metric accents rehearsing bodily patterns of gravitation (think of the recurrent first beat in 3/4 time that coincides with a falling movement of the body, the weight on the heel, then on the ball of the foot, that evolves into a rising movement at the end of the first beat). Of course, this is very much a cultural issue, since such irregular rhythms do not at all preclude such recollections for cultural participants in, for instance, Eastern European folk music.

Another issue here, however, is a symbolic-numerical issue. It is certainly no accident that Seidl uses prime numbers to illustrate the idea of rhythmic regularity. In Western music, metrical patterns have been dominantly binary (2/4, 4/4, etc.) and ternary (although the dominance in modern music tends to be decisively binary). The penchant for the binary can hardly be disconnected from ideals of perfect ratio and perfect symmetry in Western culture—and the psychological "fact" that the mind tends to group phenomena in twos and threes, so that even a uniform repetition of sounds would end up being processed mentally in binary or ternary fashion. However, in prime-number meters like the 5/4 and 7/4 that Seidl suggests, a perfect division into twos or threes cannot be made. In 5/4, for instance, the division would be two and three; two movements at work in the same metrical unit, which bars the occurrence (and, possibly, one's perception) of a stable, equivocal pulse.

Then again, prime-number meters may not merely occasion a felt rupture in one's temporal-spatial orientation otherwise taken for granted, so that the world of sensible, perceivable forms is—if only for a moment— under erasure. Prime numbers also intimate the "beyond" of the sensible world in a symbolic fashion. Indivisible (except by one and themselves) prime numbers have been familiarly associated with the singular, the one—

the ungraspable absolute. As such they are likely figures (literally speaking) of the sublime: they can be seen as *indices* of the sublime in their very incomparability, which is to say their inability to be factored: their resistance, so to speak, to being (de)composed into smaller parts. They are the very equal of the idea of a whole without composite units that remains beyond imaginative scope. Thus, one may conclude, irregular rhythms that are based on prime numbers latently *perform* the movement of the sublime not only in their possible straining of temporal-spatial orientation but also because they imply or enfold the "aspect" of the incomparable that is, precisely, the hallmark of the idea of the infinite as that which surpasses every measure, every standard of sense, and extends (like the irregular sequence of prime numbers) without end.

This is, then, where the sheer power of metaphor can take us: a program of the musically sublime, directions included, written on the vestiges of Schopenhauer's musical ruin as a playful figure of speech. For all Seidl's, Nietzsche's, and Wagner's efforts to ban the imaginary, unarchitectonic music is, in the final analysis, built on a trope that feeds on association and imaginary image making to come to life: the frozen cadenza (music) as the inverted other of frozen music (architecture). The musically sublime is, to that extent, built on a chain of "accidents" insofar as the idea of unarchitectonic music as a musical practice and even a musical "law" originated *in* its accidental, tropological dispersion.

What Seidl's argument suggests—and what composers like Ferruccio Busoni would imply in their inveighing against "architectonic" or "symmetric form"—is the interesting possibility that the musically sublime does not derive from music's syntactic parameters (cf. rhythm) but from its very *(tone-)materiality*.[29] The emphasis on the receding of symmetric form, and metric regularity in particular, suggests the scenario of a musically sublime that revolves around the *break-through of the matter of sound*.

Potentially, despite Seidl's overt (Hegelian) fascination with the supersensible, this could create an opening to a more recent, postmodern reading of the sublime proposed by Jean-François Lyotard. This reading relocates the sublime within a sphere of immanence instead of transcendence. Insistently, Lyotard recasts the moment of the sublime as the "happening" or "arising" of an unformed, boundless matter as sound, color or, more in general, openness and indeterminacy.[30] Indeed, where Lyotard touches on the sublime as a musical moment, he speaks of the timbre, the "unformed matter" of sound that dodges aesthetic determinations: the nuance of sound would bypass the mind insofar as it cannot be grasped, controlled, or repeated *in the act of listening* (*TI* 155–57). As an arising, it partakes of a flush of the here and now—of *this* nuance—and refuses to be born as form. As such, I will argue in the next chapter, this nuance performs what Seidl called *Formwidrig-keit* or form-contrariness in relation to the sublime: a form that harbors un-form, that is in conflict with itself and contradicts the senses in such a way that it constantly suggests its own impossibility (*ME* 46). Form-contrariness thus signals the limits not merely of what "form" can do and comprise but also what the mind can form or grasp.

4. Sounds Like Now: Form-Contrariness, Romanticism, and the Postmodern Sublime

In *The Inhuman*, Jean-François Lyotard invents a string of associations with the German *gehorsam sein*: to be obedient, or, literally translated, to be able or tending to hear. "To obey," Lyotard suggests, "is *gehorchen*. *Gehören* is not far, to pertain to, to depend on an agency, to fall into a domain, under an authority, a *dominus*. And *zuhören*, to lend one's ear." There is, Lyotard continues, "an inexhaustible network linking listening to belonging, to the sense of obligation, a passivity I would like to translate as *passibility*" (*TI* 178). As a concept, passibility nicely merges "possibility" with the idea of something coming to pass or being allowed to pass through. In Lyotard's book, being in a state of passibility means being in a mental state that hinges between activity and passivity, neither and both, a state of being open (mentally, bodily, creatively) so that something unexpected may arise. It is a "soliciting of emptiness," an "evacuation" of preconceptions and intentions, in short a state of indeterminacy in which one's mind is suspended so as to allow something un-thought (a word, phrase, color, sound that "doesn't yet exist") to come to pass (*TI* 19). And then, "it" happens, gracefully—or not.

Passibility could well be the key term for the postmodern sublime feeling: this feeling no longer exclusively turns on a mind suspended by shock but on a mind willingly suspending its own intentions to welcome the unknown. If and when an alien, un-thought event happens is contingent, yet it is this very contingency that makes up its sublimity as an *occurrence*: something that appears all of a sudden out of nowhere. This is the wonder of the postmodern sublime: a philosophical wonder celebrating *that* there is something rather than nothing, but also a creative wonder "belonging" to the painter, thinker, or composer who has suddenly hit on a new turn.[1]

It is significant that Lyotard should embed this concept of passibility in an aural network and in turn signify this network ethically in terms of dependability, obedience, and obligation: what is at stake here is not just the ability but also the demand to hear, to be receptive. Indeed, being receptive to an otherness that the mind cannot (yet) quite "place" or contain is what the postmodern sensitivity revolves around here: the sublime is invasive as it makes the soul or *anima*, as Lyotard calls it, aware of its own dependability on an "outside." It is not itself, as a core already available, but an other that propels its animation and apparition. Thus, the soul *is* not, "does not affect itself, it is only affected by the other. . . . Existing is to be awoken from the nothingness of disaffection by something sensible over there" (*PF* 243). The soul is *called upon*, in the very ancient sense of being implored or invoked, and in this calling senses its precariousness. It senses its vulnerability in the absence of an absolute foundation or autonomous "existence": it is contingent, relying, so to speak, on an intrusive violence that poses as external (an "over there") but is at the same time internal (an "already there") in its constitutive force. Responsiveness thus plays a crucial role in the postmodern sublime.

This urgency of responsiveness is reinforced in Lyotard's essays on Barnett Newman's abstract expressionist rerenderings of the pictorial sublime (*TI* 78–88, 89–107). Consistently, Lyotard here describes looking at the fourteen *Stations of the Cross* (1958–1966) in terms of the waiting and suspension he associates with hearing: "I (the viewer) am no more than an ear open to the sound which comes to it from out of the silence; the painting is that sound, an accord" (*TI* 83). Newman's paintings become aural events insofar as they embody happenings that occur suddenly, unforeseen. They do not "depict" the sublime but make it happen in their material occurring: if there is any "subject matter" in these paintings, Lyotard suggests, "it is immediacy. It happens here and now" (*TI* 82). These paintings do not show things; they present the act of becoming apparent: they offer the sublime performatively.

Self-pronouncements: the very possibility of self-presentation or self-performance is here intimately tied to a refusal to figure in the sense of realistic pictorial figuration creating the illusion of a three-dimensional space. That is to say, for Lyotard it is their apparent barrenness that allows these paintings to behave "aurally," to become events that *happen* materially, surface only, without a message or an afterthought, and affect the viewer in their happening *as* happening.[2] This is what—in Lyotard's texts—distinguishes the postmodern from the romantic sublime: postmodern is what wrecks and breaks the familiar forms that have been used to figure the unpresentable as an "over there," something residing beyond the horizon of sensuous grasp; it is the breaking itself of such familiar forms. The postmodern sublime is thus not a sublime of transcendence and figuration but a sublime of barrenness and performance; it *does*, minimally (*TI* 98).

Though this barrenness performs the sign of a break with past conventions, I will nevertheless frame it in this chapter with a romantic concept already encountered in the previous chapter: form-contrariness, or the possibility of form becoming un-form, undoing itself. My suggestion will be that form-contrariness cuts both ways in the romantic and postmodern "directions" of the aesthetics of the sublime. As we will see, this concept can operate as a suggestion of excess that cannot be heard but is felt as being "there" nonetheless, and as an interruption of form *per se*—the coming forth of matter itself without a beyond being thought in the background. Focusing on both romantic and (post)modern musical practices, my aim will be to show that Lyotard's binary distinction between the romantic and postmodern sublime is finally untenable.[3] Despite their obvious differences, both directions are nevertheless also reflexively inversed in their shared, "form-contrary" engagement with the matter of sound.

Second, I will explore the pattern of Lyotard's postmodern sublime feeling as a feeling that is "monochromatic," so to speak, in its insistence in the sphere of sensibility. It is a critical feeling that refuses or indeed precludes a turning from imagination to reason—as the Kantian model has dictated for so long—and in this respect would seem to question implicitly the narrative frame of the sublime feeling. However, even if this decapitated feeling depends on contingency instead of causality, it never quite opens the possibility of a simultaneous rather than successive occurring of pleasure and pain. Even where Lyotard invokes the concept of the *différend* to represent the sublime feeling as a double bind, this double bind has the nature of an unbridgeable abyss rather than an oscillation between two intensities that are mutually exclusive yet inexorably intertwined.

Form-Contrariness and the Sublime of Immanence

The *Chorus Mysticus* of Franz Liszt's *Faust* Symphony (1853)—as heard in Leonard Bernstein's and Kenneth Riegel's particularly dramatic recording of it[4]—features a male choir that is only harmonized when it sings about the transcendental attraction or "pulling" of the eternal-feminine: "Das Ewig-Weibliche/*Zieht uns hinan*" [The Eternal-Feminine/*Draws us heavenward*]."[5] Starting on a parallelized octave on C, which is to that extent unharmonized, and singing, almost declaiming throughout in bare, parallelized octaves, the choir's transition to C major enacts a moment of fulfillment

(17′08″, 17′29″). It is, of course, the fulfillment of the male-connoted subject that at last finds peace with itself by submerging in the edifying power of love. The eternal-feminine is, indeed, the redemption of this subject: as a transcendental force this is not simply a figure of "woman" but a male-constructed feminine object-offering posited as an intermediary of heaven, signaling hope and the possibility of inner harmony. According to Liszt's (notoriously undependable) writings on the matter, the eternal-feminine constitutes nothing less than a "third principle" in the mental life of male subjects that, apart from "obscure thoughts" (thinking) and "decisiveness" (acting), embodies the "need for an endless, indeterminate feeling."[6] Reduced to representing and, indeed, awakening an aspect of the male subject, the eternal-feminine is not just there on its own—it is there for *him*.[7]

And yet it is other, as a force affecting the subject from the outside and above. In the *Chorus Mysticus* this is most clearly enacted in the upward movement of the flutes, oboes, clarinets, and, especially, the harp (from 22′56″ onward) that will culminate in the C major chord of the organ. From 23′13″ (corresponding to m. 790) there is a steadily developed *crescendo* (rehearsing earlier phases of intensification) reinforcing this ascending gesture to an almost unbearable degree: in the end I am enveloped in an intensity of resonances in relation to which no "greater" can be imagined. Even as a resisting listener, weary of grand gestures that extol equally grand responses, I have a very real sense of being brought to the limit, a sense of progressing to an impossible point beyond the capacity of hearing, of a sonorous panorama extending to its outer reaches. And then—silence, brief and hasty, as if the panorama were suddenly locked away, not for human ears, impossible to retain: the mystical here coincides with the fermata.

Writing in a Wagnerian philosophical tradition, Arthur Seidl in his nineteenth-century dissertation on the musically sublime invokes the idea of such a steady crescendo to illustrate the effect of the sublime in music. In a more or less Kantian fashion, Seidl posits the sublime as a way out of the world of sensibility: the emphasis is on *Erhebung* through a painful encounter with something that defies—yet also stretches to its outer limits—the formative power of the imagination.

Upholding a typically metaphysical frame to think the sublime, Seidl's argument boils down to the idea that the "constitutive moments" of the sublime are binarily opposed to those of the beautiful: the latter feeds on "regularity, symmetry, harmony, etc.," the former on "amorphousness, disproportionality, lawlessness [*Regellosigkeit*], asymmetry, disharmony, etc." (*ME* 31). The binary is, however, difficult to sustain: the sublime may be all that, all these negatives of the formative, but as an artistic or artificial sublime it needs forms nonetheless—if only to set itself against it, to suggest a dramatic break that can only be realized effectively (and affectively) in the very understanding that forms have been ripped to pieces, do no longer count, are no longer valid, have been transcended or surpassed. In the formless the formative and formatted are, in one way or another, always already presupposed. This may equally lead one to conjecture that the beautiful (associated with forms) is, in one way or another, always already presupposed in the sublime as a force that announces the absence or beyond of forms. The former is not so much the unconnected other of the latter but rather *animates* the "presence" of the sublime (as Philippe Lacoue-Labarthe might say) *as* a "presence" that *de-limits*: there is, precisely, no possibility of the sublime (in art) without the possibility of limitation set against it.[8]

It is, therefore, no surprise that Seidl reverts to the idea of mediation to think the sublime in a formal or artificial setting. There is a compromise here: an object, which is to say a *figured* apparition, can take on such huge proportions that it may suggest an idea of absolute, rather than relative, greatness in the mind of the beholder. This idea is born out of an interaction between the object, which is never unlimited in "fact" but intimates the unlimited in its limitation, and the subject willing and able to process this intimation. This paradox therefore belongs to the artificial sublime: "the object already incites in the subject the mood [*Stimmung*] of the sublime through the particular nature of its shape [*Gestaltung*], through its own form": the shaped is an incentive for transcendence (*ME* 34).

It is this interaction between limitation and de-limitation that Seidl calls form-contrariness. This concept gestures the virtual presence of a negative presentation: a given form is here negated by the idea of a beyond-form to which it gives rise. There is something working against form that, precisely, reinforces its evocative potential.

Now, the difficulty for a declared Schopenhauerian-Wagnerian philosopher of music is to present music at once as form, as part of a "phenomenal" artistic practice, and as the objectified beyond-form of the Will. Does music need the principle of form-contrariness to evoke the sublime, when all it needs to do to *become* sublime is to cast off an illegitimate architectonic aspect enforcing a rhythmic regularity? Was not music already "in essence" the sublime incarnate (chapter 3)?

Indeed—but there is always the second-best: there is the convenient suggestion to distinguish the sublime *of* music from the sublime *in* music (*ME* 93–117). The former refers to a coinciding of the sublime and the musical (to which I will return below), while the latter refers to a "mere" figuring of the sublime through more or less conventional musical forms that—in no way different from other artistic forms—have the ability to intimate a presence of inordinate might or expansion. Here, the musical effect depends greatly on an engagement of imagination to try to progress actively beyond the set and heard limits of a musical occurrence. (Seidl presents this engagement of imagination as, precisely, being short-circuited when the sublime *of* music is at stake: the "out-sight" here associated with imaginative activity must be disrupted in favor of an aural seeing or blind hearing that would obliterate the visual altogether [chapter 3]).

A movement from a Schopenhauerian to a Hegelian perspective is fruitful in this respect. For what Seidl calls the sublime *in* music is in effect what Hegel has referred to in the *Science of Logic* as the "bad infinite"; an infinite progress of the imagination, a repetitiveness or indefinite egress that never quite (absolutely) negates the negation that is finitude.[9] Thus, Seidl points to the effects of excessive loudness and speed, of sharp dissonances, and of a long-built crescendo effectuated by an ever increasing tone mass. The "ever increase" in this instance depends on the felt awareness of an incurable lack—not an affirmative, absolute fulfillment: inspired by the increase of sound, the imagination is "incited to apprehend ever more, and to ascend ever higher. It even rushes ahead of what is given, what is concretely available [in the tones produced], progresses further and further on its own, and finally loses itself in an indeterminable, infinite height, that is to say, progresses up to an unbounded, omnipotent intensity, which leaves objective reality far behind" (*ME* 93–94).

There is a progression here that rehearses itself without end—and sustains the illusion of indefiniteness: the massive crescendo gives rise to an idea and even a response exceeding its own form by intimating unaccomplishedness. "Putting forward" the infinite, this crescendo, *as* postponement, embodies the possibility of endless extension. In this process, imagination would proceed *on its own*, as if fired by the intensifying movements of the music, into a realm that leaves the actual sound-world behind. It loses its sensible footing.

Paralleling the "bad" (or, for Burke, artificial) infinite, the sublime in music is thus effectuated through an ever increasing stretching of the scope of imagination, until it is lost in its own excessive activity (instead of the Kantian realization of a supersensible capacity of reason giving rise to the idea of infinity as absolute totality). It is the outcome of an imagination gone mad with the possibility of its own excess: the side effect of a delirium (*ME* 95–96).

Form-contrariness thus embodies a *technique* or perhaps even a *mechanism* of deception that presents the possibility of error—the imagination imagining to have transgressed the limits of sensibility while "in fact" endlessly appending, rehearsing sensible impressions—but also the possibility of destruction. Limitation is a condition of possibility for formation; limit, as Paolo Zellini has put it, "is what makes every object exist concretely, by constantly endowing it with the proper form and individuality." Disrupting this order of limitation brings "reality back to an amorphous and disorganized state, in which each thing loses its recognizable form as a concrete entity."[10] De-limitation thus interrupts formation and recognition: there is "not-something" to be heard or seen—it is a force of disorientation.

Amorphous states are difficult to imagine in music (one could perhaps think of the insistent and out-shaping tremolos in Alexander Scriabin's *Vers la flamme*, op. 72)—and yet. According to Lyotard, strategies of de-limitation and material interruption are typically performed in the experimental currents of the avant-gardes. These currents would perform in a very modern way the struggle with form and beyond-form that already surges in eighteenth- and nineteenth-century poetics and aesthetics of the sublime. "Modern," in this instance, refers to *a refusal to form* in recognizable, realist modes. Indeed, for Lyotard this locates the avant-gardes within the aesthetics of the sublime rather than that of the beautiful. This is their origin.

It is for this very reason that Seidl's romantic concept of form-contrariness—no matter how Hegelian his approach—may be of interest to Lyotard's postmodern reworking of the sublime. Form-contrariness illuminates and readjusts, I would like to suggest, central issues in Lyotard's essays on the sublime, insofar as it does not naïvely suggest an absence of form but rather a form that is making itself impossible: a formal undoing of form. Art, including avant-garde art, can never quite remove form. It is, quite clearly, always against the background of formal conventions that the avant-garde succeeds in performing possibilities of un-form. In turn, however, juxtaposing Seidl's concept with Lyotard's theory of the sublime may infuse form-contrariness with a critical urgency that redirects it from an "old" transcendentalism toward a "new" discourse of immanence. This is, at least, one of the objectives of Lyotard's project: to retrieve the sublime from the beyond of sensibility and to reposition it in the here and now—even though this here and now never simply opposes but rather reframes the beyond of the senses.

꙳

In *The Inhuman*, Lyotard argues that avant-garde art—as an art of experimentation—no longer evokes the sublime in a context of nostalgia. Nostalgia here specifically denotes the desire for an absolute that is deemed not so much absent as lost: a presence that transcends the self and the senses but that may once have been familiar to, perhaps even identical with, the self (compare chapter 2). Lyotard associates this desire with the romantic sublime. Thus, in romantic evocations of the sublime such as Caspar David Friedrich's landscape paintings, there is the clear sense of a presence "behind the curtain"—a presence that cannot be presented or appropriated but that is nevertheless felt to be there, intimated in distant horizons, desolate trees and ruins, or mountaintops. The crescendo in Liszt's *Chorus Mysticus* can be framed in a similar way: the music constantly gestures to a beyond of itself, a place of transcendence where the self might merge with a redeeming force of the supersensible.

By contrast, the sublime of the (pictorial) avant-gardes is a sublime without nostalgia: "they do not try to find the unpresentable at a great distance, as a lost origin or end, to be represented in the subject of the picture, but in what is closest, in the very matter of the artistic work" (*TI* 126). This means that the (pictorial) avant-garde is part of the romantic engagement with the sublime, especially its concern with representational limits, but it at once departs from this engagement by disowning the very possibility of a *lost* origin or end—this end is lost from view in artistic modes that no longer presuppose a world outside of their very own materiality, their own immanence.

However, if the postmodern sublime no longer pines after an unreachable beyond or a lost past, it also shares with the romantic sensibility the necessity of a radically open future. Even so, in Lyotard's postmodern framing, the indeterminacy relative to such an idea of a radically open future concerns a specifically material indeterminacy: if this future bears on an infinite, it would be a *plastic* infinity. In *The Inhuman*, witnessing to the indeterminate quite simply means that the "basic" preconditions and presuppositions of art are *subject to doubt* and that it is this doubt the artist must testify to:

> The doubt which gnaws at the avant-gardes did not stop with Cézanne's
> "coloristic sensations" as though they were indubitable, and, for that matter,
> no more did it stop with the abstractions they heralded. The task of having
> to bear witness to the indeterminate carries away, one after another, the barriers set up by the writings of theorists and by the manifestos of painters

themselves. A formalist definition of the pictorial object . . . was soon overturned by the current of Minimalism. Do we have to have stretchers so that
the canvas is taut? No. What about colors? Malevich's black square on white
had already answered this question in 1915. Is an object necessary? Body art
and happenings went about proving that it is not. A space, at least, a space
in which to display, as Duchamp's "fountain" still suggested? Daniel Buren's
work testifies to the fact that even this is subject to doubt. (*TI* 103)

Thus, Lyotard continues, "the investigations of the avant-gardes question
one by one the constituents one might have thought 'elementary' or at the
'origin' of the art of painting. They operate *ex minimis*"—whether minimalist or not (*TI* 103). Their work is in question because it refuses to be reconciled with "elementary criteria." It materializes what, and indicates that,
these criteria repress.

In this setting, form-contrariness could be rewritten as a going against the
traditional conditions of possibility of any given art form: it makes impossible or questionable a continuation of existing schools and programs. Thus it
heralds the new but latently also opens the prospect of *nothing* ever being
formed again: the very prerequisites for such formation have been subverted. Thus conceived, form-contrariness will be linked to the shock of
the new: the surprise that in the absence of absolute foundations something
new and unforeseen by artistic rules suddenly happens *after all*. Or the threat,
conversely, that no such possibility will ever announce itself again: nothing,
the neuter, remains when *anything*, no matter what, could be made.

Plastic indeterminacy—the distinguishing mark of the postmodern sublime—thus entails a "positive" (the freedom from constraints) and a "negative" (the risk of the unknown and the risk of paralysis) all at once. As such,
the postmodern sublime may be no more than a formal rehearsal of the existential shock of the sublime that faces one with one's own mortality. While
in Burke's theory the subject is momentarily faced with a possible discontinuation of life and is subsequently distanced from it, Lyotard posits the threat
of a possible discontinuation of art, which is then once again dispelled by
art itself: "Art, writing give grace to the soul condemned to the penalty of
death, but in such a way as not to forget it" (*PF* 245; see also *TI* 99–100).
This is not to say that all avant-garde art can by definition occasion (or relieve) the specifically existential terror that Lyotard takes up from Burke.
Rather, it is to say that avant-garde art exemplifies the Burkean privation of
continuation (of life, light, or certainty) in its disruptive, self-questioning
strategies, in thematizing or making explicit the suspension of—what Lyotard calls—the *It happens* in the realm of art. Or, differently said, not the

depiction of a spectacle of death, or some other terror-inspiring scene, but the staging of the disruption *per se* associated with the idea of death is what links the avant-gardes to the intensifying shock of the sublime.

In this respect, though some worlds apart, there is a parallel between Seidl's and Lyotard's respective theories of the sublime. Or, to rephrase this, Lyotard's suggestion that the postmodern sublime is not *outside* the work "itself" is not a matter of reference but a matter of matter itself and this has an elective affinity with Seidl's advocacy of a sublime *of* rather than a sublime *in* music: not a sublime that is inferred from certain musical strategies, that is "outside" of musical matter, but that is inherent in music's very texture: its sound color. Despite their obvious differences (Seidl still represents a metaphysical tradition, while Lyotard works within a more deconstructive frame), both locate the happening of the sublime *in the offering of the occurrence itself*—whether specifically musical (in Seidl's case) or "creative" in general. We could thus even venture to label Lyotard's postmodern sublime a sublime *of* art, and in our blending of Seidl's form-contrariness with avant-gardist negative presentations, relocate form-contrariness in the sublime *of* rather than in the sublime *in* art. We could then rewrite form-contrariness in relation to the postmodern sublime as a technique or mechanism that less makes the supersensible present within the forms of the sensible than it announces or embodies a friction within the sensible *"itself."*

Thus Lyotard rearranges a romantic "beyond grasp" within the here and now. He re-presents it as a *material* excess that the mind cannot digest and appropriate. In this context, Lyotard uses the concept of "matter" in an ontological sense as the matter given to perception: the matter of data that in Kantian philosophy is "represented as what is *par excellence* diverse, unstable, and evanescent" (*TI* 140). This matter is difficult to capture in its "raw" state—a logical problem pertaining to the Kantian fact that the mind can only process objects that conform to the mental forms and categories regulating perception and cognition. Thus, matter "in itself," not yet subjected to these forms and categories, will bypass or resist perception and cognition: it cannot (yet) be made into an object. Another way of putting this is that as an "in itself," not yet touched and shaped by the formative and cognitive faculties, matter can only "exist" when these faculties are momentarily suspended: "forms and concepts are constitutive of objects, they produce data that can be grasped by sensibility and that are intelligible to the understanding, things over there which fit the faculties or capacities of the mind. The matter I'm talking about is 'immaterial,' an-objectionable, because it can only 'take' place or find its occasion at the price of suspending these active powers of mind" (*TI* 140).

This is an obvious variation on the well-known theme "death is where the mind is not." The mind must somehow be "mindless" to be touched by a material event that *is*, on its own, rather than just being material for perception and cognition. Thus it could be suggested that the difficulty of grasping this occurrence of matter in itself is what replaces the Kantian difficulty of grasping ideas of reason in the postmodern sublime. Indeed, to make matters simple, in Lyotard's rewriting of the sublime matter is what comes "before" the forms of sensibility, just as ideas of reason come "after" or are "above" these forms in Kant's analytic of the sublime—matter here is the bare fact, and we wonder *that there is*, before a *what is* has been determined.[11]

Seen in this light, form-contrariness may not just be rewritten as an *artistic* technique or mechanism but may also pertain to an "aspect" of matter in an ontological sense—its radical alterity from the forms of imagination and understanding. We will revisit this ontological form-contrariness later in this chapter. First, it is urgent to show how form-contrariness in the "immanent" sense may throw a different light on, precisely, romantic musical practices. As we have seen, Lyotard reserves the "immanent" sublime quite strictly for (post)modernist experiments, and with respect to music in particular ventures to locate the "beginning" of such experimenting with Wagner and Schoenberg—with a view to chromaticism and free tonality, no doubt.[12] Just as strictly, I have shown, he distinguishes between the "postmodern" artistic sublime as the artistic act of fracturing as such and the "romantic" artistic sublime as the artistic act of depicting rupture while still holding fast to illusions of stability and totality. It remains to be seen, however, if this strict distinction will hold in the face of diverse romantic musical assays that foreground sonic ruptures and excesses *per se*: it is in the peculiar sounding of tones that the sublime here announces itself sonically. It is, therefore, here necessary to turn to music as a cultural practice rather than a metaphor: in which different and specific ways do (fragments of) romantic musics enact the sublime as the breakthrough of matter? What does that tell us about the postmodern sublime in general as a philosophical concept that is "musically" informed?

To illustrate my point—an illustration that has the nature of a speculative proposal—I have focused on two paradigmatic extremes in romantic music. On the one hand, I reread the bombast of virtuosity, personified in Franz

Liszt and typically arousing wonder and admiration from contemporary listeners as his theatricalized body stretched beyond its apparent limits.[13] My rereading is geared toward the insight that the sublime here—in the middle of a cult of bombast and staged awe—does not so much manifest itself in grand and transcendental movements but in a rather more subtle, elusive gesture: in a making strange of the matter of sound. Liszt's *Totentanz* in its piano solo version will be my starting point, in a recording by Arnaldo Cohen, which thoroughly foregrounds these sonic explorations.[14] On the other hand, I focus on smaller romantic forms—miniatures, fragments—tending toward musical experimentation.[15] In the smallest of forms, the sublime is traditionally not thought to be at issue, yet I will argue that disruptions of forms and conventions here stage a sublime that Lyotard calls postmodern. Frédéric Chopin's Prelude in A Minor, op. 28 is my focal point, in a recording by Martha Argerich that carefully reinforces its peculiar aporia's.[16] This may be an unsurprising if not a hackneyed choice, as the Prelude has often been invoked in criticism as a "sign" of the musical uncanny.[17] Nevertheless, despite, or rather because of this, the Prelude is central to my argument. As I will show, what is at issue here is not a series of unsettling disruptions *per se*: it is the way in which they frame and foreground a *sonic event* that redirects the romantically sublime toward a most minimal occurrence. This is why I have analyzed these examples in their aural mediation; in the act of listening to them, rather than reading them.

Romantically Sublime

In the eighteenth century, Handel, in becoming a "Man-Mountain," embodied the (Longinian) sublime.[18] In the mid–nineteenth century, Liszt—following Beethoven—continued the honors, most notably as a pianist. As William Gardiner portrayed Liszt in the *Leicester Chronicle* after a performance in September 1840:

> Like Beethoven, he [Liszt] describes the grand evolutions of nature by the power of sound. He can raise a storm about him, which he finds in the *hurly-burly* of the instrument, so frightful, that he is obscured and lost; but as it dies away, he reappears through a mist decked in the most radiant of colours. The rapidity with which he showered down a succession of minor thirds, through all the semi-tones . . . resembled the fall of a cataract into an abyss—producing whirls of thunder, on the lowest depths of the scale. This stroke of sublimity was strikingly shown in the elevated aspect of his countenance.[19]

The entire palette is there—as well as the familiar structure of elevation through near defeat: violent activity in nature, an inability to see clearly, and a seeming surrender to uncontrolled noise—but then a grand resurrection invigorated by the very close call of defeat: "man" transcending and controlling a sonic spectacle of nature's awful force.

Transcendence, however, here also obtains a very specific connotation of corporeal difficulties overcome. It is the act of pianistic execution itself: an act exceeding the apparent limits and restrictions of the body, even of nature itself (as one critic noted for the *Lincoln, Rutland, and Stamford Mercury* of September 4, 1840), that traditionally aligns Liszt with the (Longinian) sublime:[20] the violent feat of virtuosity.[21] Yet, as Heinrich Heine had already suggested in 1837, this feat, to be truly up to the sublime, requires another kind of transcendence—one of spirit over machine and mediation. Virtuosity should cover its tracks as a bag of physical tricks:

> all virtuoso *tours-de-force*, which only attest to difficulties overcome, are to be
> rejected as useless sound and to be relegated to the realm of the magician,
> the performer of horseback-tricks, the sword swallower, the balancing arts.
> . . . It is sufficient that the musician has complete control over his instrument,
> that one completely forgets the material mediation [*materiellen Vermittelns*]
> and only the spirit is audible [*vernehmbar*].[22]

The virtuoso is associated with the stuntman, with the circus, with the tricks of the body that explicitly point to a thriving on risk taking, on obstacles overcome, on a performance that, as Susan Bernstein has so aptly analyzed, *is* the body, its apparent limits, and the way in which these limits can be tested, stretched, or transgressed. Indeed, Bernstein suggests, the chief nineteenth-century anxiety about virtuosity in music is that it fully exposed instrumental music's physical "material origins."[23] This is how music highlighted the body.

For Heine, however, Liszt dematerializes, so to speak, this danger: one no longer senses the effort and the mediation.[24] There is, here, not a display but a true sublimation of physical exertion: a process, to echo Nietzsche, building on forgetfulness—forgetting the body in its virtual withdrawal brought about by muscular ease.[25] Still, one should note that ironically, or even inevitably, this simulation of effortlessness easily threatens to collapse into the very possibility that Heine denounces: the identification of man and musical machine.

As Heine himself observes on the issue in 1843, after having noted the debilitating effect of the pianoforte's pervasive presence in almost every Parisian household: "Technical ability, the precision of an automaton, the identification with the stringed wood, the sounding instrumentalization [*tö-nende Instrumentwerden*] of human beings is now appreciated and celebrated as the highest."[26]

The anxiety brought about by the detached mechanism of the keyboard—Heine tellingly makes a distinction with the violin—relates to an identification of the player with the instrument in terms of flawlessness: the absence of digressions, inconsistencies, and labored effects. In this way, however, the mental and physical accomplishedness allowing pianists like Liszt to dispel any impression of difficulties overcome becomes at once beyond human (lifted above the standard of bodily limits, almost a paradoxically physical enactment of the Kantian sublime) and inhuman (automatic, detached, a spectacle to be paralleled in the manual mimicry of pianolas).[27] A neat distinction between the two here collapses, making for an uncanniness that recalls nineteenth-century thrills of dolls and monsters brought to life, of the undead resisting a binary distinction between "dead" and "alive," "programmed automaton" and "free" being. Oscillating between the superhuman and the inhuman, between transcendentalism and mechanicism, virtuoso performances may thus perhaps be said to invoke a technological sublime *avant la lettre*: a sublime that does not revolve around the indeterminacy associated with the infinite or the realization of some moral destiny but around the apparently boundless capacities of a man-machine, displaying ever newer and ever more fabulous technical possibilities without the slightest effort, electrifying (in Heine's machine-age words) the masses through its "demonic nature."[28]

Yet significantly, this demonic aspect was not even reserved to the automatic side of the virtuoso: it was also the exceptional "liberties" the virtuoso displayed in the aural-visual spectacle of the concert or recital that had a potentially unsettling ring to it. Richard Leppert has aptly noted:

> The virtuoso was a troublesome paradox: he was the literal embodiment of extreme individuality, but one that ran the risk of exceeding the demands of bourgeois decorum, reserve, and respectability. Put differently, the extreme individuality of the virtuoso might as easily be read as the self-serving and solipsistic excess of the old aristocracy—except that virtuosos were performing for money in a new market economy of the arts. . . . For some—those carried away—the sublime was experience vicariously; others were convinced that they were simply being taken to the cleaners.[29]

The extreme (moral) individuality and the suggestion of superhuman force, of courage perhaps even, distinctly echoes—though also in a rather distorted way—the autonomy celebrated in the Kantian dynamical sublime: not merely a sublime of transcendence but one centering on a display of daring and apparently immaterial artistry. Telling, in this respect, is the response of a contemporary listener who likened Liszt to a "conquering military leader" producing "a revolution of feelings in our breast," uplifting and fulfilling the mind.[30]

Not simply opposed but rather precisely implicated within this sublime of awe and wonder—cunningly staged—is, however, another sublime dimension in relation to Liszt. Performance, especially virtuoso performance, relies on sound effects, and it is in the peculiar production of these sound effects that a sublime of immanence, rather than transcendence, can announce itself. If the virtuoso as performer embodied something uncannily in between man and machine, there is, in Liszt's piano music, also a sonic uncanniness that defies aural resolution—even though a familiar form of variation and development is still there to couch the rupture.

Interestingly, in the *Totentanz* this very primary uncanniness is occasioned by what would have seemed to be merely ornamental figures: glissandi. Variation 2, at 3'22"–3'37" (corresponding to mm. 91–95), offers a typical example of the piercing sonorous effects Liszt could produce on the piano.[31] In 1860, Adolph Kullak still referred to the glissando (literally, a "gliding sound") as "purely decorative," "outmoded" (with the exception of Liszt's piano works, he adds), and "cheap."[32] In the *Totentanz*, however, the glissandi are not so much decorative as instrumental and vital to the articulation of a process of dynamic intensification. This process sets in at the very beginning of Variation 2 (2'55"; m. 75), gradually sliding out into the intensive ending of this Variation.

As if a Variation within a Variation, 3'08"–3'22" (corresponding to mm. 83–90), both reflects and inflects 2'55"–3'07" (corresponding to mm. 75–82): the still (diabolically) playful sextuplets are changed into pounding triplets (the "trumpets"), the bass is lowered an octave and inverted (the rhythmic movement being down-up instead of the other way around), and out of it emerge the glissandi like a frenetic, shrieking resonance. More and more, in 3'22"–3'37", as the volume increases, it is the cascading sound of the glissandi that dominates the music in wavelike movements. Their peculiar texture—and their sharp sonorous contrast to the (fractured) theme played in the bass—has no mere ornamental function here but rather defines this last part of the second variation as a palette of different sonorous varieties. More so, the sound of the glissandi cannot well be placed or contextualized as a recognizably pianistic sound or as any other familiar musical sound. When played vibrantly, the glissandi are hard to clearly make out, sounding like a strange zooming that scratches in between the chords.

Thus it is not just an excess of resonance but a resonating otherness that obstructs the easy formation of a sound-image here. Interrupting the loud but nevertheless easily graspable bass chords like a fierce wind blowing in and out, the glissandi cut through the music, continuously threatening to drown it out in their high, resonating intensity. Listening, the effect is once more of something erupting—a break in the (sonorous) context—and what erupts is an auditory matter that approaches the so called "dirty timbre" often encountered in twentieth-century pop music.[33] Indeed, if I have described the sonic impression of the glissandi in terms of scratching, sliding, or zipping in and out, it could be effectively compared to the intrusive, grating sound of scratched vinyl as heard in much Western pop music of the 1980s. As such, Liszt's liberation of the matter of sound from the constraints of agreeable form posits a typical counterexample to the dominant, Hanslickian idea(l) of the musically beautiful: not the lure of formal proportionality but the interruption of sonorous materiality (a return of the repressed, one might say), not the containment of the beautiful but the excess of the sublime here brings home music's "vital issue." This is closely related to what Charles Rosen has identified in *The Romantic Generation*: Liszt typically valued realization over conception, the sonic event over structure.[34] With Liszt, as Rosen puts it, the "piano was taught to make new sounds. These sounds often did not conform to an ideal of beauty, either Classical or Romantic, but they enlarged the meaning of music, made possible new modes of expression." This would even make the seemingly vulgar and banal central passage of the Hungarian Rhapsody no. 10 into a "dazzling" feast of unsuspected pianistic noises and tone colors (492).

There are numerous other examples in the Lisztean canon—ranging from the spectacular to the experimental, though with Liszt the two precisely never cancel each other out—that perform in music such a return of the repressed of the matter of sound. The first section of the *Funérailles* (1845–1852) and even more so the opening chords and tremolos (roughly the first thirty seconds) of the *Marche Funèbre* (1867) from the third *Années de Pèlerinage* illustrate the point: the first already gestures toward the radical foregrounding of sonic waste and excess in the latter—registered so deep in the bass as to create a constant and palpable second, aural dimension that is, of course, the peculiar effect of overtones Wagner associated with the musically sublime in his *Beethoven* essay. Here, one can imagine an amorphous matter breaking through the bounds of form—an excess of resonances usurping formal demarcations that facilitate the musical imagination—as constituting a sublime moment: a rupture challenging one's auditory stronghold. A rupture, too, that makes one hear the thing itself, in a Lacanian sense of the term: the piano, the metal, the limits and outbreaks of pianistic sound—so much so that one feels compelled to register the material singularity of its happening: *this* performance on *this* piano, or *this* recording, even these loudspeakers. Every change would seem to make a world of difference—the traditional dependence on score and structure here becomes problematic. In this respect, Liszt's music requires a different approach, one that at least takes into account the instant, material conditions of possibility of sound production—and also the impossibility to fully capture or recover its very instance.

The return of the repressed is a familiar gesture in the "negative" romanticism of Liszt. It typically manifested itself musically in contradictions or violations of "good form."[35] Thus Heine (who once compared Hector Berlioz to a "skylark of the size of an eagle, such as existed in a primordial, lost world") referred to the "fiery instrumentation," the "poor sense of melody," and the "little beauty" in works like Berlioz's *Symphonie fantastique* or the colossal *Requiem*. Indeed, there would be a sense of the "colossal and monstrous [*Ungeheuerlichkeit*]" here.[36] In the writings of Liszt (co- and substantially rewritten by the princess Caroline von Sayn-Wittgenstein) on Berlioz and his *Harold* symphony, such monstrosity gained an artistic legitimacy. Defending the romantic, even Longinian *adagium* that the aurally transgressive in musical practice is permitted in view of the greater good of music's "progressive development," Liszt presented the mutilation of the ear as nothing less than a mutilation of the past to open the possibility of the future (a view that of course runs parallel to nineteenth-century perspectives on nationalism and cultural progress).[37] If Berlioz's soundscapes were—to use a phrase of Lyotard's—"monsters" in the public taste, their monstrosity was the sign of a future advent: a "new" music or musical destiny that yet remained incomprehensible (*TI* 125).

Heine's use of the term *Ungeheuerlichkeit* is instructive in this respect. Literally translated, *ungeheuer* would mean the monstrous, gruesome, and unheard of. As Rudolf Otto, however, showed long ago in *The Idea of Holiness*, the term had at least since Kant been (mis)used and "rationalized" as the uncommonly great in terms of size.[38] In a corrective rereading of the term, he claims that *ungeheuer* has to do with something more subtly disturbing. To this end, he points out that the Greek *deinós* comes closest to the *Ungeheuere* in German. Here, *deinós* basically signifies the "uncanny [*Unheimliche*] of the numinous": of, briefly phrased, the radically other and mysterious, an unknowable secret inspiring fearful trembling and exerting an irresistible fascination at the same time, repellent and attractive at once.[39] This "double-content" or "contrast-harmony" [*Kontrast-Harmonie*] of the numinous has its aesthetic equivalent in the sublime [*Erhabene*], conceived negatively as a sublime of terror and astonishment. Here, however, this negativity embodies a subtle shock, a sinister rippling rather than a dramatic interruption. Seen in this light, the *Ungeheuere* in music could refer to a music that is unnerving not so much in the sense of frightening an audience for a dramatic purpose (as, say, in Mozart's *Don Giovanni*) but to the sonic effect occasioned by a music that somehow does not sound "right."

A most poignant romantic instance is Chopin's Prelude in A Minor, no. 2, op. 28, characterized by an internally divided movement. This chiefly concerns the dichotomy between melody and accompaniment: the design of the former, as Lawrence Kramer has shown, is incongruous and asynchronous with that of the latter, the harmonic progression in the bass seeming to lead a life of its own.[40] Most obviously, however, the Prelude derives its eeriness from the repetitive dissonant chords in the left hand that, since the tonic is only fully revealed in the closing bars, remain indeterminable and inexplicable until the very end. It "hears" as if something is withheld, never quite breaking through, creating a tension of unease that is not so much resolved as cut short abruptly in the closing cadence.

Insofar as the *Ungeheuere* refers to the uncanny or *Unheimliche* of the numinous, the Prelude enacts what Sigmund Freud has called the coincidence of the *Heimliche* with the *Unheimliche*.[41] As we know, this coincidence consists in the fact that *heimlich* has a contradictory connotation of, first, homely or familiar and, second, surreptitious, suppressed, something kept from sight: a secret (*Geheimnis*) one cannot put one's finger on. In this second connotation, *heimlich* easily collapses into the not-in-orderness of the *Ungeheuere* and *Unheimliche*: something spooky, "not right," causing unease and fright.

The Prelude makes audible this interrelation between the homely and uncanny. On the one hand, its harmonic movements are stealthy, secretive, and concealed, as if hiding or withholding something. This becomes especially clear in the disruptive silence at 1'33"–1'36" (corresponding to m. 19), breaking off the (already once silenced) harmonic progression in the bass before it has had a chance to bring forward its full articulation in A minor.[42] On the other hand, it is this strategy of evasion and suppression that renders the chords heard in the accompaniment so peculiarly strange and other:

when hidden or suppressed, as the Freudian dictum goes, what would have been familiar or homelike (in this case literally the home key) becomes strange or *unheimlich*. This not merely refers to the Prelude's tonal ambivalence, which lasts to the end. Most significantly, when finally A minor makes itself heard in the tonic cadence, it sounds outlandish rather than homelike. In the context of the preceding (which now turns out to have been a long and winding journey home), "home" (the tonic) is somehow also "other": having been held back so persistently, it intrudes on, instead of having motivated, the music heard.

Perhaps a traditional analysis of the Prelude will indicate a deeper coherency, rendering the tonic cadence less unexpected than it seems to be in the hearing of it. Yet the point is its very aural irresolvability. Listening to the Prelude, what strikes one is an aural incongruity that cannot be made to disappear. As Kramer has put it, the Prelude "*sound*[*s*] abnormal, and cannot be made to sound otherwise": it *aurally* defamiliarizes music in its dominant conception.[43] Likewise, Michael Rogers has emphasized the "crucial, but puzzling pitch events" in the Prelude, although he tries to rationalize them by uncovering a deeper structure involving golden sections.[44] Nonetheless, insofar as nineteenth-century critics like Seidl plead for a specifically musically sublime, works like the Prelude in A Minor illustrate the point: it is unnerving not because of the sordid ideas it gives rise to but because of its own awkward and discomforting sounds that cannot be easily placed within familiar (nineteenth-century) musical hearing schemes. In this respect, the Prelude premediates the sublime in its postmodern sense: it invokes otherness in its mode of presentation, not by way of association.

As such, interestingly, Chopin's Prelude embodies a certain tendency in romantic music toward a sublime of immanence that is at once a sublime of transcendence: it performs aurally a gesture that recedes from comprehension and that remains, as such, undetermined. *For that reason* it gestures toward the sublime: it effectuates a break—however minimal—in the sensation of musical sound, in the way these sounds *touch* their listener. (The same can be signaled in Chopin's Etude in E Minor, opus 25, or the Etude in B Minor, opus 25, and likewise in Liszt's *Nuage gris* [1881], the *Bagatelle Without Tonality* [1885], or *Unstern* [1880–86]).

Significantly, there is a similar tendency in Chopin's Prelude in E-flat Minor, op. 28: due to the absence of a clearly articulated melody (it is nothing more than the constant repetition of the same formula), this Prelude enacts the very essence of "preluding" or "foreshadowing" in a movement without finality.[45] Here aural irresolvability is not due to tonal ambivalence but to the felt awkwardness of sonic fugitiveness. Verily a musical ruin, as Robert Schumann once typified the Chopin Preludes, the Prelude aurally foregrounds a resistance to teleological form: as in twentieth-century minimal or repetitive music, it acts out a process of minimal transformation and modulation. It is the very aimlessness of this process—ending where it started—that problematizes an aural synthesis here: you hear a rush, quickly, increasing and subsiding, and that is it. Not a grating rupture or an uncanny recurrence but the impression of an aural density that constantly resists clear articulation (due to the required speed) and threatens to disband into small, internally strained sound clouds: this emphasis on the sheer, material energy of occurring itself, already fracturing in the moment of its appearance, is how the E-flat Minor Prelude enacts the sublime in a postmodern or immanent sense. Again, it is the very matter of presentation that unsettles the score here.

Thus romantic experimentations with sound effects and formal fragmentation—however isolated I have regarded them here—make us aware of the possibility that the postmodern sublime is not just a latent presence or energy in modernist art and music. Precisely because music revolves around movement, moreover, it is most apt at "illustrating" (even if this only amounts to an approximation) the happening of the sublime in its immanent version: the latter is not a given, not a place one can turn to for inspection, but a dynamic, as sudden and fragile as it is singular and elusive. Therefore, as we will see in the next section, the postmodern musically sublime *in effect* embodies the mere trace of a retreat: the retreat is what we register, while the happening itself evaporates during its own occurring. This evaporation, and the indeterminacies implied in it, is what is at stake—among others—in post-1945 experimental music. How does this music foreground the occurrence of the *now* as an inevitable departure? How does this relate to the form-contrariness registered in romantic music? How would this inform Lyotard's conception of the postmodern sublime? Is it the outcome of a "musical" philosophy?

Instantly Sublime

As we have seen, a binary distinction between the romantic and postmodern sublime—as Lyotard repeatedly suggests—is difficult to maintain: as much as the romantic sublime may represent a nostalgic sublime, romantic music can nevertheless stage a sublime of sound in its very matter, rather than intimating an ideational beyond. There are different romanticisms and different romantic sublimes (even, as we have seen with respect to Liszt, in the very same composer), and experimenting with musical matter is not restricted to twentieth-century musical avant-gardes alone. Arguably, the experimenting with sonorities in, say, Liszt's *Totentanz* is of a different category than the typically "minimal" or even ironic happening of sound in the modern (Claude Debussy, Anton Webern, Edgar Varèse) and postmodern (John Cage, Morton Feldman) ages. And yet there is a connection: the foregrounding, in one way or another, of sonic intensities. Perhaps a fitting characterization of this connection would be a "reflexive reversal" (in a mechanical sense of the term): whereas material disruptions in romantic music are still dramatic interruptions, these interruptions become the *basis* of a music that seeks to establish sound as its very parameter in the experimental avant-gardes of the earlier twentieth century. Moreover, and perhaps even more crucially, while romantic music is still set in a space-time that is presented as "given," as a stable framework that somehow always already exists, it is in the experimental music of John Cage and Morton Feldman that every sound implies, literally carries with it, its own space-time: every sound appears under its own conditions. Or even more radically: every sound appears under the conditions of an accidental occurrence—it may happen, or not.

In this section, I will argue that this practice of the accidental not only coincides with Lyotard's notion of the postmodern sublime but in fact molds and performs it. The very crux of the postmodern sublime is the ungraspability of the random occurrence of an instant that is never quite a moment in time: *now*—a moment already beginning to disappear as it is being pronounced. It is this random occurrence and this decaying of becoming that is embodied in the aural planes and strategies staged by Cage and Feldman respectively:

> Each moment presents what happens. I [Cage, KBW] / derived the method
> I use for writing music / by tossing coins / from the method used in the
> Book of Changes. / It may be objected that from this point of view / any-
> thing goes. / Actually, anything does go but only when / nothing is taken as
> the basis. / In an utter emptiness / anything can take place. / And, needless
> to say, / each sound is unique (had accidentally occurred while it was *being
> played*) / and is not informed / about European history and theory . . . [46]

As we will see, it is not hard to imagine a parallel between Lyotard's immanent sublime and these accidental styles of the twentieth-century avant-gardes. If this sublime is not "far away" but "right here," in the now here happening, this *now* is a matter of chance: whether it occurs, and how, no one can predict—as an event, it refuses programming or control. Thus, Lyotard elaborates on Martin Heidegger, the occurrence of "now" is "infinitely simple, but this simplicity can only be approached through a state of privation. That which we call thought must be disarmed" (*TI* 91). Thought must leave the known and "received" behind, discard programs that appear to guarantee continuation, and open itself up to sheer, undetermined potentialities (*TI* 91). In this space of privation the "now" may occur as *event*: it happens *to* the mind in its evanescence (*TI* 18–19). The question I would like to pose is: how do aural experimentations with chance and indeterminacy (re)inform this event-philosophy?

The sublimity of "now" as the instantaneousness of the instant, and the (im)possibility of being *touched* by that instantaneousness, remediates a crucial issue in the Western philosophy of time that was already raised by Saint Augustine: the problem that we can never measure, or even grasp and retain, now-time.

> How, then, do we measure present time, when present time has no duration? It must be measured while it is in the process of passing. It cannot be measured after it has passed, because nothing then exists to be measured. But while we are measuring it, where is it coming from, what is it passing through, and where is it going? It can only be coming from the future, passing through the present, and going to the past. In other words, it is coming out of what does not yet exist, passing through what has no duration, and moving into what no longer exists.[47]

The present would have seemed so real, so *now*, so *present*, in contrast to the past that is gone and the future that is not yet. Yet what part of the present, Saint Augustine wonders, *are* we measuring when we want to measure it? It is a present that has already come to pass, a present now past. Seen in this light, William Barrett has noted long ago, it "begins to look . . . as if the present . . . would turn into an indivisible and unreal, because unexperienced, knife-edge between the past and the future, both of which are nonexistent." And it also begins to look as if the present is not the "ultimately real present" but rather already an abstraction (instead of a "basic datum").[48] Even where, Barrett continues, "such tiny flickerings of consciousness may occur, they may flow by relatively unnoticed within a larger structuring present that is indeed much more the controlling present before my mind."[49] In other words: the present is already a projection of a certain order; it is already, in Kantian terms, the product of a synthesis. *That* present is a present we can describe and remember, but the minimal, singular "flickerings" and variations of consciousness happen as they pass—and are hardly retainable. They are hardly "catalogued" *as such*, as the manifold data of consciousness.

This is what Lyotard suggests when pointing out that the sublime does not reside beyond consciousness but rather occurs within it as a nonreducible and nonrepeatable minimal event. It is also what Cage may have had in mind in attempting to release the sounding of (no matter what) sounds from any structural or formal continuity: we, Western listeners, have grown deaf to singular soundings because we are so conditioned to hearing sounds *musically* in meaningful structures. Seeking to interrupt this peculiar deafness, to appeal to a (dormant) sensitivity that may be affected by the "tiny flickerings" of sonority in their singularity, Cage staged a prototypical "space" of the postmodern sublime: "you make a little clearing where the penumbra of an almost-given will be able to enter" (*TI* 8–23, 19).

The half-shadow of something not-yet: in Cage's sound world this would be the foregrounding of a sonic potentiality that was always already "there" but could not be perceived *as such*. Sounds "in themselves," come into their own, as Cage quotes Christian Wolff, are "given no impulse by expressions of self or personality." Such sounds have no intentions or purposes; they are indifferent, inarticulate, to the extent that they lack reference, meaning, and address.[50] They have no place in a story or a program, they just sound; that is all. Thinking of ways to differentiate classical from contemporary music and listening, Cage proposes that the latter is not (yet) subject to "classifying": "all you can do is suddenly listen / in the same way that when you catch cold all / you can suddenly do is sneeze."[51] You do not hear a sound in relation to other sounds (as in a harmonic interval), in relation to a designated referent, or even an imagined addressee—your ears are instead tuned to the mere occurring of this sound *qua* sound. It could, for that matter, be any sound that comes along and already fades as you start to listen to it. (Yet even then I have trouble hearing sounds as sounds come into "their own." The "composer" may have detached himself from traditional ways of music making but I may still be preconditioned by traditional ways of music listening and unknowingly bring to these sounds not only memories of music heard before but also traces of listening conventions that cannot be wiped out just like that. Hearing sound as "sound alone," unburdened by expressive conventions, and hearing it completely newly, barely, disinterestedly, requires an act of faith.)

It was, perhaps, with $4'33''$ (1952) that this sonic release was first realized most effectively: it offered a minimal frame (the setting of a conventional public listening) and empty structure (covering three parts of fixed lengths) in which any sound might come to pass. $4'33''$ was an exercise in response-ability: rather than participating in a structure of oversight and anticipation, or not participating at all, listener-viewers would have (as Cage puts it in "45' for a Speaker") to "keep the head alert but / empty. Things come to pass, arising and disappearing."[52] Here, not a preconceived pattern but simply *each moment* "presents what happens": sounds are determined by their instantaneous becoming, rather than their notation, in an open arrangement.[53] This renders such happenings impossible in terms of repeatability: *as* they are staged in an empty structure, they are affected by their immediate setting. *This* concert hall, *these* listeners, looking at and listening to *this* performer, who is performing *here and now*, in these surroundings—these "factors," open to chance, codetermine if, how, and which (if any) sounds will arise.[54]

This urgency of singularity and, in relation to it, the possibility of an accidental, immediate listening that comes before meaning making, is also a central issue in Lyotard's reflections on the sublime and the wonder of the now here happening. In fact, I would suggest that Cage's experimental musical actions and many of the lectures and writings from his *Silence* premediate (in the sense of "remembering before the fact") Lyotard's meditations on the sublime as the instantaneousness of the instant. (Indeed, in *Peregrinations* Lyotard confesses to having studied "the Epicurean *ataraxia*, the Stoic *apatheia*, the extreme Stoic *adiaphora*, the Zen not-thinking, the Taoist nothingness, etc." that indirectly and [as for the latter two] directly inform Cage's near impossible aesthetics of the event in itself. Indeed, in the same text, Lyotard refers to Cage's *Silence* as opening up the "ethical" aspect of this momentary aesthetics. Significantly, he later adds to this secret interest in the lure of a pregnant emptiness that the "experimental musician is going to start on his way without the goal of concluding or resolving his experiences, but rather with the intention of becoming unencumbered enough to meet events").[55]

Thus, Lyotard suggests that not a big, overwhelming musical gesture but the nuance of a sound, its most minimal aspect, its timbre (its material but provisional and incidental "impress") constitutes the punctual presence of the sublime. This "punctuality" is not to say that the sublime is always in time but, precisely, too soon or too late for us—and as such *never* in diachronic time but always already outside of it, briefly skirting it at best. The *being affected* with this brief skirting, inexplicably and almost imperceptibly, is a sublime feeling in its postmodern sense. It is a sense of *quod* (that) rather than *quid* (what), a sense perhaps most sharply illustrated by those *déja-vu* sensations stimulating the mind in the imagined certainty that one experiences something familiar, already seen, rehearsed, without yet knowing what it is precisely. Here, the sense of the sublime is a hint of something not yet formed that can only occur *as such*, *as un-form*, before the mind has been able to organize any directed response. Indeed, *in* the very failure of the mind to regulate the "data" of experience the sublime announces itself. So it is, according to Lyotard, with the nuance of sound:

> For if the matter of sound, its nuance, can reach the subject, this is at the cost of surpassing, or "subpassing," its capacity for synthetic activity. This would be a definition (a negative one indeed) of matter: *what breaks the mind.* . . . The nuance, as non-formalized matter, escapes the syntheses, both of apprehension and of reproduction, which usually see to the grasping of sensory matter to ends of pleasure (through forms), or of knowledge (through schemata and concepts) . . . that sonorous matter which *is* the nuance is there only to the extent that, then and there, the subject is not there. (*TI* 156–57)

The matter of sound is literally a material "in itself": it does not figure or represent anything, it just occurs, momentarily, outwitting the mind, foreclosing a "proper" schematic digestion. Leaving no "evidence" in its trail, it is as if this sound, *as such*, had never happened. For indeed, to speak with Feldman, what we can perceive of this sound does not lie in its projection, its "appearing," but in its decay: "this departing landscape, *this* expresses where the sound lies in our hearing—leaving us rather than coming towards us."[56] Where sounds are concerned we are always already doomed to make do with traces: hearing sounds as such, in their immediate appearing, may be more complicated than Cage had imagined. Their appearing at once marks their disappearing and it is only the course of the latter—the history of a retreat—which we register: their inception, the movement of their launching, remains for ever beyond the grasp of sensible perception.

Feldman's *Piano and Orchestra* (1975)—which offers something of a return to conventional notation in the service of sound-color differentiation—foregrounds this indexical affect, as I would like to call this touch that is always too late but attached nonetheless.[57] *Piano and Orchestra* re-presents music as a plane of discrete happenings that resonate yet never precisely repeat each other. These happenings occur in between silence as the colors of an eerie, suggestive palette changing slowly, softly, constantly—minimally.

There are chords that change chromatic matter, that change in length or in intensity but otherwise remain static; there are single notes echoing and responding in different instrumental sonorities; there are scraps of melodic "lines," threatening pulsations in the bass, and recurring "motifs" or brief movements in ever changing contexts. You feel that this is a music demanding a listener willing to "walk around": to listen not statically and with a single, linear focus but to focalize the aural plane from different angles. This multiperspectival access only works to reinforce the impossibility of a "total view": there is no encompassing structure in which to assimilate and appropriate these sound-events. They cannot quite be predicted but are rather constantly dispersing; there is no melodic or harmonic "law" dictating that after this tone should come that one.

Indeed, there is no sense of direction or finality, as the pauses constantly abort the possibility of a "self-evident" progress. As a listener, you are on the alert, but your precariousness is only increased by what I would like to call the immaterial inception of the sound-events you are witnessing: the inaudible beginning and occurring *as such* of each event through a thickening of texture (layering) that facilitates insistent reverberation. This is, at least, what *Piano and Orchestra* highlights compulsively in its peculiar mode of sonorous projection: this is a music that, except for a few instances, consistently tries to undo its own starting points, to displace its attacks, as if it were simply floating in a static space-time. The ingenious use of framing reinforces this impression of absence: almost each sound emanates from a silence rather than a preceding tone that, as silence, cannot be heard. In this way, *Piano and Orchestra* makes audible not simply silence "itself" but the movement of the audible surging as the trace of an inaudible, instantaneous occurrence that cuts time but never enters its bounds.

This paradox of sonorous inception that cannot be heard is, no doubt, the same paradox as the paradox of the *now*: the presence of the immediate present is a presence continuously lost. This is how Feldman's sounds perform the postmodern sublime: a minimal occurrence that carries with it the history of a lack, rather than a grand gesture that points toward a supersensible destiny. And yet there may be the clear sense of having been affected, brushed by (the aftermath of) an aural event.[58] In various essays from the late 1980s, Lyotard connects this "gift" (*donation*) of being affected to a precariousness of being given over to an external force, however minimal it may appear. This force is typically imagined as a flash bursting through a neutral continuum—there is an emptiness that is suddenly enlightened with energy: "Sensation makes a break in an inert non-existence. It alerts, it should be said, *exists* it. . . . Even in its most lively exaltations, the soul remains moved, excited by something outside, and it remains without autonomy" (*PF* 243). It is likely that Lyotard here elaborates on Sigmund Freud's speculative discourse on the beginning of life as a shock out of lethargy in *Beyond the Pleasure Principle*—a beginning despite itself that is always already given over to its own undoing, and keeps repeating and undoing itself. I will return to this speculation in detail in the next chapter, but here it should already be stressed that for Lyotard the soul that is touched (pleasantly in the feeling of the beautiful, or pleasantly-unpleasantly in the sublime) is no longer the self-sufficient "principle" Kant had presented it to be. It is now animated from without, time and again.[59]

In *Piano and Orchestra*, this gesture of an external animation that cuts the calm is performed a number of times (most dramatically toward the end) in unusually loud, abrupt, and sharply articulated sound events—the calm is never quite silent, never quite unsuspecting, dreading even, yet the brass-dominated intrusions still come as violent surprises. As a listener, you are awoken, suddenly, to be let go again, as if a quickening breath had come to pass through you. This breath, as Lyotard has remarked, may itself be inaudible *as* animation, but it is "not perishable either": it may well be the very stimulus or impetus of the sounds arising in its wake (*PF* 233).

This view on animation renders nothingness constructive rather than destructive alone: it is the endless, groundless ground of existing—and to that extent abundant, prolific. As such, this double animation foregrounds a crucial aspect of the postmodern sublime: it embraces, one might say, a productive nihilism that emphasizes the constant and inevitable interplay between nothing(ness) and something(ness). Thus, insofar as the sublime features the shock of the new in art, in *The Inhuman* anaesthesia or disaffection, forgetfulness, nothingness intersects with the *aistheton* or being affected, being touched (by an "outside"), insofar as the anaesthetic becomes a paradoxical *condition of possibility* of creative processes. Only when nothingness, emptiness, *suspension* reigns, can something arise—and the wonder of something suddenly occurring can happen.

In "Lecture on Something " (in *Silence*), John Cage had already suggested such an intertwining of nothingness and somethingness, the latter emerging out of the former and the former always remaining "present" within the latter as an unidentifiable or mute affect:

It is nothing that / goes on and on without beginning or middle or ending. Something is / always starting and stopping, rising and falling. The nothing that / goes on is what Feldman speaks of when he speaks of being sub- / merged in silence . . . So that listening to this music one / takes as a springboard the first sound that comes along; the first / something springs us into nothing and out of that nothing arises the / next something; etc. like an eternal current. Not one sound fears / the silence that extinguishes it. And no silence exists that is not pregnant with sound.[60]

Nothing has a clear etymological trace of "not one": a plurality. This is what Lyotard hints at when he denotes nothingness not as an uneventful space but as a *potentiality*. Paralleling silence with nothingness, Cage likewise refers to the former as a charged space, "pregnant with sound" we have not heard yet. Thus sound and silence are intertwined; something is in nothing, nothing is in something, insofar as sounds are "present" potentially in silence, just as silence remains present as an anesthetic trace in the occurrence of sound ("Every something is an echo of nothing").[61] Redirecting this to Lyotard, sound/silence would be a perfect metaphor for the occurrence of the instantly sublime: an unexpected, uncalculated happening that interrupts *and* revivifies (aural) sensibility.

Thus, as we have seen, the occurrence of the postmodern sublime—as the instantaneousness of the instant, the wonder *that* "it" happens—comprises both a negative and a positive moment. The Dutch philosopher Renée van de Vall has described these respective moments in relation to Barnett Newman's *Vir Heroicus Sublimus* (1963) in terms of visual disorientation and reorientation, and the same terms can be transposed to the aural field in this instance.[62] Thus, in *4′33″* there is a negativity of disorientation in the shock of silence being suddenly revealed as a reservoir of sounds, and the perplexity, however brief, of no longer sensing a stable distinction between silence and sound. This may obscure conventional landmarks of aural processing, creating a shift in one's familiar ways of aural "positioning." One does not know what to listen for, one has lost a sense of aural direction, since now sounds are not produced from a single, designated (and visually privileged) source—they could come from anywhere, and be anything, ever changing as singular instants. There is no point in shaping them as coherent forms or processes, and this precisely prevents a "regular," masterful listening.

Frustrating as this may be, this process can nevertheless also entail a positive moment of reorientation: the joy of sensing new ways of listening that are less totalizing than imaginative and affective, a reorientation in musical space without the filters of exclusion animating dominant Western listening schemes. Affected, you have (however briefly) seen through these filters. They have become useless—music is now heard as *event*: as a possibility that could occur anywhere in any circumstances. Thus, the shock of the new may give way to a delight of the new as that potential of endless possibilities already discussed above: emptiness into fullness, frustration into elation. As Lyotard puts it in *Postmodern Fables*: "The *anima* is threatened with privation: speech, light, sound, life would be absolutely lacking. That's *terror*. Suddenly, the threat is lifted, the terror suspended, it's *delight*. Art, writing, gives grace to the soul condemned to death, but in such a way as not to forget it" (*PF* 245).

. . . there is not, there is, there is not, and there is, though there is not. This might sum up the "process" that Lyotard rewrites as the postmodern sublime. But is it a process that does justice to the paradox of the sublime as an unsolvable conflict of pleasure and pain, an unsolvable conflict of apparently opposed intensities that are nevertheless constantly acting on each other? Indeed, is the "plastic sublime"—the sublime that almost automatically switches color from nothingness as threat to nothingness as opportunity—*as such* not in conflict with Lyotard's conflating of the sublime with the *différend*?

Differend

Though not always mentioned in so many words, the *différend* or differend constantly hovers at the background of Lyotard's reflections on the sublime and the avant-garde. The differend bears on a conflict that forecloses mediation, on an irreducible difference. As I will show, Lyotard's rereading of the Kantian sublime feeling in terms of such a difference recasts it as an unsolvable feeling, hovering between pain and pleasure and never quite "deciding" in favor of the latter. Indeed, with the help of Lyotard's notion of the differend I will suggest that what is conventionally conceived of as the turning from pain to pleasure in the sublime feeling is really an impossible turning: the bridge from the former to the latter turns out to be impassible. It remains to be seen, though, if this impassibility can also "account" for a different unsolvability that is inherent in the paradox of the sublime feeling: the "fact" that it involves apparently opposed intensities that are not so much worlds apart but that collapse into each other.

Simply phrased, the differend may be said to pertain to a conflict (legal, historical, political, personal, etc.) between two parties that is not a litigation. This means that a differend is not a dispute allowing both parties the recourse to a legitimate defense. Rather, one of the parties, the wronged party, is deprived of the possibility to express a wrong he or she has suffered. He or she is deprived of this possibility because the conflict at hand is resolved in the idiom of the party that has caused or was responsible for this wrong in the first place: "I would like to call a *differend* [différend] the case where the plaintiff is divested of the means to argue and becomes for that reason a victim. . . . A case of differend between two parties takes place when the 'regulation' of the conflict that opposes them is done in the idiom of one of the parties while the wrong suffered by the other is not signified in that idiom."[63]

A differend thus occurs when one is denied the possibility of a (legal or "legitimate") response: the possibility of voice. There is, for Lyotard, a hegemonic force at work here that resists and represses the release of heterogeneity: of a plurality of voices, phrases, and phrase regimens allowing for an equal plurality of perspectives. If there is only one phrase regimen, only one mode of discourse that circulates as legitimate, others become inarticulate and inaudible. Imagine you are trying to "make a case" against an oppressive party and being forced to do that in the language or idiom of that oppressor—a perfect crime.

In *Lessons on the Analytic of the Sublime*, Lyotard makes explicit the "working" of the differend in the Kantian sublime feeling: this feeling is here represented as being only apparently harmonious yet irredeemably differential in nature. Indeed, he argues, at the heart of the Kantian sublime there is a differend, and this differend is constituted by the problematic encounter of the infinite (which reason can think but imagination cannot form) and the finite (which imagination can form). What, in Lyotard's view, happens in the Kantian sublime is that reason challenges "the thought that imagines" to present with forms the absolute—which is, of course, an impossible challenge, since the thought that imagines works by virtue of limitation: "Presentation cannot grasp an infinite of givens at one time in a single form. If it is asked to present more, it comes up against a maximum, its 'measure' which is the subjective foundation of all magnitude. This measure is the absolute of the thought that presents . . . the absolute 'aesthetic' magnitude that is possible."[64]

What is waiting to be formed, waiting to be phrased, here is a not-something or a not-given beyond all comparison. This absolute cannot be made present in the "idiom" of the thought that imagines, which has been challenged or violated by reason to do so all the same. One could say with Lyotard that here two absolutes meet: on the one hand, "the absolute whole when [reason] conceives," and on the other, "the absolutely measured when [imagination] presents" (*LA* 123). This is thus a meeting of two aspects or abilities of thought. The one is able to think limitlessness, the other encircles finitude(s), gathers together and retains what it can comprehend at once in a form (form being limitation), putting at a distance or putting apart (*absonderen*) what exceeds its power. Thus, what causes the conflict or *Widerstreit* in this meeting is not merely the limitlessness demanded by reason but also the absolute limit of presentation against which imagination, as it were, bumps itself.

Now, if a differend or irresolvable conflict arises between the faculties of reason and imagination respectively, this is not simply to be ascribed to the "incommensurability of their respective causes (in the juridical sense)"— that is to say, to the fact that the former is turned to the conception of an absolute whole while the latter can only grasp and form a limited whole (*LA* 151). Rather, a differend can be felt (in thought) when, precisely, imagination is challenged, or demanded, to remove "itself from its finality . . . to put itself at the measure of the other party [reason]"—and fails signally (*LA* 151). It can be felt in what Lyotard reads as a forced and failed transition from the empirical to the supersensible, from concepts of the understanding to ideas of reason, from frustration to elevation. Indeed, a *failed* transition, and nothing more than that: while Kant compensates for imagination's pain in an ultimate awareness of moral freedom, Lyotard emphasizes that there need *not necessarily* be and perhaps *cannot be* a transition from the empirical to the supersensible, from indeterminacy to resolution, in the experience of the sublime. The "fact" that the Kantian subject changes from the perspective of sensibility to the perspective of reason in the experience of the sublime does not mean that the gap between sensibility and reason is, in any way, bridgeable or passable. Indeed, Christine Pries has argued, due to their mutual incompatibility, there is an abyss between the two excluding any "settlement," which makes it impossible for ideas of reason to be ever realized within the image-forming domain of sensibility.[65] The so-called harmony of the faculties thus covers up an internal conflict that remains—and, according to the tenets of the first *Critique*, remains irresolvable.[66]

Thus, instead of a transcendental resolution there may be but a negative presentation "resulting from" the sublime feeling: a "trace of a retreat," a trace of a failure or pain that "something" cannot (yet) be formed (*LA* 152). This trace *makes explicit* the differend that has occurred between reason and imagination. It exemplifies an unbridgeable gap between the two and, more than that, attests to the absurdity of the demand of reason to present the absolute. After all, to offer a negative presentation is really to say: I cannot (yet) form, this demand is beyond my means and quite senseless, too, because to form the limitless is, in the end, to not-form at all. Seen in this light, Lyotard observes, "[n]egative presentation" is . . . merely the demonstration of the inanity of the demand that the absolute be presented" (*LA* 152). Even more importantly, this negative presentation makes one aware that an injustice has been done: reason, as we have seen in chapter 2, has made an unjustified claim to imagination to transcend, deny itself. Imagination has been violated and this is what the negative presentation ultimately shows. Seen in this light, a transition from frustration to resolution is not merely not guaranteed in the (Kantian) sublime; it can also be necessary to not achieve a resolution when a differend has occurred.

Contrary to Lyotard, however, I maintain that this differend is not maintained but covered up in the Kantian sublime in a final, harmonious moment of closure-in-transcendence. For Kant, after all, the "injustice" done to imagination is as it were lifted in the realization of a supersensible destiny that is judged as delightful for the *entire province of mind*. Differently said, the differend is here sublimated or forgotten in an overall, subjective finality: Kant postulates the pain of imagination as being transformed in a necessary, intermediate pain, a pain, indeed, indicating that imagination and reason have worked together in achieving a delight that lifts the Kantian mind as a whole. One could thus consider this moment of a final judgment for the entire mind as a "third instance" that solves the conflict between the sensible and the supersensible after all—but it is clearly a solving at the expense of the former. The sensible is cast out of the redeeming projection that the Kantian subject has made to fit itself.

Nevertheless, Lyotard's concept of the differend is instrumental to critically think the sublime feeling anew as a feeling defined or "made up" of two opposed intensities: as an irreducible difference, the differend concerns two coexisting "parties" whose conflict cannot be solved in either direction without an injustice being done. Or as James Williams has put it, Lyotard takes to and rethinks the feeling of the sublime as a feeling that would stop any "false bridging between absolute differences."[67] The effect of the interruption of the sublime concerns a felt gap between two "sides" or "positions" that cannot be integrated as one, and *it is this gap that halts the mind*.

By way of illustration, Williams points to William Turner's *The Devil's Bridge, Pass of St. Gothard* (1802). This painting captures the bridge over the soaring depth as a "fragile line thrown between great alps that threaten to

stretch, twist and throw it into the abyss at the faintest change in the tumul-
tuous skies. There is a bridge, but not one that you feel is passable. It is a
sign that there is hope in fording the waterfall that has cut an irreparable gulf
into the mountain, allied to a sign that hope is in vain."[68]

In this way, Turner does not resolve but exploit a contradictory, simultaneous feeling of hope (passability) and despair (impassability). Thus, the
guaranteed passage from frustration to self-elevation in the traditional sublime is here exchanged for a sustained ambiguity: a sustained feeling that a
conflict cannot be resolved, a limit cannot be transcended, or a bridge cannot be passed. We have seen something similar in Chopin's Prelude, which
performs an irredeemable disjointedness, figuring the homely and un-
homely at once.

This felt unsolvability between two intensities, it seems to me, divulges
an aspect of the postmodern sublime that is not necessarily implicit in the
sublime of immanence discussed in the previous sections. There, we have
seen a Lyotard who reanimates the eighteenth-century concept of the sublime as a fear of nothing happening turning into (and being lifted by) the
wonder of *it happens*; here we see a Lyotard who rereads the transition from
fear to wonder as an impassable transition. The reason for this may be that
the sublime feeling as differend depends, so to speak, on the tragedy that
befalls sensibility in the Kantian sublime. It is, that is to say, the transcendental framework of the Kantian sublime that allows an affect to be thought
that makes felt a gap between the sensible and the supersensible spheres. In
the immanent sublime, such gaps are less pronounced: the conflict between
the sensible and supersensible is here no longer at issue insofar as the latter
(as the ungraspable) has been included in the former as the pre-sensible or
the anaesthetic. There may be a tension between the pre-sensible and the
sensible, but the bridge between them is not impassable. Indeed, we have
seen, the former may be included in the latter and presents, in any case, a
"state of mind" that can be relieved by the latter. Thus, Lyotard's reworking
of the sublime points into the direction of an affect of succession (there is
not [i.e., fear], there is [i.e., wonder], etc.) and an affect of hesitation: in
between hope and despair, fear and wonder, without a means to negotiate
between the two extremes.

On the face of it, this rendering of the sublime feeling as a "sign" of
the differend rearranges the sublime feeling as an irresolvable double bind,
undermining as it does "the precept of logic that we cannot be in a state of
simultaneous hope and despair."[69] Since, however, this idea of a double bind
is tied too intimately to the transcendental problems that are at stake in the

Kantian sublime—namely, the conflicting positions of imagination and reason, *whereby reason is the dominant party*—this double bind is not typical of
the Lyotardian sublime "at large." The reason *that* the perspectives of reason
and imagination cannot be mediated without causing an injustice is, precisely, that there is a homogeneous tendency here to filter out the sensible
in self-transcendence. In the immanent sublime there may still be a differend
insofar as "something"—a breath, a sonorous inception, or an instant—
cannot be phrased or presented, *but the heterogeneous field* of which the immanent sublime partakes *also always holds out the possibility of something occurring
after all*. That is to say, there is solace to be found as well in the open space
of nothingness. As Lyotard puts it in *Postmodern Fables*, with "the appearance
of [an] audible sound, a promise is made. This sound promises that there
will be other sounds. Hence that there will be something rather than nothing" (*PF* 228). That, however, would solve the irresolvable after all—even
though the threat of nothingness, the "terror of being annihilated," remains,
inaudibly (*PF* 228).

We are therefore left, on the one hand, with a critical feeling tied to a
transcendental dilemma and, on the other, a seemingly resolved—because
successive—feeling of tension and relief ("it's *delight*") stirred by the threat
and consolation of matter "happening" (*PF* 245). Neither of these modal-
ities of the postmodern sublime, I believe, does full justice to the irresolvability and conflicting simultaneity of the musically sublime as I have traced
it in the previous chapters. The latter does not because it feeds on the possibility of closure in the form of a fear-relieving delight—however feeble that
relief may be—and the former does not because the paradoxical complexity
of the sublime is not quite due to an irremediable conflict *alone*. Thus, the
Burkean double feeling of the infinite intertwines a pleasure of tensionlessness with a pain of tension: it is a Janus-faced experience pointing forward
and backward at the same time, in which a strain of unfulfillment intersects
with a joyful suspension of change or development. Similarly, in Usher's
reading of the sublime feeling as a mighty unknown want and in my reading
of *Sehnsucht* as an unresolved experience of the infinite, a (sustained) lack
of fulfillment makes for a pain of want but also, at once, for a pleasure of
deferral.

What I would therefore like to propose is that the resistance to closure
typical of the sublime feeling is not so much due to an unbridgeable difference but to a difference that manifests itself as an *interlocking* of two conflicting intensities. It is not a matter of an unsolvable opposition *per se*, but an
unsolvable opposition that is, as it were, entangled or ensnared in itself: a

deadlock or an untiable knot rather than an abyss with two opposites standing on either side. Seen in this light, I argue in the next chapter, the paradox
of pain and pleasure in the experience of the musically sublime can be fruit-
fully reconsidered in terms of *différance*: as an endless shimmering of unstable
intensities, without a binary opposition of two constant, self-same "principles" being thought in the background. Instead, the one "principle" can be
said to be *always already at work in the other.*

5. Anxiety: The Sublime as Trauma and Repetition

The sublime is not only duplicitous in its paradox of pleasure and pain, but also in its "double mode" of a quieter and a more violent sublime: what John Baillie called the sedate sublime and the sublime mixed with pathos— and what Kant, of course, called the mathematical and the dynamical sublime.[1] Usually, critics interpret these two varieties of the Kantian sublime experience as pertaining to theoretical or speculative and practical reason respectively. They can, however, also be elucidated by pointing to the eighteenth-century cult of the sublime as being a cult of empty and vast but also of wild and violent nature: nature that appears boundless, without end, and nature that appears threatening, without shelter; nature that cannot be grasped, and nature that cannot be controlled. In a Kantian setting, encounters with these spectacles of apparent otherness are only superficially fateful. Like the pool of Narcissus, they are in the end the reflections of a desiring subject. Indeed, these spectacles are but reifications of the boundless scope and stern autonomy of reason—real and unreal at the same time, inflated like the subject who, as Adorno once remarked, "puffs himself up as if in spite of everything, as the bearer of spirit, he were absolute. He thus becomes comical."[2] He becomes a bloated reversal of his own fragility and nothingness.

And yet—one always senses a fatal subtext in Kant's third *Critique* threatening to undermine the grand gesture of self-delusion that decides the sublime, warring forces of pain and pleasure. This fatal subtext is, of course, the irresolvable breach between imagination and reason: the impassable bridge between the sensible and the supersensible. In Kant's analytic, however, this breach is nonetheless passed over under the law of subjective finality—it is conveniently reversed into a flexible change in perspective.

Lyotard, we have seen, tries to retrieve this subtext by rewriting the sublime affect in terms of the figure of the *différend*: an irresolvable conflict or opposition. Conversely, however, I would here like to redress the Kantian analytic by rereading the movements of the mathematical and dynamical sublime as movements of liminality: movements at the limit that do not accommodate an eventual breakthrough because they are split and halted by an internal duality. Thus, building on recent readings of the sublime in terms of trauma, I reconsider the dynamical sublime in terms of a traumatic encounter that cannot be retrieved and transcended. Not because the subject is invaded by an external presence that its mnemonic networks cannot handle, but because the boundaries between subject and object have dissolved: the latter is subjected to openness, to an absorption or total identification that briefly suspends the possibility of the subject.

Aesthetically, such traumatic effects are only virtually possible: literally at one remove and mediated as special effects—framed, designed, created. Yet as I show, it is precisely this aspect of formality that allows us to understand the break of trauma as a break that requires a form or frame to effect its undoing in the first place. As the irruption of otherness, the traumatic feeds on the context it displaces; the one cannot be thought without the other. This is perhaps why, artistically, traumatic events may be impossible to capture *as such*, but at the same time the movement of trauma as a break in the context of "ordinary" experience can be most accurately performed. Indeed, as a dislocation of familiar, controlled practices of experience, trauma may defy representational limits and conventions yet at the same time parallel the disruptive movements of modern art that tend to scatter the registers of their very conditions of possibility. In view of this typical double bind, I have chosen to analyze the interruption of the traumatic as an aural event in a romantic musical work I have here dissociated considerably from its historical footing. I have done so for three reasons. First, since it is part of my project to involve romantic music in postmodern rewritings of the sublime, and in turn to show how our present-day conception of the postmodern sublime can be reshaped by looking at romantic music, it is necessary that I frame my rereading of a postmodern musically sublime with a romantic musical instance—and vice versa. Second, and as part of the above consideration, in my analysis I address (though never more than implicitly— anything more would be beyond the scope of this chapter) an interaction between romantic and postmodern preoccupations with the past. Elsewhere, I have already suggested that the affective paradox of the sublime *only* becomes feasible in the felt presence of an intrusive yet irretrievable past.[3] Here, I will analyze how, precisely, romantic music may intervene in contemporary theories of trauma as the helpless rehearsal of a constantly lost past. The specificity of the analysis, as I hope to show, is urgent in rethinking the sublime in terms of trauma. To trigger such a rethinking, I focus on the

Andantino of Franz Schubert's Sonata in A Minor (D. 959). Featuring a sudden chromatic dispersal within a diatonic continuum, the Andantino's middle section performs a break in the context that precludes mending. This is not, however, because the break (chromaticism) and the context (diatonicism) embody separate positions on either side of an abyss, but because the breaking matter is here always already part of the context it scatters.

My rewriting of the mathematical sublime is loosely connected to the Burkean experience of the artificial infinite, and it will be considered in critical relation to the Freudian repetition compulsion and Jacques Derrida's figure of *différance*. As we know, *différance* holds difference and suspension in one: a movement that fails to crystallize as unity in an unequivocal direction. Old as this figure now may be, it effectively spells out (if not epitomizes) the self-defeating gesture of the experience of the artificial infinite: a gesture split internally between a forward- and backward-moving tendency. As I will argue, it is this double tendency that marks the sublime feeling as a feeling that cannot be one. I explicate this impossible unity of the "quiet" sublime feeling in an analysis of twentieth-century repetitive music. This music often tends to intimate an indefinite expansion through a movement of return and repetition, and in this way upsets familiar distinctions between progress and regress, tension and relief. Approaching works such as Terry Riley's *In C* (1964) in this way, I hope to show that the pattern of repetition is, so to speak, a fatality of the sublime that is inherent in its very destiny of liminality. Rehearsal and repetition, dislocation and suspension: these concepts project the dynamics of a musically sublime that works as forcefully in romantic "assays" of the distant past as in postmodern experimentations of the recent past. This is not a sublime that is bounded or determined historically: it is not a place, or a definition, but a labyrinthine process—the inability to pass beyond the fold of an ever recurring temporality.

In the Manner of an Unconscious Affect: Trauma and the Sublime

In *Songs of Experience* (2006), Martin Jay has mapped the rich variety of the concept of "experience" in American and European philosophy, history, and critical theory. In sum, "experience is a term rife with sedimental meanings that can be actualized for a variety of different purposes and juxtaposed to a range of putative antonyms."[4] On the one hand, it may refer to knowledge gained from specific matters, from empirical observation; to the outcome of Kant's triple synthesis of the senses, imagination, and understanding; or to an "integration of discrete moments of experience into a narrative whole."[5] In this sense, "experience" has the connotation of something masterful—literally a mastering in the sense of learning from trials and testing, but also in the sense of a controlled, integrated process of perception that fits the kind of causal structures that organize reality.

On the other hand, "experience" refers to a lived experience in the sense of "living through" something: an *Erlebnis* or a "distinctive and characteristic mode in which reality is there-for-me."[6] As we know, Walter Benjamin distinguished *Erlebnisse* (here, sensory experience) from *Erfahrungen* (here, experience "proper" or active experience) by associating the former with involuntary and the latter with voluntary memory.[7] Thus *Erlebnis* signals an experience that is not an experience "proper" since it has somehow, and paradoxically so, been experienced unconsciously. By contrast, as Jay puts it, "*Erfahrung* . . . involve[s] the ability to translate the traces of past events into present memories but also to register the temporal distance between now and then."[8] *Erfahrung* thus entails the possibility of narrative recall which *Erlebnis*—with its typically shocklike intrusions—lacks. The latter is of the category of the immemorial.

Of these two, it is the brief, untenable, and paradoxically unforgettable aspect of *Erlebnis* that would intersect with the sublime feeling as I have traced it in the writings of Lyotard, the early Nietzsche, and Wagner. Wagner situates the sublime feeling in a time and place that is beyond consciousness, while Nietzsche rereads the sublime in terms of *Rausch*—an unlived experience of the disintegration of the "I," which is, to that extent, also a disintegration of experience as constitutive of that very same "I." The moment when the "subject" partakes of an infinite life-Will is also the moment when this subject is under erasure. This erasure detaches the Dionysian *Rausch* from the sphere of experience "proper": the two are separated by a gulf of oblivion that cannot be mediated or traversed. This is, we have seen, what Lyotard has reiterated time and again in his essays on the sublime: where the sublime is, the subject is not. There is a differend between the ego and the sublime, as the shock "proper" of the latter is of a non-time preceding the binding of the ego.[9]

An experience that is not an experience, or, as Lyotard would say to emphasize the absence of the subject in this "experience," a phrase that remains inarticulate, a phrase without an addressor.[10] "Phrase" here refers to a "sentence" as a syntactically independent grammatical unit, but also more inclusively to an event that is not necessarily linguistic: "phrase" refers to any happening that opens up a four-cornered universe of addressor, addressee, sense or meaning, and referent.[11] Or, as Claire Nouvet has put it very clearly, "someone (addressor) says something (meaning) about something (referent) to someone (addressee)" (even though we should be aware that a phrase is not so much an event "emanating" from a subject but rather a more or less contingent happening in the manner of a Heideggerian *Ereignis* that, however, presents itself without being able to be represented).[12] Silence could be a phrase, any possible gesture could be a phrase, and even a mere signal could be a phrase: they are articulate, as Lyotard uses the term, in opening up a quadruple universe. The inarticulate phrase is inarticulate insofar as it *does not* open up such a universe—it does not seem to "come" from a sender or "reach" an addressee, and it lacks referentiality. As Anne Tomiche has put it in a most perceptive essay on Lyotard: "the inarticulate phrase . . . is thus a nonsignifying, nonaddressing, and nonreferenced phrase. However, it points to a meaning of only one type: a feeling (of pleasure and/or pain: anxiety, fear, and so on). The inarticulate phrase thus does not 'speak of' anything but 'says' (without articulating) that there is something without signification, reference, or address . . . it happens as a pure 'it happens.'"[13]

Another way of putting this is that the inarticulate phrase "happens" in the manner of a Freudian unconscious affect.[14] It makes *sense* but only in the sense of a sensibly perceived feeling of pleasure or pain—it does not say what or why that feeling is or where it comes from. And in a way it cannot: as an unconscious affect, Lyotard elaborates on Freud, the inarticulate phrase is of a different order than words and ideas: a pre-egoic order that suspends the possibility of an addressor and addressee—the possibility of a communication that is "sent" and "received." Or, as Tomiche puts it, the "status of the affect is . . . that of a 'pure' presence" that defies the order of representation: the affect offers itself to consciousness insofar as it can be perceived as pleasure and/or pain, but it also bypasses consciousness since it "remains unrecognized or misconstrued."[15] The unconscious affect is thus an affect without an apparent cause: it is a feeling that cannot (yet) be referred or attached to an object or idea. If it is a substitute of something, it "does not let itself be recognized as substitute."[16] This is because the affect has a deferred origin: its "original" context is detached, and the energy of the affect is concentrated on a different scene in which it is manifested to consciousness.[17]

Such a missed encounter can be called *traumatic* insofar as it revolves around an encounter between two "times" or "scenes" that cannot be made to correspond or connect. One could, for that matter, suggest that the affect (or affect-phrase as inarticulate phrase) *passes through* yet cannot be included and processed within the representational bounds of consciousness.

As a deferred experience (of the sensory kind), it is somehow stored differently: it came "in" to a mind helpless to respond and came "out" with a cunning detour.

The term "trauma" of course invokes a gap or open wound—as the open space between two times that cannot be traversed—and this openness, we have already seen above, also prominently involves a dislocated or suspended subject. Trauma, as Dori Laub has put it, "is marked by its lack of registration" insofar as the subject is reduced to fragmentation in an encounter with a violence it cannot fend off.[18] Thus conceived, traumatic events are events for which no context is (as yet) available to deal with them in an effective way: to place these events, to associate them with previous experiences, and to thus integrate them in existing meaning schemes. They are, as yet, mute.[19]

In perhaps a rather superficial way, the "procedure" (in the very literal sense of going forward) of such events coincides with the Burkean existential and the Kantian dynamical sublime: both revolve around a painful helplessness, a loss of control, and a threat of annihilation. Granted, the difference would be that in Burke's and Kant's accounts of the sublime it is *distance* that plays a crucial role in transforming pain into pleasure, while traumatic events are, precisely, marked by a lack of distance. Such events are not only "too much," they are also too close, as the subject or ego *qua* mediating force is short-circuited. By contrast, mediation plays a crucial role in Burke's sublime of terror and Kant's sublime of will-power insofar as the terror affecting the subject is never more than imaginary: the subject imagines itself being faced with a mortal danger and is only overwhelmed from a safe distance. Indeed, it is the consistent awareness of one's own safety that would "prevent" these experiences of the sublime from becoming traumatic experiences.

However, Frank Ankersmit has recently made the intriguing suggestion that precisely the *indirectness* of the experience of the sublime points to a connection with trauma. Thus, he argues:

> When Burke speaks about "tranquility tinged with terror" this tranquility is possible (as Burke emphasizes) thanks to our awareness that we are not *really* in danger. Hence, we have distanced ourselves from a situation of *real* danger—and in this way, we have *dissociated* ourselves from the object of experience. The sublime thus provokes a movement of de-realization by which reality is robbed of its threatening potentialities. As such, Burke's sublime is less the pleasant thrill that is often associated with it than a pre-emptive strike against the terrible.[20]

Not a cozy shivering in the full awareness of one's own safety but a "pre-emptive strike against the terrible": the de-realization of a scene or object that is brought about, precisely, by the inability to process this scene or object unproblematically and uninterruptedly. A reality "too much" and "too close" in this way becomes a reality dispossessed ("robbed of its threatening potentialities") and dissociated. This means, as Ankersmit proposes, that the sublime, like trauma, can be said to be "both extremely *direct* and extremely *indirect*."[21] Both trauma and the sublime refer to an experience that is too direct because it precludes the go-between of "normal"—i.e., active—assimilation. At the same time, however, such an experience is "abnormally *indirect*": "we cannot face this directness and, precisely because of this, we dissociate ourselves from it and thus remain, in a way, external to it. From the latter perspective, both sublime and traumatic experiences strangely present themselves to us as if they were somebody else's experience."[22]

This "paradox of directness and indirectness" sheds an entirely different light on the "as-if factor" of the sublime feeling in its traditional connotations: the suggestion of a *transferred* terror (i.e., a terror that does not affect the subject but another, or affects the subject only from a distance) predominant in theories of the sublime from Addison to Kant here explicitly becomes an *unclaimed* terror, a terror that is and cannot be fully owned, as if it were "somebody else's experience." Or differently said, the "safe distance" claimed for the subject in the experience of the sublime is in Ankersmit's analysis not a sign of the subject's mastery but of his or her powerlessness and "vacant" mind. It points to a dissociation that puts a scene, object, or event of terror at a distance because it has already come too close.

However, *to whom?* To the subject, who is absent? Is there still a self (subject) and other (intrusion) to be thought in the experience of trauma and the traumatic sublime? Has not the distinction between self and other, inner and outer, collapsed when the self as mediating buffer has been entirely absorbed in what Ruth Leys has called an "abysmal openness"?[23] Is it, for that matter, still possible to relate trauma and the traumatic sublime to specifiable objects when the difference between subject and object has subsided so that no "object" or "subject" can be thought—let alone identified? Is there, indeed, a psyche inside overwhelmed by an outside in the unclaimed experience of trauma when the subject has been (momentarily) suspended?

I will answer these questions in this section by following the thesis proposed by Ruth Leys that traumatic experience can never be disconnected from a primary, total identification that she (in imitation of René Girard and Mikkel Borch-Jacobsen) refers to as *mimetic* (TG 32). By pursuing the "thread" of mimetic identification as a complete absorption of subject and object, Leys argues convincingly that trauma is not simply a happening from without but one always already *preceding* and *instating* the subject. This will help us to see how the shock of the sublime—framed as a traumatic shock— can be rewritten as a dislocated and deferred experience of openness.

"I am not aware . . . that patients suffering from traumatic neurosis are much occupied in their waking lives with memories of their accident. Perhaps they are more concerned with *not* thinking of it."[24] As we know, in 1920 Freud speculated on trauma and the death drive in relation to a repetition compulsion (*Wiederholungszwang/trieb*) he had observed in World War I survivors with an otherwise "normal" psychic apparatus. Exposed to unimaginable and unendurable terrors and strains in the trenches, they were haunted in their nightmares and symptoms by a continuous return to the overwhelming, terrifying, or catastrophic scenes and events they had encountered. What intrigued Freud about the repetition compulsion in traumatized soldiers was that it had nothing to do with repression. As Caruth puts it, he was astonished by the fact that the recurrent nightmares of these soldiers could not be understood "in terms of any [repressed] wish or unconscious meaning" but rather constituted "purely and inexplicably, the literal return of the event against the will of the one" inhabited by that event. "The traumatized," she continues, "carry an impossible history within them, or they become themselves the symptom of a history that they cannot entirely possess."[25]

For now, let me not comment on the assumption—implicit in Caruth's lucid explication—that trauma involves the attack on an already available self, and that, consequently, this trauma is separate from that self: an alien force coming in to take possession of another, self-subsistent psychic apparatus. This is perhaps what Freud's text on trauma and repetition warrants, insofar as it repeatedly phrases an opposition between inside and outside in terms of "the interior of the apparatus" and "external stimuli" or "excitation from outside" respectively (*BP* 33). Indeed, the Freudian concept of trauma revolves around a breach in an "otherwise efficacious barrier against stimuli"—and it is this breaching that explains the incessant and involuntary return of something not suppressed yet (un)forgotten.

Basically, Freud's argument runs that the compulsion to repeat is but the attempt at mastery of a *belated experience*. It is, in Freud's terms, the mastery of an excess of stimuli that could not be processed or assimilated because the psychic apparatus was not prepared for it, because, indeed, the "organ of the mind" lacked "any preparedness for anxiety" (*BP* 36). Interestingly, what is thus at issue here is that according to Freud "the last line of defense" against an excess of external stimuli is paradoxically the *preparedness to be shocked* (36). In proper Freudian parlance, this means that anxiety [*Angst*], which for Freud already signals a mentally preparing for and expecting a possible danger ("though it may be unknown"), constitutes the last protection against fright [*Schreck*], which signals "the state a person gets into when he has run into danger without being prepared for it; it emphasizes the factor of surprise"—trauma thrives on the unexpected (11). As such, the repetition in traumatic neurosis concerns the repetition of a preparedness that is yet to be prepared.

Thus, the symptom resolves—quite painfully and incessantly—the trauma: the constant return to a traumatic encounter paradoxically concerns the developing "of the anxiety whose omission was the cause of the traumatic neurosis" (37). One is always fighting the last war—but of course, the apparatus does not know *that* it is, again and again (and always too late) creating a "last line of defense" in the form of a felt anxiety that had to have signaled an imminent danger. The apparatus was not even "logged on" to begin with.

Does this mean that the traumatic memory is literal: a literal, instead of a narratively adjusted, rehearsal of an isolated past? That this is a relic of the past in the psychic apparatus that has been miraculously left untouched by the networks and processes of consciousness? That, in sum, there is a piece of past *an sich* in the traumatized unavailable to the victim/survivor but, as it were, there for the taking in a hypnotic reiteration of that past? Bessel van der Kolk and Onno van der Hart have argued in this manner, stating that trauma's dissociative (instead of associative) "entering" mode ensures its unavailability through conscious recall (or, for that matter, repression) but also its persistent presence.[26] The traumatic memory is, in the terminology of Pierre Janet, a "fixed idea": a piece of truncated memory that cannot be made into a story to be recounted and related, adapted and assimilated to other stories.[27]

To think such a possibility—an almost Schopenhauerian possibility of a slice of reality *an sich* residing within the mysterious recesses of the subject—is to start from the assumption that the psychic apparatus and the traumatic event are fundamentally alien to each other: that there is something from without hiding within that has somehow retained its literal form and left its "original" imprint. Yet the difficulty is (as we have seen with respect to the deferred action of unconscious affects) that there is no way of telling how cause and effect relate to each other here. Indeed, the mere motivation to think *in terms of* cause and effect is overturned in the strange economy of unconscious affects and traumatic disorders. As Brooks Brenneis has put it, "nowhere is there attached to the various habits, routines, and repetitive twitches of our lives a label that identifies them as responses to discrete past events"—it is as if we are dealing with signifiers without, or constantly postponing, a signified.[28]

How, then, can a trauma be recognized? How do we isolate the literal as distinct from the distorted (i.e., "normal" neurosis)—and how do we unearth the "cause" as fossilized precisely as it once occurred? In much relevant literature on psychic trauma the faith in the ability of such an unearthing is typically voiced in terms of a dialectic reversal: the unforgettable becomes the memorable through the talking cure or the cathartic hypnotic cure—through, let us say, a staged rather than a compulsive rehearsal of a past infliction.[29] The trauma becomes part of a "lived," transforming time, instead of possessing the subject in an unknown past that constantly suspends the future.

Yet, the success of integration remains questionable. Van der Kolk and Van der Hart have, for that matter, already indicated that though a trauma can be "cured"—and hence resolved or transcended—the patient often continues to live in two parallel worlds (the world of trauma and the world of narrative memory) that cannot be wholly reconciled.[30] The cathartic release of a painful intrusion that can be related to the traditional sublime feeling as a relieving, "narrative" moment of closure can thus not be implicitly thought in relation to trauma. Indeed, Leys has argued, such closure is often thwarted due to "the inherent irretrievability" of the traumatic event.[31] The main obstacle here appears to be that (as Freud observed) even after a therapeutic retrieval the patient lacks "conviction as to the reality of the reconstructed traumatic scenes."[32] These scenes still appeared as other rather than one's own and to that extent continued to resist active integration. Thus, the "abnormal indirectness" of the trauma is sustained, even in its "removal": *this is not happening to me.*

Not to me—the phrase becomes most acute when we consider the possibility that the breaching of the protective shield is not a breaching of psychological defense mechanisms alone but at once a breaching of the shield protecting the unity of the ego. Traumatic shocks, that is to say, relay the *unbinding* of the ego: the latter, we have seen above, cannot defend the fort (*TG* 28–29). Now, while binding—as the binding of subject to object—

with Freud is mostly an affair of Eros or desire, Leys points to the presence in Freudian theory of a binding that would come before and persist within libidinal bonds. This is *"feeling,* a term that overlaps with a whole group of psychological concepts, such as sympathy and mental contagion, and implies an entire theory of *imitation* or "mimesis" (30). Thus we have entered the theater of mimetic identification, oscillating between the tenderness and aggression belonging to possession and consumption: mimetic identification is cannibalistic as it devours what it covets or wants to be. Thus, the theater of identification is by no means reserved for libidinal dramas. It emerges, as Jennifer Bean puts it, "not as the result of the subject's unconscious desire for a loved object, but rather as an imitation by one 'self' of an 'Other' that to all intents and purposes is indistinguishable from a primordial identification in which the organism first *acts* like, and only later desires, the outside or Other."[33] (Think here, of course, of the Lacanian mirror stage, which likewise features an introjection of an other, an image one literally lives up to.) Thus, there is a primordial tendency that precedes self-other distinctions and, as such, troubles a "proper" constitution of the self: no self without an other; indeed, what is familiarly thought of as self is nothing but an open site where acts of assimilation may take place. As Leys emphasizes, this process of primary identification can never be remembered by the subject because it "precedes the very distinction between self and other on which the possibility of self-representation and hence recollection depends" (*TG* 32). Identification as a primordial process only asserts itself through deferred action: the "assemblage" of the self *in* and *as* a subjection to others that makes possible *in the first place* the coming into being of the subject.

According to Leys, traumatic encounters rehearse this presubjective, subjugating state: that is to say, the subject's *"originary* "invasion" or alteration." The lack of inscription typical of trauma could thus be ascribed to a *vacuity* in a helpless permeability and responsiveness to stimuli that comes before "all self-representation and hence to all rememoration" (32). Thus the traumatic event—in the sense that Lyotard would use the latter term, which is to say not as presupposing a subject but rather as triggering the *anima* in the first place[34]—is immemorial not just because the cognitive and mnemonic networks cannot deal with it but because it "triggers the 'trauma' of emotional identification" that precedes representation (*TG* 33). Seen in this light, traumatic events connote a dislocation in a very real sense, insofar as they put the subject out of place: they usher a disruptive and no less violent release of *unbinding.* Thus, Leys observes, trauma involves binding and unbinding at the same time: the traumatized soldier "who is so antimimetically withdrawn from the world that he is completely numb to it is simultaneously so . . . identified with it that the boundaries between himself and others are completely effaced" (35). He has absorbed this world, he has incorporated its perils so as to reiterate them time and again, but in order to survive has at once dissociated himself. This trancelike detachment mimics the primordial openness that incubates the subject and (as a subjective suspension) forecloses remembrance. As such, trauma and the repetition compulsion not only come *before* but also *with* the subject: the latter comes to be through rehearsal.

Traumatic Breaks, Sublime Happenings: Schubert's Andantino

Suspension and affect: a site or situation where subjectivity is not yet (or no longer) and an intensity without a determinate origin. Interminability is the name, or the problem, that links the traumatic to the sublime: like the traumatic event, the sublime event in its Burkean-Wagnerian-Nietzschean-Lyotardian senses revolves around suspension (the vacant mind as a site of intrusion) and affection (a touching that is beyond will and consciousness, that will not be narrativized). Ankersmit in fact goes so far as to state that trauma "*is* the sublime and *vice versa* and at the bottom of both is an experience of reality which shatters to pieces all our certainties, beliefs, and expectations."[35] At least, as a cultural concept, traumatic experience can be posited as a twentieth-century alternative version and questioning of the eighteenth-century Enlightenment sublime. As such, it is notably no longer directed at grand and violent nature with a triumphant, autonomous subject towering above it, but at massive, manmade atrocities (World War I, the Holocaust, Hiroshima) attesting to the utter failure of the humanist project. Instead of an experience of elevation, this twentieth-century alternative to the traditional sublime feeling signals precisely an inability to overcome and come to terms with events that (still) defy imaginative and also conceptual grasp. Anxiety, that "superfluous" intensity to come to terms with an affect that cannot be recovered, epitomizes this twentieth-century sublime.

Much has been written on the topic,[36] but here I will restrict myself to the way in which the particular *movement* or *pattern* of the traumatic experience can be taken as a starting point to (re)read the sublime feeling as an affect that cannot be unequivocally or satisfactorily resolved—that, indeed, contradicts its own resolution. Instead of closure and transcendence, there is here a pattern of potentially endless repetition; instead of the proverbial cathartic moment, the subject is trapped in an experience that is inaccessible (forgotten) and irremovable (unforgettable) at the same time.

The following problem, however, immediately arises in this transference from the real of the psychopathological to the "as if" of the aesthetic: (how) can the traumatic become an aesthetic effect if we conceive of such an effect as a sensuous address? If, as Ankersmit contends, the sublime *is* the traumatic and vice versa, the question of the "appearance" of the traumatic and the provocation of traumatic affectivity in art is not even a question to be critically probed—the two are simply interchangeable. This, however, would be bypassing the obvious fact that art (also) allows for other than purely pathological impacts and resonances. Of course, in terms of intrusion and violent surprise the traumatic has long constituted a dimension of the aesthetic—think of the dramatic tool of catharsis, the exploration of fright, transgression, dismemberment and mutilation in art since the renaissance,[37] or even the radical, twentieth-century avant-garde gestures to break with the past, to cause a breach that would shatter the known, figurated world and allow the past (i.e., tradition) to make itself apparent only in indirect, negative allusions.[38]

Yet as *affection*, rather than enactment, the traumatic only passes into the zone of the aesthetic when it is mediated as a special effect: when it is framed, staged, designed, provoked, performed—in short, set and calculated. Granted, mediation is always already part of trauma, as the latter can be brought to bear on a primordial mimetic identification: the subject is a special effect of a traumatic openness to otherness. But the calculation I am here referring to is perhaps less submissive, in that it is aimed at an optional, specifically situated "assault" on the senses: a dramatic interruption in a mode of looking, listening, or touching in—I would like to say—a *permissive* virtual setting. Within these parameters, I will here approach the traumatic as a musical event from the following perspective: how can the paradoxical, traumatic pattern of mimesis and intrusion be thought as a movement that *makes sense*, that addresses itself to the senses, in a framed environment of staged performance and listening? Indeed, how can the traumatic—as a special effect—become a missed encounter in such an environment; how can sounds produce an impact that is delayed or deferred in the process of listening, so that the traumatic can be recast as a specifically aural experience?[39]

In *The Romantic Generation*, Charles Rosen has argued convincingly that involuntary memory is not a modernist but a romantic invention. From Raymond de Carbonière's travelogues from the end of the eighteenth century to Robert Schumann's nineteenth-century song cycles, intrusive memory features prominently as "the unfinished workings of the past in the present."[40] For example, the postlude of "Die alten bösen Lieder"—the last song of Schumann's *Dichterliebe* cycle—literally echoes the piano part to the final section of "Am leuchtende Sommermorgen" (the twelfth song from the same cycle). Rosen rightly maintains that this return is "unmotivated by any convention of form or even by the demands of the text." It appears "spontaneous, an involuntary memory, governed by a law of its own": a movement that returns, for apparently no necessary, logical reason whatsoever.[41] Still, this return is not without a dramatic function within the song cycle as a whole and the last song in particular. Revolving as it does around the attempt to bury the past—to bury the "old and evil songs, / the dreams so evil and bad" in a heavy coffin to "sink my love / and my sorrow in it"—Schumann's piano setting undermines the song's resolution. In reinvoking the postlude of the twelfth song, and reinvoking it apparently despite itself, the last song at once rebuts the resolve to bury the past and sink it deep in the sea: after the words are voiced, the past returns unbidden.[42]

More than a decade before Schumann's *Dichterliebe*, Franz Schubert's Piano Sonata in A Major featured such unbidden returns by means of dramatic contrasts in its middle section.[43] Together with piano pieces such as Chopin's Ballade in F Major op. 38, which was published in the same year as Schumann's *Dichterliebe*, this sonata frames a provocation of shock through the sonorous staging of unbridgeable gaps and irreconcilable frictions. As I will argue, the Sonata's Andantino evokes a sense of the sublime in terms of the traumatic through its montage of fissures in sonority, tempo, and tonality. Framed in between two other movements that would seem to hold its sudden violence in check, the Andantino nevertheless threatens to rip itself apart in an apparently aimless assault that runs its course through undirected scales and unexpected sound attacks. In this way, the Andantino *enacts* a traumatic encounter while at the same time causing a breach in an aural sensibility attuned to tonal gravitation and affective coherence.

Evidently, the very possibility of this breach to be enacted rests almost entirely with its performance. (*Almost*, insofar as the rupture is not only an aural but also a visual event: it is visible as a movement of mass, speed, density, and breakthrough.) Significantly, most recorded performances tend to level or cover up the breach in the Andantino. Thus, many performers (such as Paul Lewis or Maurizio Pollini) are inclined to use the pedal all too generously, to tone down dynamics, and to speed up lightly so as to subdue the sharpness of the contrasts and dissonances in the Andantino's middle section.[44] An impressive exception is Radu Lupu's interpretation, which is at once light and pronounced. Lupu is one of the few performers who takes the staccato indications in the bass of the opening measures seriously and extends this strategy to the middle section—there is no excessive resonance and no downplaying here to curb the sharpness of the scales and the chords. All notes can be heard discretely in their undirectedness, rather than being subdued into murky parts of a whole that is still presented as a graspable, "surveyable" figure. Likewise, the echoes in the recuperation have a convincingly accidental ring—due to Lupu's calculatedly indifferent touch, their appearance is not exploited sentimentally, and thus brought out all too purposefully, but rests involuntary, as if sounding impersonally, accidentally. In the following, I have therefore based my analysis on Lupu's performance.

The Andantino starts with one of the most beautiful-melancholic themes in romantic piano literature: a lamenting melody in the right hand and a smoothly swinging figure in the bass. Seemingly harmless, and very much in the nature of a song, there is nevertheless something deadly about the Andantino's opening (0′01″–2′17″) (corresponding to mm. 1–68): it is a music that continuously turns back on itself. Thus, on the one hand, the melody constantly spins round and reiterates its initial notes, held in suspense, always moving in on itself again. Similarly, the swinging figure in the bass sustains and echoes itself throughout the first movement, in this way creating a similar suspension of progress and development. But after 2′17″, the music wanders away toward the edge of an abyss.

This edge is first of all marked by a transition from F-sharp minor to the distant key of C minor at 2′42″ (m. 85). Rapidly, the sounds now lose their own ground and disintegrate into an explosion via chromatic steps between 3′05″–3′37″ (mm. 101–122). What follows is a series of freakish improvisations and outbursts patched together without any thematic coherence or harmonic development. Here, the middle section can be seen to enact as *process* the course of dislocation described above with respect to trauma: if functional harmony accommodates identity in the very literal sense of one and the same, by promoting the dominance of one (melodic) voice, and if, moreover, this single voice matches its accompanying chords through the corresponding laws and hierarchies of tonality, the middle section performs a rupturing of identity in a double way. On the one hand, the single voice of the opening song is unbound into a plurality of chromatic signals, undoing the discrete unity typical of diatonic foregrounding. At the same time, the ruptured matching between foreground (melody) and background (accompaniment) between 3′08″–3′26″ (mm. 103–115) fissures the blocked unities that functional harmony builds on. Thus, in the absence of functional harmonic parameters, the possibility of identity and the boundaries between self (diatonicism) and other (chromaticism) are destabilized.[45] That is to say, the otherwise rigid and enclosed forms of functional harmony have here become permeable: suffused with an "alien" heterogeneity that these forms can no longer rationalize, and that is *only* violent and chaotic within the parameters of tonality, their differentiation is no longer feasible. This heterogeneity, in its turn, is not a completely alien force, attacking the tonal system from the outside. It is rather a demon that returns: chromaticism is always present within and behind diatonicism; the latter is nothing but a cut or figuration out of the former. Thus, what happens in the middle section is that the unheard and unseen background of diatonic intervals—the chromatic scales—floods and disbands the foreground, the *gestalts* it normally allows to be singled out. The eruption is thus in fact an old echo, at once within and without the system it attacks.

At 3′24″ (m. 114), the right hand builds up a climax that is suddenly cut short: what would have been the climax on E is unexpectedly without an accent, the sequence now falling apart into the chromatic triplets and their tremolo counterparts in the bass between 3′24″–3′27″ (mm. 116–19). There is an obstinate build-up toward a climax at 3′37″ (m. 122), but this is more like an impotent pounding out of the same chord exhausting itself out until the sharp *ffz*-halt in C-sharp minor at 3′37″. Cunningly, this chord only appears as closure and in fact heralds a new series of "break-ins." After its silence, a number of aftershocks occur until 3′53″, following the same pattern of violent outbreak and dead silence (mm. 122–30).

These repetitive *tutti* strikes constitute at once a dramatic point of rupture—the music being reduced to a broken recitative with interrupting attacks—and a breaking point where the explosive middle section is suddenly smoothed out and reversed into a transitional stage leading back to the theme of the first part. This smoothing out is notably achieved by the transformation of the intrusive "attack chords" into the softened arpeggios in the bass (3′59″–4′09″; 4′52″–5′17″; mm. 133–145) (I will return to this below). Something of a struggle remains, however, as if the music were trying to come to terms retroactively with its own irruption. With a slight hesitation, the movement then directs itself via a songlike accompaniment in sixteenths to what seems to be its initial position.

However, the beginning is not what it was before: it resonates with an echo on C-sharp, suggesting the presence of a residue that continues to make itself heard in the resounding of the initial theme—a literal resounding that (in Alfred Brendel's words) precisely "obstructs an easy return to the beginning."[46] It seems, or hears, as if something irreversible has happened that cannot be silenced in the present: a gap that cannot be bridged and manifests itself as a resonance upsetting and hovering persistently over the opening melody (4′51″–5′24″; mm. 159–75). The bass, meanwhile, does not presume its opening movement but continues to be heard in six-teenths—an echo, perhaps, of the interrupted recitative in the irruption sequence.

Accordingly, the outbreak of the disruption is evoked in the immediate similarity of 6′03″–6′30″ (mm. 195–202) to 2′05″–2′17″ (mm. 63–68), inti-mating another repetition: the return of the violent rupture. Or, more pre-cisely, as at once a repetition and a slight differentiation of 2′07″–2′17″ (mm. 64–68), the repetitive movement on F-sharp minor between 6′05″–6′30″ (mm. 196–202) suggests a movement of return instead of resolution. Despite the soft arpeggiated chords (that once again achieve little more than a super-ficial smoothing things out, a smoothing already disturbed by its own echo) and despite the almost overinsistent restatement of the tonic at the very end, was not the same octaved and repeated F-sharp minor in 2′07″–2′17″ also the onset of the violent rupture in the middle section? On this basis, Kramer proposes that the harmony in the final bars suggests that "bygone violence is cyclical, unexhausted": instead of a conclusion, the ending of the Andantino alludes to a violence always threatening to come back, to a past that cannot be transcended.[47] The music ends in the way in which it started to disinte-grate, and if it is thus a "bygone" violence that is suggested to be cyclical here, this is to say that the *return* to an "unexhausted," not-quite-bygone violence is cyclical and cannot be warded off.

This is reinforced by the following: while the sudden change from the "attack chords" to the arpeggiated chords points to some sort of immediate forgetting (a covering up, a resumption to "normalcy"), it is a forgetting that fosters its own undermining, that harbors an unforgetting. For the problem is that the seemingly unmotivated change from the final attacks between to the arpeggios at 3′59″ suggests, precisely, a lack of registration, a lack of power to assimilate and neutralize the violence: the chords con-tinue to sound, the attacks are still "there," even though they have become inaudible *as* attacks. The violence is here dispossessed, but it nevertheless continues to possess the music. This possession, I have shown, is reinforced by the fact that the "forgotten" continues to assert itself as a disturbance of the present (in the echoes and accompaniment of the resumed melody) and finally even manifests itself as unforgettable in the final plagal progression, which suggests a (cyclic) regression into a potentially still active past.

As such, the irruption of the Andantino ceases to be simply intermediary, even though this is what its traditional ABA-form suggests: beginning, middle, ending, with the wildness in between and the smoothness on the sides. Instead, however, the irruption cannot be contained and moves, as it were, to the outer side, reasserting itself within, and in fact undermining the traditional function of, the concluding part. Still, by an evident paradox, the drama of the violence wholly depends on the very presence of its ternary or narrative context of beginning–middle–ending. This context indeed conditions the possibility of the irruption to be announced *as such* and disrupts that context in the process from the inside out. Arguably, this extends to the sonata in A major as a whole, which incorporates and constitutes its own rupture without the means to wholly mend or transcend it: the last chords of the Andantino continue into the Scherzo, but this by no means "lifts," so to speak, the pressure of the irruption. It remains there, at once part of and severed from its immediate context, as a break that cannot be integrated—and it requires a Rondo to become subdued (in the sense of being withdrawn). Thus, the Andantino reveals and ruptures its own ternary structure: it collapses at the very center that—as a breaking point—becomes ex-centered in its looming return at the end.

Broken Listening

Theoretically at least, one may assume that the release of chaotic sonorities in the Andantino dislocates not only a musical structure but also an affectivity of listening that, as a cultural *modus* of listening, is tonally framed. Now, "tonality" is, of course, not a monolithic practice—already in the late 1990s William Kinderman suggested we speak of tonalities in the plural, given the heterogeneity of tonal composition practices[48]—but as a "symptom" of functional harmony it has asserted its dominance since the later sixteenth century. Indeed, not to put too fine a point on it, during the eighteenth and nineteenth centuries, "the preponderance of the canon of western music was composed . . . played and listened to, in the entrenched system of equally tempered scales and the principle of tonal harmony."[49] Despite the increased heterogeneity of cultural musical (listening) practices in the twentieth- and twenty-first centuries, the dominance of this canon in the concert hall repertoire and music education syllabi still pays lip service to a mode of listening that may be termed "narrative" in its tendency to causally link successive sonorous events and in its impulse forward toward resolution.[50] Indeed, Vincent Meelberg has contended, plotting one's way through music is a cultural practice, if not an unconscious cultural device, which successfully renders even the most undirected and "unordered" music meaningful.[51] This does not mean that music is always already narratively structured but that one can *narrativize* music in the act of listening and, through this act, forge it as a graspable whole.[52]

Scott Burnham has, for that matter, already noted that the typically Beethovean master narrative of rest-adversity-crisis-resolution exemplified by the *Eroica* Symphony has come to be normative for Western musical ("tonal") listening as a whole.[53] If, as Paul Ricoeur maintains, our experiential grasp of the world is narratively conditioned, then listening *qua* narrative listening controls the shape of musical experience as a meaningful experience that "places" or "situates" the subject with respect to sonorous spaces. Indeed, insofar as tonality easily accommodates narrative listening, it has frequently been suggested that tonality in classical music serves the same purpose as central perspective in painting: to grant the listener a secure sense of space and oversight. This is, however, not to say that narrative listening need by implication accommodate to the kind of canonical narrative "tales" associated with Beethoven's heroic style, which, Burnham thinks, may have "assumed the role of a Kantian transcendental category; ha[ve] . . . become an a priori condition of hearing music."[54] Narrative processing need not be as a rule a climaxed and unambiguously resolved processing. Yet it will be a processing based on rapid weavings and interconnections made possible by the movements of tension and respite characteristic of tonal progressions—as well as themes and modes of phrasing that easily allow a listener to project a "developed" or "evolved" process.

In tonal listening, this narrative trajectory is dominant—yet it is not a dominance that cannot be broken. Indeed, Anthony Newcomb has famously noted that if we start from the assumption that the dominant frame for musical listening is a goal-oriented or teleological listening, then much would be lost on us that is, in fact, not *as a rule* lost on us.[55] We may even enjoy nonteleological movements or processes very much. What can be stated as a minimal axiom, though, is that a teleological trajectory of listening may be interrupted within its own territory when confronted with a sonic surround that resists the instant forecasting of causal successions (i.e., narrative activity). When the mindset is tonal, due to formal triggers, when the inclination of listening is narrative in a teleological sense, a sudden and radical upsetting of musical space may well disarm tonal listening and locally erode its networks of appropriation. There, in that gap, within these networks, an open, mimetic aurality could be imagined. This would be an aurality that commands "the ear" into the projections of a sonic eruption, rehearsing its movements reflexively rather than determining them according to plan and from a safe distance. In the following I will explore the viability of such an open aurality on the basis of my own listening experience of Schubert's Andantino.

First and most obviously, a disarming of tonal listening can here be linked to a sudden undermining of a harmonic center. (Though this is surely not to say that all music dispensing with the tonic by definition brings about a break in the context of "ordinary" experience—in fact, much atonal or polytonal music will find yet other ways to sustain or, conversely, irrupt the continuity of listening. The disarming I here speak of is only effective when the "horizon of expectations" is tonally framed.) As Arnold Schoenberg once noted, tonality is "but a means to an end" insofar as it is its business "to make what happens easily comprehensible."[56] Even if one is a so-called untrained listener, unaware of the laws and progressions of tonality, the tonal center functions as an aural point of gravitation, comparable to central perspective in painting, which projects the possibility of both temporal and spatial orientation. One senses where one stands, how tension is working, and that it will be resolved. Options are restricted since, as Jacques Attali has put it so well, "the only freedom the order of tonal music left open [in the eighteenth and nineteenth centuries] was the freedom to express oneself within its rules."[57] Tonal listening is thus attuned to a system of "combinatorics—a system governing the combination of authorized sounds."[58]

It is this system that Schubert's Andantino violates in its middle section: due to a chromatic radicalization (if never a *total* breaking) of combinatorics, tonal listening here lacks a stronghold to steady its course and is, instead, overwhelmed by an excess of articulations that already shift and evaporate into different successions before they can be projected into a meaningful unity or (for that matter) a coherent contrast. The only structural stronghold left is the chromatic basslines and scales, but that is at best a weak stronghold; they operate more like a continuously shifting field than a stable focal point. Moreover, even if the presence of dissonance still always implies an awareness of a key, the key relationships here remain so unfixed and indeterminate that this awareness cannot adequately serve as the basis for a rudimentary orientation. Indeed, the harmonic fragmentation that destabilizes the Andantino at its very core radically prevents the possibility of recognizing any harmonic relationship with its opening part: the irruption cannot be recognized—and thus domesticated or contextualized—in the light of what went before. This impossibility of association already indicates the tension or high degree of difficulty that tonal listening is faced with in this instance: synthetic activity bumps against a sonorous matter that literally resists to be brought into relation (both internally and with respect to the first section) and in this way obstructs a formative activity depending on recall, recognition, and integration.

Second, the middle section resists a thematic representation: there is no possibility for a "peg" to project the music as a comprehensive totality divided into different segments or units that can be recognized and patched together. Musical memory, Schoenberg has noted, is crucial to musical grasp or comprehension and depends in its turn on repetition—the repetition of a theme, idea, or motif facilitating recognition and association.[59] Conversely, moving from one fragmented figure to another in every two measures between 3′05″–3′19″ and then regressing into disintegration, the irruption of the Andantino lacks a theme or idea that *can* at all be repeated and developed. Indeed, the very fragmenting thrust of the music seems to be directed at a thwarting of recognition, at a breaking of musical memory in its capacity to retain and relate a musical manifold so as to integrate it into a unity. This is reinforced by a performance of the Andantino by Andreas Staier on an 1825 Johann Fritz piano:[60] the bass is here so fully and richly resonant, with the right-hand chords nonetheless sharply phrased, that one's listening is split between what Anton Ehrenzweig once called the simultaneous unfolding of "competing events."[61] (A complex unfolding underscored by the richness of overtones characteristic of nineteenth-century pianos: tone color, and the nuanced differences between different tone colors, is here much more outspoken than in modern pianos.) In this chromatic setting there is no easy way to reconcile these events vying for exclusive attention within the conventions of tonal listening. Thus, and almost without being aware of it, one is given over to another mode of listening: less overweening, less focused on thematic lines and developments than wandering, groping—a reinterpreted listening that hangs suspended between the aimless modulations of dedifferentiated movements working against each other.

Between 3′34″–3′37″ (mm. 120–122), it is true, some stronghold is regained as the music works up steadily in C minor to what would seem to become a cathartic climax: a C-minor *ffz* chord. Indeed, this chord allows for a momentary sense of relief in its brief assertion of closure. However, the sense of relief generated by the assertive sounding of this chord is already subtended by a tense anticipation due to its abruptness before a dead silence: as if it were halting the preceding violence, it signals a climax, it peaks, and hangs suspended in one and the same movement. Thus it brings about a curious sense of release (tensionlessness) and indeterminacy (tension) in one. Like the extreme brevity of the Schopenhauerian sublime moment, the C-minor chord at the same time discloses and forecloses an opening to relief and reorientation as its affirmative thrust—without getting a chance to reso-nate and thus sustain its potentially stabilizing effect—then stops short in, and is indeed already dispossessed by, a vacuum that holds (tonal) listening in suspense, depriving it of the means to direct, orient, and prepare itself. This undermining of any sense of preparedness is then continued and rein-forced in the following "attack chords." Here, the repeated intrusions of the *tutti* chords—as an almost perverse echo of the C-minor chord that had briefly hinted at closure and release—reduce tonal listening to a passive as-tonishment, with the "attack chords" interrupting the continuity of a prest-ructuring and directing musical focus. For a moment, this focus is fragmented and disarmed, as it were opened and enveloped by, rather than itself actively enveloping, a sensate, discontinuous sounding.

Just as suddenly, this envelopment evaporates, but it is not a complete evaporation, not a complete defragmentation. True, tonal listening is reha-bilitated and reoriented after its own disintegration, yet it does not achieve a new and final synthesis. This is not just because the Andantino resists a final resolution in the intimated return to its own irruption, but also because the disintegration leaves a hole in the totality of the synthesis of listening. This is a gap that returns as a hallucination in the echoes hovering above the melody in the last part and continues to resist a narrative "working through." For formally there are no leads in the last part of the Andantino to place the irruption in a liberating creative gesture, to relate and assimilate it with the quiet, repetitive movements that "frame" it. Technically speak-ing, indeed, one may suggest that the rupture cannot be heard within the confines of tonal listening: breaking the formulaic scheme, the transcenden-tal category that conditions the possibility of tonal listening, the Andantino's breaking point is in excess of the habitual representations that the tonal ear is able to project. It is heard, yes, but it is at once what irrupts, disarms, and suspends the conditions of possibility of tonal listening in its domesticating and goal-oriented functionality. In this sense, tonal listening has here been

virtually traumatized: its tools, schemes, and repressions have proved ineffective to ward off a chromatic openness and appropriate it within the laws
of tonality and functional harmony. Indeed, this openness briefly absorbs
tonal listening as an activity insofar as it reduces the latter to a repetition of
its own dedifferentiation. For a moment, listening is here no longer a tonally
structuring device but a decentered affect that *becomes* its sonic surround: it
rehearses the undecidability of a chromatic alterity.

Repetition and Repetition: Rhythms of Life and Death

An echo or reiteration of the heard: this is the responsiveness of a mimetic
aurality that is *itself* never more than an interruption, an in-between space
that cannot be bridged. Repetition here surges again as the token of an impotence of some sort: the impotence of defense and resistance and the accidental merging with an overweening intensity. However, in the dialogue
between trauma and the sublime, repetition also signifies more than "just"
the mark of a failure of transcendence. Indeed, the figure of repetition holds
its own right in the aesthetics of the sublime: as we have seen in previous
chapters it signals not (only) the aftereffect of a shock of astonishment but is
also of central significance to a rather different, quiet aspect of the sublime
as an aesthetics of the infinite. Thus, we have seen, the Burkean experience
of the artificial infinite revolves around a never-coming-one-step-closer to
an end or goal in a virtually incessant rhythm of a repetition of the same.
This experience of the artificial infinite opened up the possibility to rethink
the sublime feeling as a feeling that is not one: regressive and progressive at
the same time.

In what follows, I will explore more fully this possibility of a feeling that
is not one in the context of the aesthetics of the infinite (the mathematical
sublime), rather than in the context of the aesthetics of traumatic shock (the
dynamical sublime). I will do so in critical elaboration of the claim made in
the previous chapter that the paradox of pain and pleasure in the experience
of the sublime can no longer be thought of as pertaining to a mixture of
two opposing, independent principles, but as pertaining to an intertwining
of two unstable, ambiguous intensities that are paradoxically inscribed in
each other. To probe the ways in which such an intertwining can be
thought, I will once more turn to Freud's remarks on the repetition compulsion in *Beyond the Pleasure Principle* and reread these remarks through the
critical lens of Derrida presented in *The Postcard*.[62] In his more metaphysical
moments, I will show, Freud here represents the compulsion to repeat as a

double bind pointing in two contradictory directions: backward (life negating) and forward (life affirming) at the same time, without a way to reconcile the two. It is this peculiar structure of the repetition compulsion, rather
than its specific directedness to a traumatic shock, which I will then use
to frame an alternative sublime experience caught in its own, conflicting
intensities.

Beyond the Pleasure Principle could be called the story of a vacillation that
remains unsolved: it narrates, and performs, a conjunction of the apparently
diametrically opposed life and death instincts Eros and Thanatos. The latter
bears a special significance to the title of *Beyond the Pleasure Principle*, as
Freud (hesitatingly) posits the death instinct beyond the dominion of what
he considers a general tendency toward a reduction of tension (unpleasure)
in the mental apparatus: the pleasure principle (*BP* 4). With reference to
G. T. Fechner, he then postulates a dominance of the pleasure principle in
mental life (*BP* 5). However—the pleasure principle is not alone. It is opposed, bent, and obstructed, so that "the final outcome cannot always be in
harmony with the tendency towards pleasure" (*BP* 6). Typically, the Freud-
ian-conceived mind is in (perpetual) contradiction, rather than in harmony,
with itself, with alternating intensities appearing to undermine the dominance of the pleasure principle. For what, in turn, holds in check and in fact
necessarily obstructs or suspends the imperatives of the pleasure principle is
the *reality principle*. As a "method employed" by the sexual instincts, the ego
must keep the pleasure principle at bay so as not to lose itself in the total
release of indomitable, annihilating drives (*BP* 7). Repression is the answer.
Certain instincts must be rerouted and their satisfaction suspended, causing
their "illegitimate" breakthrough to be felt as unpleasurable. In *Beyond the
Pleasure Principle*, this unpleasure felt on account of the satisfaction of an "illegitimate" instinct is called a "neurotic pleasure": a pleasure that cannot be
felt as such (*BP* 8).

As we have already seen above, what struck Freud about the traumatized
soldiers' compulsion to repeat was that it had, to all appearances, nothing to
do with repression. There was nothing secretively pleasurable about these
repetitions at all. Or, as Derrida puts it in "To Speculate—On Freud," the
demon in the Freudian repetition compulsion is "the very thing which
comes back [revient] without having been called by the pleasure principle":
the former can bypass and outwit the latter.[63] Apparently, this compulsion is
not at all tied to the life instincts attached to the pleasure principle but rather
leads a life on its own, as a death instinct located "before" or "beyond" the
plane of dominance of the pleasure principle.

What follows in *Beyond the Pleasure Principle* is not a little complicated and at times bizarre. Constantly dissatisfied with his own speculations, and then picking them up again without, once more, coming to a definite conclusion, Freud (as Derrida has observed) makes his text enact the repetitive moments it inscribes.[64] His arguments are, moreover, haunted by later nineteenth- and early-twentieth-century speculations on biogenesis that can now only be merited for their historical, rather than their theoretical, relevance. I will, therefore, restrict the following account to an elaboration of an internal duality that can be read in the Freudian pleasure principle: the opposition between life (tension) and death instincts (respite) becomes an internally divided movement of interwoven intensities.

As a backward-moving force, this death instinct initially appears to be opposed in binary fashion to the seemingly progressive force of the life instincts (i.e., the sexual instincts) tied to the pleasure principle. The former is impelled by a tendency to *return*, the latter by a tendency to *move ahead*. The former wants to destroy life and all the tensions it involves; the latter wants to preserve and develop it. Here, however, the paradox that marks Freud's account of the death instinct in its "relation" to the pleasure principle already emerges: if the latter revolves around an absence of tension, death surfaces as the ultimate "goal" of the pleasure principle, which is nonetheless the "method" of the life-greedy sexual instincts. How to think this paradox that, subverting familiar notions of self-preservation, may point the way to re-presenting the paradox of pleasure and pain in the sublime?

The answer may be epitomized in this single phrase: the idea of an awakening (to life) as a return (to death). This idea is the "outcome" of Freud's attempt to project the "inexplicable" tendency in traumatized soldiers onto a more general level of biological and psychic life. Taking, as Cathy Caruth puts it, "the literal return of the past as a model for repetitive behavior in general, Freud ultimately argues . . . that it is traumatic repetition, rather than the meaningful distortions of neurosis, that defines the shape of individual lives. Beginning with the example of the accident neurosis as a means of explaining individual histories, *Beyond the Pleasure Principle* ultimately asks what it would mean to understand history as the history of a trauma."[65]

This history amounts to the history of a traumatic awakening: a traumatic awakening to life for which there was no preparation. I do not want to tread into the more eccentric elements of Freud's biological argument here, but it should be stated that he even goes so far as to define the instinct as such in terms of the death instinct, that is, the desire to return to a state of inanimation: "*It seems . . . that an instinct is an urge inherent in organic life to restore an earlier state of things*" (*BP* 43). Seen in this light, the death instinct (the instinct as such) is not an instinct that can be reduced to the pleasure principle. Rather, it comes "before" it—even though the former shares with the latter the tendency to eliminate tension as much as possible.

Speculating (after Schopenhauer) that life is a mere detour on the way back to death, Freud also speculates that the instinct for self-preservation at once signals its other. The urge to preserve one's life, he suggests, is ultimately an urge to secure one's own "proper" death (*BP* 47). Thus the instinct for self-preservation that Burke posited at the heart of the sublime becomes at once an instinct for self-destruction: in preserving one's life, one's "immanent" death is guarded. Such behavior, Freud adds, is "precisely what characterizes purely instinctual as contrasted with intelligent efforts" (*BP* 47).

The forces of Eros and Thanatos that Freud postulates to be at work in the psychic organism thus operate in a double bind of a death instinct that moves backward and a life instinct that moves forward only out of sheer necessity to follow what is in principle (the instinct already signaling a movement of return) its backward-oriented path. One may thus presume "two kinds of processes constantly at work in living substance" that operate "in contrary directions, one constructive and assimilative and the other destructive or dissimilatory," representing the sexual "instincts" and the death instincts respectively: two rhythms simultaneously moving in their own contradictory ways, though also being constantly at work in each other through a dominant rhythm of return (*BP* 59).

Interestingly, Derrida has observed, in this double bind of death and life conventional semantic distinctions between life and death, tension and tensionlessness, preservation and destruction, pleasure and unpleasure, start to falter. For one thing, the instinct for self-preservation that—as we have seen in chapter 2 with reference to Burke's existential sublime—is familiarly conceived as the urge to protect or defend life turns out to be an urge to preserve one's own death. The sentinel of life, as Derrida paraphrases Freud, "having to become that which it 'originally' will have been, the courier of death, everything changes sign at every moment."[66] Thus, progression becomes at once a regression, development ultimately turns out to be motivated by an urge to resist change and renewal, an urge to return, the guardians of life are originally the guardians of death, the aim of life—and Freud here explicitly refers to Schopenhauer—is death, and the instinct itself, conventionally understood in terms of strife and advance, reveals itself as a rhythm of delay (*BP* 59).

By the same paradoxical logic, the complete satisfaction associated with the pleasure principle and the destruction associated with the repetition compulsion no longer appear as binary opposites but rather as two sides of the same coin. The one cannot be thought without the other: the death instinct associated with the repetition compulsion is already at work in the life instincts that work through the pleasure principle, and vice versa. If, as Freud says, the pleasure principle is a "tendency" operating in the service of a "function," and if this function is "to free the mental apparatus entirely from excitation or to keep the amount of excitation in it constant or to keep it as low as possible," then this function "thus described would be concerned with the most universal endeavor of all living substance—namely to return to the quiescence of the inorganic world" (*BP* 76). In other words, the pleasure principle operates in the service of the death instinct. If this is how the death instinct is already inscribed into the life instinct, then the latter is also at work in the former to the extent that the instinct to return is also at once the "task of living" (*BP* 77).

Reading this untiable knot of death and life instincts in terms of *différance*—difference (an apparent difference in direction: backward and forward) and deferral (a deferral as delay, as detour; the detour of life, or life as detour)—Derrida proposes to read the pleasure principle itself as a *différance* come to life. This is ultimately what Derrida detects in Freud's text: Freud reworks the apparent dichotomy between life and death instincts into an *internal duality*, an in-between space that is originary. Instead of something beyond the pleasure principle, there is something at work within the economy of the pleasure principle that, serving the "function" of the death instinct, interrupts and sustains it in its search for complete constancy and satisfaction. Hence Derrida: the pleasure principle "would not be a function but a tendency in the service of [a] general function," which is the "return to the inorganic and Nirvana . . . via the intermediary or place of passage . . . to wit the PP [pleasure principle]."[67]

The internal duality Derrida detects in the pleasure principle (and that effectively dispels the idea of two separate energies opposing each other) thus invokes a movement that constantly and aimlessly vacillates within itself, hinging between (auto)destruction and satisfaction. Back and forth, back and forth, and back in forth, and vice versa. It may well be this force or mechanism of an internal duality that ultimately accounts for the irresolvable double bind of the sublime feeling as a feeling of tension and respite at the same time. The idea of two intensities at once same and other, always already involved, precludes the comforting possibility of a dialectic resolution. At best, one could circumscribe the Freudian parallel movements of death (repetition) and life instinct (development) as a narrative of return always out of phase with itself: "It is as though the life of the organism moved with a vacillating rhythm. One group of instincts rushes forward so as to reach the final aim of life as swiftly as possible; but when a particular stage in the advance has been reached, the other group jerks back to a certain point to make a fresh start and so prolong the journey" (*BP* 49).

As such a narrative of return, however, I would like to add that if the Freudian life instincts signal an enforced tension (Freud refers to them as "breakers of the peace") and the death instinct a primary tensionlessness, the former can nevertheless *include* the latter—even if it is not an inclusion as reconciliation (*BP* 77). Recall, in this instance, the peculiar mechanism at work in romantic *Sehnsucht*. On the one hand, it involves a tension of frustrated desire, a desire that wants to go forward but cannot find, and does not even know, its object or endpoint. On the other hand, however, this tension of frustration can be deconstructed as a strategy of deferral, of suspending any kind of tension-inducing change. It has, we have seen, the character of a compulsive repetition, always looking for a way to dodge its own resolution. Thus, differently said, because desire here constantly contradicts its own end, the tension at stake in *Sehnsucht* at once harbors a tensionlessness of suspension: it allows for an infinite deferral of renewal and transformation and the "labor" involved in it.

Repetitive Music and the Sublime

It is in this way, as a Janus-faced movement tending to advance and withdraw at the same time, that the sublime feeling bends to the paradox (in John Baillie's words) of a mind "that is the subject of contradictions," experiencing "joy and grief, pleasure and pain" at once.[68] In the following pages, I will try to show how this paradoxical crossing between repetitive and accumulative rhythms can be imagined with respect to music. Translating this crossing into aesthetic terms of pleasure and pain, I show how an irresolvable deadlock of two opposing tendencies (stasis and return on the one hand, and mobility and agitation on the other) can make itself felt in the act of listening. As I argue, this felt double bind constitutes the moment of the sublime feeling as a feeling (of the infinite) that is not one. From the outset, I would like to emphasize that this does not entail a simple projection of

Freud's life/death instincts onto the sublime but rather a critical transference of their logic of *différance*.

My focus in this analysis will be on the particular strategies employed in present-day repetitive music. This choice is obvious in more than one way. To start with, in the *Enquiry* Burke of course already points to the effect of the steady repetition of similar parts to invoke a feeling of the artificial infinite. If anything, it is around this pattern that much contemporary repetitive music revolves. Hoffmann likewise highlighted the idea of an incessant return in Beethoven's Fifth, or the *Coriolan* Overture, in his discourse of instrumental music as an art destined to bring about the feel of the infinite. Second, twentieth-century American composers of minimal and repetitive music such as La Monte Young, Terry Riley, Steve Reich, Philip Glass, or Louis Andriessen (as different as they are) already reveal a fascination with limitlessness and in certain cases more specifically with the evocation of an eternal moment—a moment without beginning or ending that is felt as infinite. As much as these musical strategies of repetition and return have familiarly been linked to inductions of trance and forgetfulness,[69] I nevertheless argue the contrary: shifting in between progression and regression, repetitive music may bring about a felt paradox of contrary intensities of tension and respite that are nonetheless sonically intertwined.

There is, perhaps, a rather special connection between American repetitive music and the idea of the sublime.[70] Revolving around a direct presentation of a process of repetition of similar (and at once slightly differing) parts, much repetitive music invokes the process of infinite movement intimately tied to the sublime movement. Thus, Steve Reich has observed that his early strategy of phase shifting (two or more voices or instruments playing the same repeating pattern one or more beats out of phase with each other) can well be regarded as an "extension of infinite canon."[71] There are two or more melodic lines or patterns that are rehearsed on different levels and in different phases again and again. Unlike traditional canon, however, Reich's phase shifting induces a tension or unease due to the parts being slightly out of step with each other—there is an irresolvable friction between the different parts that constantly rub against each other from a minimal, magnetic distance. What may thus occur in the experience of listening to such phase-shifting processes is the sense of an ongoing expansion. As Reich puts it with respect to *Violin Phase* (1967), the listener "becomes aware of one pattern in the music that may open his ear to another, and another, all sounding simultaneously in the ongoing overall texture."[72] One pattern opens the way to opening of the next, and the next—it is like a hallway with infinitely opening doors. Crucially, I hear this infinite opening *as process* rather than as representation: it is the process of shifting and rehearsing *itself* that becomes the "subject" of music here.

Not all repetitive music is purely repetitive in this way (which is why Timothy Johnson has proposed the term repetitive music as technique: *as* a technique, rather than a style or "school," it can also occur in nonrepetitive music).[73] Purely repetitive music, one could say, feeds on repetition as a dysfunctional mechanism. Something like the Freudian *heimlich* becoming at once *unheimlich*, repetition here undermines the listener's perspective and thwarts her or his sense of overview, while in traditional music the use of repetition serves, precisely, to provide for such a perspective and sense of overview.[74] This is due to the fact that much contemporary repetitive music lacks (in Mertens' words) a "*narrative* and *teleological* frame" and consequently does not use the instrument of repetition in the service of this frame.[75] Simply put, the lack of a teleological and narrative frame implies that this music lacks an either implicit or explicit directedness and a plotlike development of beginning-middle-ending (rest-tension-resolution) that typifies tonal music. This undermines the secure, anticipatory perspective of tonal listening.

However, in more recent repetitive works such as John Adams' *Harmonielehre* (1985) or Philip Glass's *Itaipu* (1989) the less secure footing of repetitive listening is once again reinforced by melodic lines and thematic pegs that facilitate a sense of overview. Indeed, in both instances the listener is seduced into a sense of elevation motivated by a very strong feeling of progression. It is, moreover, not so much a temporal process as the musical evocation of a giant visual spectacle that motivates the patterns of repetition in these works. Thus, in *Harmonielehre* Adams translates a dream he had about a huge tanker in the San Francisco Bay Area suddenly taking off like a rocket into musical sounds and motions: the music evokes the sense of an impossible levitation, of something starting to heave and lift itself that is not supposed to heave and lift itself. As in the paintings of the American abstract expressionists, the fascination with the grand and majestic here persists alongside a concern with minimal presentation. Phillip Glass's *Itaipu*, a grand-scale symphonic evocation of the massive hydroelectric dam at Itaipú on the Paraná River falls into the same category. Of its four parts, especially "The Lake" evokes a tense but almost addictive sense of anticipation as it shifts from a dreamy, wavelike movement into a forward-rushing, swollen motion that, after having subsided, leads into the massive strokes of "The

Dam." Here, American repetitive music—strikingly—recaptures the experience of sublime nature and twentieth-century technological achievement in conventional terms of awe and wonder.

While the sense of impossible levitation and infinite space in *Harmonielehre* and *Itaipu* is rather unambiguous (my listening is here worked up steadily toward a climactic release), it is mostly in earlier repetitive music that a more complex and paradoxical awareness of temporal movement is foregrounded. Reich's *Piano Phase* (1967) performs a process that revolves around tension and release at the same time: a mixture of tension-elimination brought about by an incessant repetition of similar patterns in three cycles and tension brought about by a continuous change and friction (the phasing). Yet also without the instrument of phasing, repetitive music may not simply trigger a relaxing forgetfulness, a sense of timelessness, but also—and at the very same time—a sense of *endless time*.

As a focal point, I here use Terry Riley's classic *In C*.[76] Like Reich's *Piano Phase*, the simultaneity of stasis and mobility in Riley's *In C* is gestured at in its combination of a repetition of the same with a texture of continuously changing motifs—compare it to a kaleidoscope constantly changing color, with different motifs fading in and out, expanding and again retracting. However, if this constant color switching suggests a sense of motion set against a repetitive pattern, *In C* appears to be always departing without arriving in a truly "new" stage, meandering ever so slightly from within in different sonorous textures. It starts off in the manner of a regular canon, yet it never comes close to articulating a fully developed phrase. What it offers are fragments of a canon that are never integrated into an entity but constantly tend toward any such entity, here and there disintegrating into a seemingly amorphous mass resembling the preparatory tuning of instruments before a performance is about to take place. It is this sense of something impending but never arriving that typifies *In C* throughout.

Pointing to the paradoxical combination of repetition and motif shifting, Michael Nyman suggests that *In C* presents a mobility within a seemingly immobile setting: "Within a completely static musical 'environment' is perpetual motion"—or, in reverse, within perpetual motion is complete stasis.[77] The shifting motifs suggesting this motion constitute but infinitely small changes that do not signal a substantial development, motif-wise. Indeed, as the opening motifs already indicate, the substantial here makes room for what is familiarly referred to as the ornamental in traditional teleological musical structures: the "substance" of the music is its insubstantiality, its ornamental figuration that refuses to convey a fixed direction, a (subordinated) functionality. Usually, in such traditional teleological musical structures, functionality is as it were already added in the adding of a new tone that will develop—say, either away from or back to the tonic, creating a sense of tension or relaxation in the process. A tone, a motif, a phrase is in the service of a larger totality. In *In C*, interestingly, this functionality is not simply fully absent but is rather tentatively gestured toward while at the same time being short-circuited. Or, to put it differently, the sonorous space in which such functionality usually materializes is here opened only to be never purposively realized, to transpire on the spot.

Thus, in terms of temporal economy *In C* saves time but never cashes in on it. In teleological structures, the temporal economy serves to set something in advance, to hold out the prospect of a result or return. *In C*, however, does not so much refrain from temporalization as it temporalizes without yielding a plan: a plan in terms of a measure-by-measure development, a hierarchy of beats, or an all-pervasive sense of progression derived from tonal functionality. There is no breaking point, no opening in which something breaks through, as was the case with Schubert's Andantino, as there is basically nothing to break against. There is only an endless, open prediction. Indeed, one could say that *In C temporizes* in the sense of interminable delay so as to gain time endlessly and purposelessly, to never evolve beyond a stage of preparation, beyond a "being on its way."

This endless gaining of time suggests not so much a simple dulling of the awareness of (the passing of) time as it does a *quickening* of the awareness of a constant, tentative time shift that keeps deferring its own development, its own consumption. Temporalization, I have said, is not absent here, even though it is a temporalization without a plan (a purposiveness, to use Kant's phrase, without a purpose): it is gestured toward through the pulse that never stops to (literally) indicate time, in the pattern of repetition itself that never stops to suggest a "continued enlargement" within the rhythm of time, and the adding of new motifs—however small and almost subliminal the changes thus brought about may be. Interestingly, as with the Prelude to *Tristan and Isolde*, I can here never quite erase the claustrophobic sense of not being able to transcend time as constant flux—however much the reiteration of the same may tempt one to lose track and awareness of the passing of time measured into a specific direction. Paradoxically, indeed, in listening to *In C* I feel trapped in the very repetitive structure sustaining the illusion of timelessness: a sense of boundlessness is here subtended by a sense of constraint.

The constraint, in this instance, refers to an anticipation bearing on the repetitive process of interminable delay that *itself* holds stasis and mobility in one. The repetitive process here entails stasis in the sense of an absence of development, a reiteration of the same or a standing on the spot. At the same time, it suggests an infinite mobility in the presentation of rehearsing patterns that could go on for ever, multiplying *ad infinitum*, precisely because a new stage or development is interminably deferred. There remains infinite room for more in a temporal economy that continuously postpones its own realization. Listening, this indefinite extension feels as a rhythm one labors to but cannot get past: the musical imagination can put no stop, no encompassing limit, to the constant reiteration of similar "parts." Every (imagined) step forward turns out to be a remaining in place, as if one were trying to reach a horizon that recedes ever further the closer one believes to be approaching it. This is, however, precisely how *In C* can evoke the sublime in its Burkean sense of the artificial infinite. The feel of an incessant progression here too turns on an immobility brought about by the continuous return to one's initial position: a tendency to return is already at work in a tendency to move ahead as one seems to be moving incessantly (and fruitlessly) forward in, precisely, a movement of incessant return.

This forward-backward paradox typifying the experience of the artificial infinite at once indicates that a purely regressive experience is here not an issue. Listening to *In C*, the regressive and progressive rather *presuppose* and reinforce each other insofar as the former propels the latter, allowing a reiteration of the same to be felt as an indefinite extension that one cannot grasp. Or, to put this differently, while *In C*'s repetitive texture on the one hand induces an anticipation of time (literally) not coming to pass, this tension is on the other hand sustained by a regressive movement that, precisely, *reduces* tension in a rhythm of return foreclosing the "labor" of change and renewal. What this in fact means is that a tension or displeasure brought about by the feel of an unaccomplished movement here already includes the respite fostered by a (deadly) constancy: pain is interlocked with its other in a suspension without end that constantly precludes resolution, as the deferral of movement productive of a "hypnotic rest" creates at once an ever opening space, an ever expanding rhythm that one cannot put a stop to.

In this way, one could imagine a sublime feeling that does not manifest itself as an experience of liberation-by-way-of-frustration but as an experience of stasis-in-mobility or mobility-in-stasis that endlessly vacillates between pleasure and pain. It is the experience of an in-between, an experience hesitating between regression and anticipation that cannot be concluded as one: the "way back" of regression cannot guarantee a complete relief as it is itself already implied in, and propels, the "way forward" of anticipation. Embodying this paradox, *In C* makes explicit in experiential terms the ambiguity, the two-sidedness of a movement gesturing ahead without limit, without end, that is paradoxically motivated and "kept going" by a tendency to return: like the irresolvable double bind of Freud's life and death instincts, this music moves in inclining to return—the shifting motifs creating a tension that, precisely, the music seeks to ward off in a texture of constant reiteration.

Or rather, within the texture of repetition a movement is created that constantly tries to cancel itself out, to unbecome through reiteration and return, yet in this very way becomes a movement that is felt as extending indefinitely, without relief. Approaching *In C* in this way, I have not only sought to relate its politics of repetition to the aesthetics of the sublime as an aesthetics of the infinite, but also to show that on a more general level repetitive music can offer rather more than easy listening or the hypnotic leisure time familiarly ascribed to it in the critical and popular imagination. Rather, it incorporates a tense rhythm of deferral and return that encapsulates the sublime feeling as a double yet immobile movement that cannot be harmonized into a unified experience. Unity here hovers as an impossible illusion beyond the limit that this feeling can never cross on account of its fatal, internal duality.

A past that interrupts, a repetition that will not be stopped, a feeling that cannot be accomplished or unified: what would this tell us about the sublime as a critical concept? Most significantly, and also in view of what we have seen in the previous chapter, as an irresolvable feeling the sublime feeling is—in one way or another—entangled in a lost moment or an irreparable past: its focus is not simply on a future moment in which, as with Kant, a supersensible destiny will have been realized or, as with Burke, one's safety from any real danger will have been affirmed. What constantly interrupts such progress here is the counteractive pull (*Sehnsucht*, repetition compulsion) or the helpless rehearsal (trauma) of a dislocated past. Indeed, my claim would be that the affective paradox of the sublime *only* becomes feasible in the felt presence of such an intrusive yet irretrievable past.

Coda: The Sublime, Intermedially Speaking

Years ago, I was hitching with a friend on a Buginese fishing boat from Sulawesi to the island of Lembata in eastern Indonesia. One late afternoon, when the sun was at its lowest, we had spotted a whale rising up from the waters within yards before us—so close and unexpected as to almost become unreal. Dolphins regularly accompanied our boat, and the sea stretched out with nothing in sight save some deserted islands scattered here and there. It was exactly one year before the great flood devastated eastern Flores, wiping away several islands in the Flores Sea. Now, however, the sea was flat, like a pond, in a dead stillness.

Sleeping on deck, I awoke one morning perhaps half an hour before sunrise. The world was enveloped in a strange and sharp pink light that blurred the distinction between the unmoving waters and the sky. Except for the boat, nothing could be discerned, not even a little flying fish, not even a horizon. All was lost in that light, which made the sea and the sky appear as one continuum, a dome without beginning or end—immense and oppressive.

It was a sight too excessive to be digested: limitlessness does not suit the glance of an eye. It needs "something" to anchor and form its view and it needs something to recognize. For one uncanny moment it seemed as if the world was lost and this pinkish nothingness had come in its place. So I closed my eyes, waiting for the sun to shape its familiar differences once more.

There can be no doubt: even when it is only a semblance, the infinite is too much for us. Nothing, according to Charles Baudelaire, "cuts deeper . . . than the infinite," even though it is a cutting that seems pleasurable and painful at the same time.[1] The pleasure consists in a momentary loss of self, in losing one's "gaze in the endlessness of the sky and the sea," perhaps experiencing a sense of forgetfulness as one drowns oneself out in this empty space, or a sense of freedom in the wide and open expanse ahead. Yet on the other hand, this emptiness remains frustratingly excessive and inaccessible: "the depth of the sky confuses me. Its unending clarity exasperates me.

The insensitivity of the sea, the immutability of the spectacle revolts me."[2] If the infinite beckons, it also resists; the indefinite clarity of the sky and the sameness of the sea: the speaker cannot stand it, for all it does is bring home the impassable gap between that unchanging stillness and his "incurable existence."[3] The infinite is longed for, but when it appears—though it can never appear in so many words—it cannot be endured.

And so the speaker is trapped in a peculiar double bind: seeking to fuse with the vast expanse he is contemplating, this fusion can only be "there" when he is not "there"—when his (sense of) self is suspended, under erasure. If such moments prove ultimately untenable due to their extreme brevity, here the feel of the infinite proves untenable because it undermines itself from the inside out: it breaks precisely when it peaks. The spell of forgetfulness is broken by the very bliss it occasions: "the energy is so voluptuous that it creates a sense of discomfort, a positive suffering"—the pleasure is too much, too intense.[4] Instead of intensifying any sense of oblivious unification, this pleasure intensifies the frustration of being cast out, of being "there" after all. It awakens, precisely, a painful consciousness of separation and of a powerlessness to sustain one's own absent-minded extension in empty space. It is then, having caught but a glimpse of the infinite, that the speaker revolts and confesses: "The quest for the beautiful is a duel whereby the poet cries with horror before he is defeated."[5] The experience of the infinite is a failed experience that collapses when a sense of intense pleasure is contradicted from within: just when this pleasure is at its highest it becomes a painful suffering. Pleasure here thus "occurs" in conjunction with pain, the former already bears the latter, just as the pain still includes the pleasure in being its intensification.

As I have tried to show here, it is in this way—in a way that resists the deciding of pain into pleasure—that the sublime feeling can be thought as a paradoxical mix of intensities. Mixture, mélange, Derrida has said, is madness, but it is in the experience of the sublime that a mad mixture manifests itself, displacing the subject as a subject of contradictions rather than affirming it as a subject of autonomous integrity.[6] A mad mixture, too, manifesting itself in the paradox that the sublime at once feeds on and breaks through the terms set for mediated, masterful experience. If the sublime signals an irremediable rupture it is never a rupture "on its own" but a rupture that is inextricably intertwined with the forms, bounds, and contexts conditioning the possibility of experience violated by it: the sublime may break through the mediating, narrative networks of experience, but it is always and already within the context of these mediations that the sublime can manifest itself as break or rupture. It needs and is interlocked with that which it does violence to—and it is perhaps due to this very interlocking that the sublime feeling can, in the end, not be a neatly structured experience of beginning-middle-ending but rather one of "mad" simultaneity.

Performing a break within rather than without mediation, it may be fruitful to relate the sublime to a concept that has gained prominence in contemporary criticism: the intermedial. Philosophically, the intermedial signals an in-between space and movement, a *milieu*, that has not (yet) been decided. Literally signifying a "middle of the middle" or an "in-between mediation," the intermedial performs a force that cannot be reduced to existing categories and classifications. The intermedial is always what we discover on hindsight, after its occurrence: the intermedial uncovers identification as an aftereffect. This not only applies to new medial practices that have been hypostatized retroactively into bounded practices (such as "concrete poetry," "sound poetry," or "postdramatic theater"). It can also be brought to bear on a *position* relative to readers, viewers, listeners, or somewhere in between them: the intermedial as a middle ground between subject and object that resists integration because it cannot be reduced to either. There is an interaction between the two that cannot be registered because this interaction is not yet a bounded feeling but rather a mere potentiality—an intensity, in other words, that has not yet been checked against previous experiences so as to make it retrievable and recognizable.

Surely, this is not the place to enter into the complex debate on intermediality and affectivity. I do want to make clear, however, that the sublime feeling as I have tried to rewrite it "musically" is, very strictly speaking, not a feeling or an emotion but precisely an *affect* that hovers in an undecidable, in-between space. I use affect here in a specifically Deleuzian sense, which is to say an affectation that the subject cannot master because it comes before all subjective mediation.[7] Affect is the name for the impressions of intensities that are unrepresentable to the extent that they exceed the stratum of experiential possibilities. They are often referred to as prepersonal but this is not to say that affects are restricted to a historical time that has occurred only once (which is to say, the time "before" the subject). Rather affects are to be conceived in terms of a recurring dynamic; they may happen again and again in those in-between moments and spaces in which the subject is momentarily suspended, put out of place. One could call them tremors or movements not yet actualized insofar as they are registered automatically and involuntarily—they are beyond conscious intention and control.

Seen in this light, there are many intersections between trauma and Deleuzian affect—indeed, one could call traumatic experience an affect especially in view of its bodily registration and "remembrance" of shocking
events. Like Deleuzian affects, traumatic experiences are registered as bodily
intensities, registered by skin and muscles, and not yet actualized by conscious schemes and networks. However, the inherent unaccomplishedness
of affects is not necessarily restricted to the kind of violent intensities familiarly associated with the traumatic. It may, by contrast, also be brought to
bear on the more quiet interruptions of consciousness, such as the idle per-
ceptions of daydreaming or the more subtle dislocations of perceptual orientation in the scene I have described above. Affect, to my mind, is really the
dynamic of occupying an unclaimed space that suddenly falls open in between the mental projections and colonizations of everyday life—violently
or gently. Because of this double participation, "affect" is a most appropriate
concept to analyze the sublime in both its dynamical and mathematical
guises: it already effectively brings home the problem that the sense of the
sublime is never more than the (after)effect of an untraceable interaction.
There is but one question: how could the internal duality, the movement,
of the sublime feeling be preserved in a radically immanent universe?

Notes

Introduction

1. For more on the music festivals during the Terror, see James Johnson, *Listening in Paris: A Cultural History* (Berkeley: University of California Press, 1995), chap. 7. For more on terror, the sublime, and the French Revolution, see Caroline Weber, *Terror and Its Discontents: Suspected Words in Revolutionary France* (Minneapolis: University of Minnesota Press, 2003).

2. Johnson, *Listening in Paris*, 126.

3. Ibid., 127.

4. Edmund Burke, *Enquiry Into the Origin of our Ideas of the Sublime and Beautiful* [1759] (Oxford: Oxford University Press, 1990), II, sect. XVII, 76. Hereafter *ESB*. All further references will be given in the text.

5. Immanuel Kant, *Kritik der Urteilskraft* [1790], ed. Karl Vorländer (Hamburg: Felix Meiner Verlag, 1990). Hereafter *KU*. All further references will be given in the text. The translations are my own, though I have also consulted the translation by J. C. Meredith in *The German Library* series. See for this, "Critique of Judgment," in *Immanuel Kant: Philosophical Writings*, ed. Ernst Behler (New York: Continuum, 1991), 129–246.

6. I use "him" in this instance since Kant had a male subject in mind for the experiencing subject of the sublime. This is basically so because the Kantian experience of the sublime requires a well-developed reason, and in Kant's phallogocentric perspective it is only men that should develop their reason and train themselves in the kind of spiritual autonomy that allows them to rise above the fears and desires attached to their sensuous, body-bound self. Indeed, Christine Battersby has remarked that for Kant a "man proves his superior moral excellence by his ability to experience the sublime." See Christine Battersby, "Stages on Kant's Way: Aesthetics, Morality, and the Gendered Sublime" in *Feminism and Tradition in Aesthetics*, ed. Peggy Zeglin Brand and Carolyn Korsmeyer (University Park, Penn.: Penn State University Press), 96.

7. For more about the theological resonances of the landscapes of the sublime, see Marjorie Hope Nicolson's classic *Mountain Gloom and Mountain Glory: The Development of the Aesthetics of the Infinite* [1959] (New York: W. W. Norton, 1963); Simon Schama, *Landscape and Memory* (London: HarperCollins, 1995); Claudia Bell and John Lyall, *The Accelerated Sublime: Landscape, Tourism, and Identity* (Westport, Conn.: Praeger Publishers, 2001).

8. Neil Hertz, "The Notion of Blockage in the Literature of the Sublime," in *Romanticism*, ed. Cynthia Chase (London: Longman, 1993), 85.

9. Petrarch climbed the two-thousand-meter-high Mont Ventoux in 1336, describing the experience in a letter of April 26, 1336. See "The Ascent of Mont Ventoux" [1336] in *Petrarch: Selections from the Canzoniere and Other Works*, trans. Mark Musa (Oxford: Oxford University Press, 1985), 11–19.

10. Ibid., 15–17.

11. Paul Guyer has already perceptively noted that the sublime with Kant must be "contrasted to nature rather than ascribed to it": the sublime experience is here not an experience *of* but an experience in *opposition to* nature. See Paul Guyer, *Kant and the Experience of Freedom* (Cambridge: Cambridge University Press, 1996), 263.

12. John Baillie, *An Essay on the Sublime* [1747] (Los Angeles: William Andrews Clark Memorial Library of California, 1953), 4.

13. Ibid., 8.

14. Ibid., 11.

15. See Theresa de Lauretis, *Alice Doesn't: Feminism, Semiotics, Cinema* (Bloomington: Indiana University Press, 1984).

16. The term "existential sublime" derives from Paul Crowther and refers to the central (moral) aspect of the Burkean sublime: that it invigorates one's sense of being alive: "a spectacle of mortality—of life under attack or threat—rejuvenates our sensibility. In such an experience, the present moment of consciousness—our very sense of being alive—is intensified into a felt quality, precisely because it is underscored by some actual or represented negation of life." See Paul Crowther, *Critical Aesthetics and Postmodernism* (Oxford: Oxford University Press, 1996), 127.

17. This dynamic of tension and respite, or imminence and distance, was in fact already outlined by John Dennis in the early eighteenth century in his *The Grounds of Criticism in Poetry*. Thus, Dennis maintained that no passion is attended by a greater joy than terror, because this joy "proceeds from our reflecting that we are out of danger *at the very same time that we see it* [i.e., the terror-inspiring object or scene] before us." This evidently antedates Burke's famous dictum that terror (for him, as for Dennis, the strongest passion of all) can become delightful when "it is not conversant about the present destruction of the person" (*ESB* IV, sect. VII, 123): when, that is to say, a threat is kept at bay and terror disappears into relief. See John Dennis, *The Grounds of Criticism in Poetry* [1704], in *The Critical Works of John Dennis*, ed. Edward Niles Hooker (Baltimore, Md.: The Johns Hopkins Press), 1:361. Dennis's significance to eighteenth-century theories of the sublime is little realized today but his presence in the British debate is not to be underestimated. Indeed, Dennis predates many of the observations made in Burke's *Enquiry* concerning the central role of terror to, and the interplay between negative and positive affects in, the sublime feeling.

18. Samuel Holt Monk, *The Sublime: A Study of English Critical Theories in Eighteenth-Century England* [1935] (Ann Arbor: University of Michigan Press, 1960).

19. Here is a selection of the contemporary studies on the sublime I have consulted: Frank Ankersmit, *Sublime Historical Experience* (Stanford, Calif.: Stanford

University Press, 2005); Andrew Ashfield and Peter de Bolla, "Introduction," in
The Sublime: A Reader in British Eighteenth-Century Aesthetic Theory, ed. Andrew Ash-
field and Peter de Bolla (Cambridge: Cambridge University Press, 1996), 1–16; Bill
Beckley, ed., *Sticky Sublime* (New York: Allworth Press, 2001); Mark Cheetham,
Kant, Art, and History: Moments of Discipline (Cambridge: Cambridge University
Press, 2001), chap. 4; Paul Crowther, *The Kantian Sublime: From Morality to Art*
(Oxford: Clarendon Press, 1989); Paul Crowther, *Critical Aesthetics and Postmodern-
ism*; Peter de Bolla, *The Discourse of the Sublime: Readings in History, Aesthetics, and
the Subject* (Oxford: Blackwell, 1989); Martin Donougho, "Stages of the Sublime in
North America," in *MLN* 5 (2000): 909–40; Frances Ferguson, *Solitude and the Sublime: Romanticism and the Aesthetics of the Individuation* (New York: Routledge, 1992);
Rodolphe Gasché, "The Sublime, Ontologically Speaking," in *Yale French Studies*
99 (2001): 117–28; Paul Guyer, *Kant and the Experience of Freedom*; Masahiro Hamashita, "Genealogy of the Aesthetics of the Sublime: To Addison and Shaftsbury"
KCS 38 (1992): 105–27; Neil Hertz, "The Notion of Blockage in the Literature of
the Sublime"; Jonathan Hess, *Reconstituting the Body Politic: Enlightenment, Public
Culture, and the Invention of Aesthetic Autonomy* (Detroit, Mich.: Wayne State Univer-
sity Press, 1999); Tamar Japaridze, *The Kantian Subject: Sensus Communis, Mimesis,
Work of Mourning* (Albany, N.Y.: SUNY Press, 2000); Lawrence Kerslake, *Essays on
the Sublime: Analyses of French Writings on the Sublime from Boileau to La Harpe* (Bern:
Lang, 2000); Jeffery Libret, ed. and trans., *Of the Sublime: Presence in Question*
(Albany, N.Y.: SUNY Press, 1993); Steven Z. Levine, "Seascapes of the Sublime:
Vernet, Monet, and the Oceanic Feeling," in *New Literary History* 2 (1985): 377–
400; Jean-François Lyotard, *Le Différend* (Paris: Éditions de Minuit, 1983), Jean-
François Lyotard, *The Differend: Phrases in Dispute*, trans. George Van Den Abbeele
(Minneapolis: University of Minnesota Press, 1996); Jean-François Lyotard, *Peregri-
nations. Law, Form, Event* (New York: Columbia University Press, 1988); Jean-
François Lyotard, *L'Inhumain. Causeries sur les temps* (Paris: Galilée, 1988); Jean-
François Lyotard, *The Inhuman: Reflections on Time*, trans. Geoffrey Bennington and
Rachel Bowlby (Cambridge: Polity Press, 1991), Jean-François Lyotard, *Leçons sur
l'Analytique du sublime* (Paris: Galilée, 1991); Jean-François Lyotard, *Lessons on the
Analytic of the Sublime*, trans. Elizabeth Rottenberg (Stanford, Calif.: Stanford Uni-
versity Press, 1994); Jean-François Lyotard, *Moralités Postmodernes* (Paris: Galilée,
1993); Jean-François Lyotard, *Postmodern Fables*, trans. Georges van den Abbeele
(Minneapolis: University of Minnesota, 1997); Jean-François Lyotard, *Karel Appel:
ein Farbegestus. Essays zur Kunst Karel Appels mit der Bildauswahl des Autors*, trans.
Jessica Beer (Bern: Verlag Gachnan & Springer, 1998); Kirk Pillow, *Sublime Understanding: Aesthetic Reflection in Kant and Hegel* (Cambridge, Mass.: The MIT Press,
2000); Jan Rosiek, *Maintaining the Sublime: Heidegger and Adorno* (New York: P.
Lang, 2000); James Williams, *Lyotard and the Political* (London: Routledge, 2000);
Renée van de Vall, "Silent Visions: Lyotard on the Sublime," in *The Contemporary
Sublime: Sensibilities of Transcendence and Shock* (Cambridge: VCH Publishers, 1995),
69–75; Thomas Weiskel, *The Romantic Sublime: Studies in the Structure and Psychology
of Transcendence* (Baltimore, Md.: The Johns Hopkins University Press, 1976);

Rachel Zuckert, "Awe or Envy: Herder contra Kant on the Sublime," *The Journal of Aesthetics and Art Criticism* 3 (2003): 217–32.

20. Jean-François Lyotard, *The Inhuman*, 124–28. Hereafter *TI*. Further references will be given in the text.

21. For Renée van de Vall, see note 19. It is interesting to note here that John Dennis already related inspiration and "poetical genius" to the sublime by defining the former as "the expression of a furious joy, or pride, or astonishment, or all of them, caused by the conception of an extraordinary hint." (Hint is derived from Middle English *hinten*, "to seize"). What may happen in the creative process, Dennis argues, is that the poet suddenly hits upon a thought or image that surpasses everything she had expected or intended to present. The soul is "transported upon it, by the consciousness of its own excellence, and it is exalted . . . and lastly . . . the soul is amazed by the unexpected view of its own surpassing power." Something new and unforeseen happens that overtakes the soul, arrests it in astonishment, but then exalts and elevates it: it is awed by the consciousness of the depth and extent of its own creative capacity. See for this the extract from John Dennis's *Remarks on a Book Entitled Prince Arthur* in *The Sublime: A Reader in British Eighteenth-Century Aesthetic Theory*, 30–31.

22. Frances Reynolds, *An Enquiry Concerning the Principles of Taste, and the Origin of our Ideas of Beauty, &c.* [1785] (Los Angeles: The Augustan Reprint Society, William Andrews Clark Memorial Library, 1951), no. 170, 17–18.

23. For the rise to prominence of instrumental music in the eighteenth century and the liberation of music from language during that same era, see John Neubauer, *The Emancipation of Music from Language: Departure from Mimesis in Eighteenth-Century Aesthetics* (New Haven, Conn.: Yale University Press, 1986); Kevin Barry, *Language, Music, and the Sign: A Study in Aesthetics, Poetics, and Poetic Practice from Collins to Coleridge* (Cambridge: Cambridge University Press, 1987); Claude Lévi-Strauss, *Look, Listen, Read* [1993], trans. Brian C. J. Slinger (New York: Basic Books, 1997); Mary Sue Morrow, *German Music Criticism in the Late Eighteenth Century: Aesthetic Issues in Instrumental Music* (Princeton, N.J.: Princeton University Press, 1997); Thomas Downing, *Music and the Origins of Language: Theories from the French Enlightenment* (Cambridge: Cambridge University Press, 1995); Daniel Chua, *Absolute Music and the Construction of Meaning* (Cambridge: Cambridge University Press, 1999); Berthold Hoeckner, *Programming the Absolute: Nineteenth-Century German Music and the Hermeneutics of the Moment* (Princeton, N.J.: Princeton University Press, 2002); Richard Littlejohns, "Iniquitous Innocence: The Ambiguity of Music in the *Phantasien über die Kunst* (1799)," in *Music and Literature in German Romanticism*, ed. Siobhán Donovan and Robin Elliott (Rochester: Camden House, 2004), 1–12.

24. See Mieke Bal, *Quoting Caravaggio: Contemporary Art, Preposterous History* (Chicago: University of Chicago Press, 1999); Mieke Bal, "Narrative Inside Out: Louise Bourgeois' Spider as a Theoretical Object," *Oxford Art Journal* 2 (1999): 101–26; or Mieke Bal, *Traveling Concepts in the Humanities* (Chicago: University of Chicago Press, 2002).

25. The specified recordings in chapters 3, 4, and 5 can be easily obtained from many of the popular online music-downloading services (iTunes, Napster, Rhapsody).

26. See Albrecht Riethmüller, "Aspekte des musikalisch Erhabenen im 19. Jahrhundert" in *Archiv für Musikwissenschaft*, 1 (1983): 38–49; Theo Hirsbrunner, "Das Erhabene in Bedrich Smetanas 'Mein Vaterland' " in *Archiv für Musikwissenschaft*, 1 (1984): 35–41; Claudia Johnson, " 'Giant Handel' and the Musical Sublime," *Eighteenth-Century Studies* 4 (1986): 515–33; Mary Sue Morrow, "Of Unity and Passion: The Aesthetics of Concert Criticism in Early Nineteenth-Century Vienna," *Nineteenth-Century Music* 3 (1990): 193–206 (esp. 202–206); Elaine Sisman, *Mozart: The "Jupiter" Symphony No. 41 in C Major* (Cambridge: Cambridge University Press, 1993); Alexander H. Shapiro, " 'Drama of an Infinitely Superior Nature': Handel's Early English Oratorios and the Religious Sublime" *Music and Letters* 2 (1993): 215–45; Michael Fend, "Literary Motifs, Musical Form, and the Quest for the 'Sublime': Cherubini's 'Eliza ou le Voyage aux glaciers du Mont St Bernard' " *Cambridge Opera Journal* 1 (1993): 17–38; Lawrence Kramer, *Classical Music and Postmodern Knowledge* (Berkeley: University of California Press, 1995); Charles Rosen, *The Romantic Generation* (Cambridge, Mass.: Harvard University Press, 1995); Elaine Sisman, "Learned Style and the Rhetoric of the Sublime in the 'Jupiter' Symphony" in *Wolfgang Amadè Mozart: Essays on His Life and His Music*, ed. Stanley Sadie (Oxford: Clarendon Press, 1996), 213–38; William Kindermann, *Beethoven* (Oxford: Oxford University Press, 1997); David. P. Schroeder, *Haydn and the Enlightenment: The Late Symphonies and Their Audience* (Oxford: Oxford University Press, 1997); James Webster, "The *Creation*, Haydn's Late Vocal Music, and the Musical Sublime," in *Haydn and his World*, ed. Elaine Rochelle Sisman (Princeton, N.J.: Princeton University Press, 1997), 57–102; James Webster, "Haydn's Aesthetics," in *The Cambridge Companion to Haydn*, ed. Caryl L. Clark (Cambridge: Cambridge University Press, 2005), 30–44; James Webster, "The Sublime and the Pastoral in *The Creation* and *The Seasons*," in *The Cambridge Companion to Haydn*, 150–63; James Webster, "Between Enlightenment and Romanticism in Music History: 'First Viennese Modernism' and the Delayed Nineteenth Century," *Nineteenth-Century Music* 2–3 (2002): 108–26; Reinhold Brinkmann, "In the Times of the 'Eroica,' " in *Beethoven and his World*, ed. Scott Burnham and Michael Steinberg (Princeton, N.J.: Princeton University Press, 2000), 1–26; Michael Fend, "Die ästhetische Kategorie des Erhabenen und die Entdeckung der Alpen in der Musik," in *Schweizer Töne. Die Schweiz im Spiegel der Musik*, ed. A. Gerhard and A. Landau (Zürich: Chronos, 2000), 29–43; Matthew Riley, *Musical Listening in the Eighteenth Century: Attention, Wonder, and Astonishment* (Aldershot: Ashgate, 2004); Abigail Chantler, *E. T. A. Hoffmann's Musical Aesthetics* (Aldershot: Ashgate, 2006). It is significant to point out here that many of these studies have been triggered and informed, directly or indirectly, by the important collection of source readings presented by James Day and Peter le Hurray in the early 1980s: James Day and Peter le Hurray, *Music and Aesthetics in the Eighteenth and Early Nineteenth Centuries* (Cambridge: Cambridge University Press, 1981).

27. Claudia Johnson, "'Giant Handel' and the Musical Sublime," 515–33.

28. In *Handel: A Documentary Biography*, ed. Otto Erich Deutsch (London: Black, 1955), 715.

29. Charles Burney, *Musical Performances in Westminster-Abbey and the Pantheon in Commemoration of Händel* [1785], reprint of the original edition (Amsterdam: Frits A. Knuf, 1964), 15.

30. MS letter undated, in the Osborn Collection, Beinecke Library, Yale University, quoted in David P. Schroeder, *Haydn and the Enlightenment*, 126.

31. See also Jonathan Culler, "The Hertzian Sublime," in *MLN* 120 (2005): 971–76.

32. Webster, "The *Creation*, Haydn's Late Vocal Music, and the Musical Sublime," 60.

33. Ibid., 64.

34. Ibid.

35. Ibid., 70–92.

36. Compare this to Sisman's illuminating article on originality and genius in "Haydn, Shakespeare, and the Rules of Originality," in *Haydn and His World*, 3–56.

37. Sisman, "Learned Style and the Rhetoric of the Sublime in the 'Jupiter' Symphony," 225.

38. Ibid., 225.

39. Ibid., 232.

40. Ibid., 235.

41. Ibid., 236.

42. Ibid.

43. Brinkmann, "In the Times of the 'Eroica,'" 1–26.

44. Carl Dahlhaus, *Klassische und romantische Musikästhetik* (Laaber: Laaber Verlag, 1988), 101, my translation. Scheibe's text was published in 1739.

45. Johann Georg Sulzer, *Allgemeine Theorie der schönen Künste* [1794] (Hildesheim: Georg Olms Verlagsbuchhandlung, 1969), IV, 478–479.

46. Brinkmann, "In the Times of the 'Eroica,'" 13.

47. Ibid., 5.

48. According to Daniel Chua, the politics of gender played a considerable role in this: previously connoted as "feminine" as an art of entertainment, an ornament, the late eighteenth and early nineteenth century witnesses a masculinization of instrumental music, particularly the symphony, as a vehicle of the sublime. Sublime attributes of power and shock no doubt aided significantly in this reversal. See for this Daniel Chua, *Absolute Music and the Construction of Meaning*, 136.

49. Brinkmann, "In the Times of the 'Eroica,'" 4.

50. Ibid., 15.

51. Edward Young, from *Conjectures on Original Genius* [1759] in *The Sublime: A Reader in British Eighteenth-Century Aesthetic Theory*, 114. On Beethoven and genius, see also Tia De Nora, *Beethoven and the Construction of Genius: Musical Politics in Vienna, 1792–1803* (Berkeley: University of California Press, 1997); Peter Kivy, *The*

Possessor and the Possessed: Handel, Mozart, Beethoven, and the Idea of Musical Genius (New Haven, Conn.: Yale University Press, 2001).

52. Gilles Deleuze and Felix Guattari, *Qu'est-ce que la philosophie?* (Paris: Les Editions de Minuit, 1991); Gilles Deleuze and Felix Guattari, *What Is Philosophy?*, trans. Graham Burchwell and Hugh Tomlinson (London: Verso, 1994), 23.

53. Thomas Burnet, *The Sacred Theory of the Earth* [1690–1691], ed. Basil Wiley (London, Fontwell: Centaur Press, 1969).

54. James Usher, *Clio, or a Discourse on Taste* [1769] (Bristol: Thoemmes Press, 1998). Hereafter *CD*. Further references will be given in the text.

55. Arthur Schopenhauer, *Die Welt als Wille und Vorstellung* [1819] (Frankfurt am Main: Suhrkamp, 1986); Arthur Schopenhauer, *The World as Will and Representation*, trans. E. F. J. Payne (New York: Dover Publications, 1958). Hereafter *WW*. All further references will be given in the text. Richard Wagner, "Beethoven" [1870], in *Richard Wagner: Dichtungen und Schriften: Beethoven, Späte Dramaturgische Schriften* (Frankfurt am Main: Insel Verlag, 1983), 9:38–109; Richard Wagner, *Beethoven*, trans. William Ashton Ellis [1896], at *The Wagner Library: Edition 1.0*, available online at http://users.belgacom.net/wagnerlibrary/prose/wlpro133.htm (visited February 6, 2008). Hereafter *B*. Further references will be given in the text. Friedrich Nietzsche, *Die Geburt der Tragödie aus dem Geiste der Musik* [1871] (Frankfurt am Main: Insel Verlag, 1987); Friedrich Nietzsche, *The Birth of Tragedy out of the Spirit of Music*, in *Friedrich Nietzsche: The Birth of Tragedy and Other Writings*, ed. Raymond Geuss and Ronald Speirs, trans., Ronald Speirs (Cambridge: Cambridge University Press, 1999), 1–117. Hereafter *BT*. Further references will be given in the text. Arthur Seidl, *Vom Musikalisch-Erhabenen. Prolegomena zur Aesthetik der Tonkunst. Inauguraldissertation der Philosophischen Fakultät der Universität Leipzig zur erlangung der Doktorwürde vorgelegt von Arthur Seidl* (Regensburg, 1887). Hereafter *ME*. Further references will be given in the text (my translation).

56. Toon Tellegen, *Misschien wisten zij alles. Alle verhalen over de eekhoorn en andere dieren* [*Perhaps They Knew Everything. All Stories of the Squirrel and Other Animals*] (Amsterdam: Querido, 1995), 430–32, my translation.

57. Ibid., 40.

1. Empty Signs and the Burkean Sublime

1. For more on Alexander and John Robert Cozens, see Jean-Claude Lebenzstejn's excellent *L'art de la tache: introduction à la "Nouvelle méthode" d'Alexander Cozens* (Éditions du Limon, 1990); or Isabelle von Marschall, *Zwischen Skizze und Gemälde: John Robert Cozens (1752–1797) und das englische Landschaftsaquarell* (Munich: Scaneg, 2006).

2. Alexander Cozens, *A New Method of Assisting the Invention in Drawing Original Compositions of Landscape* [1785] (London: Black, 1952), p. 169.

3. Martin Jay, *Downcast Eyes: The Denigration of Vision in Twentieth-Century French Thought* (Berkeley: University of California Press, 1994).

4. However, this is not to state that the empty sign of music was, in any way, unproblematic in eighteenth-century critical theory (in Great Britain, France, and Germany). As is well known, well into the eighteenth century the assumption that instrumental music signified "nothing" often caused it to be ranked as the lowest of all arts. Immanuel Kant's rejection of music in the third *Critique*, arguing that it was not a cultural art since musical mediation would not involve any concepts, is most (in)famous in this respect. In Britain, too, critical theorists were weary of music's alleged "empty" sign. James Beattie, whom I will discuss later in this chapter, is an example: in his earlier work he still considers music without words "imperfect"— yet not much later, he turns that imperfection into music's advantage. This conversion is symptomatic of eighteenth-century aesthetics of instrumental music. For more on this see: J. L. Winn, *Unsuspected Eloquence*; John Neubauer, *The Emancipation of Music from Language*; Kevin Barry, *Language, Music, and the Sign*; Mary Sue Morrow, *German Music Criticism in the Late Eighteenth Century*; Thomas Downing, *Music and the Origins of Language*.

5. Mary Shelley, *Frankenstein, or, the Modern Prometheus* [1817] (Harmondsworth: Penguin, 1985), 57–58.

6. John Dennis, *The Grounds of Criticism*, I, 363.

7. The concept "idea" is here used empirically. Thus, in good Lockean fashion, "idea" broadly connotes that which the mind perceives in itself or is an immediate object of perception, thought, or understanding. As Stephen Priest has put it, in the Lockean tradition, "idea" basically "includes not only our notions of a mental image and a concept, but also our notion of an experience. An idea for Locke is any mental content whatsoever. It is the medium of thought and what our minds are stored with." It should, moreover, be borne in mind that in the Lockean scheme of things only ideas are perceived directly: one's interactions with the world are never interactions with things in themselves but with one's ideas or representations of things. See Stephen Priest, *The British Empiricists: A Critical Introduction to the Leading Thinkers and Key Ideas of the British Philosophical Tradition from Hobbes to Ayer* (Harmondsworth: Penguin, 1990), 62.

8. Angela Leighton, *Shelley and the Sublime: An Interpretation of the Major Poems* (Cambridge: Cambridge University Press, 1984), 3–4.

9. Nevertheless, Amal Asfour and Paul Williamson have argued that eighteenth-century theories of vision were not only informed by Lockean empiricism but also by Berkeleyan idealism. In this mixture of perspectives, seeing was just as "learned," just as much dictated by convention, as speaking and reading was. This would complicate the status of pictures as immediate and precise, transparent reflections of the real and problematize the eye as the site of human knowledge. See Amal Asfour and Paul Williamson, "Splendid Impositions: Gainsborough, Berkeley, Hume," *Eighteenth-Century Studies* 4 (1998): 403–32.

10. Jacques Derrida, *De la grammatologie* (Paris: Éditions de Minuit, 1967), 203–34; Jacques Derrida, *Of Grammatology*, trans. Gayatri Chakravorty Spivak (Baltimore, Md.: The Johns Hopkins University Press, 1997), 141–64.

11.   See W. J. T. Mitchell, *Iconology: Image, Text, Ideology* (Chicago: University of Chicago Press, 1987), 124. An earlier analysis of Burke's theory of words and pictures already appeared in 1940: Dixon Wecter, "Burke's Theory Concerning Words, Images, and Emotion," *PMLA* 1 (1940): 167–81.

12.   Almost fifty years earlier, George Berkeley had in fact represented the functioning of words in a similar vein. As he put it in the Introduction to the *Principles of Human Knowledge* (1710): "the communicating of ideas marked by words is not the chief and only end of language, as is commonly supposed. There are other ends, as the raising of some passion. . . . I entreat the reader to reflect with himself, and see if it doth not often happen either in hearing or reading a discourse, that the passions of fear, love, hatred, admiration, disdain, and the like arise, immediately in his mind upon the perception of certain words, without any ideas coming between. At first, indeed, the words might have occasioned ideas that were fit to produce these emotions; but, if I mistake not, it will be found that when language is once grown familiar, the hearing of the sounds or sight of the characters is oft immediately attended with those passions, which at first were wont to be produced by the intervention of ideas, that are now quite omitted. May we not, for example be . . . threatened with danger sufficient to excite a dread, though we think not of any particular evil likely to befall us, nor yet frame to ourselves an idea of danger in abstract?" George Berkeley, "Introduction," in *Principles of Human Knowledge* [1710] (Oxford: Oxford University Press, 1996), 19–20.

13.   Kevin Barry, *Language, Music, and the Sign*, 3. It should be noted here that Herbert Schueller already made a similar claim in "The Pleasures of Music: Speculation in British Music Criticism, 1750–1800," *The Journal of Aesthetics and Art Criticism* 3 (1950): 155–71, and in "'Imitation' and 'Expression' in British Music Criticism in the Eighteenth Century," *The Musical Quarterly* 4 (1948): 544–66.

14.   Barry, *Language, Music, and the Sign*, 3.

15.   James Harris, *Three Treatises. The First, Concerning Art, the Second Concerning Music, Painting and Poetry, the Third Concerning Happiness*, in *Music and Aesthetics in the Eighteenth and Early Nineteenth Centuries*, ed. Peter Le Huray and James Day (Cambridge: Cambridge University Press, 1981), 36–39.

16.   Abbé Dubos, *Réflexions critiques sur la Poësie et sur la Peinture* (Paris: École nationale supérieure des Beaux-Arts, 1993); Abbé Dubos, *Critical Reflections on Poetry and Painting* in *Music and Aesthetics*, in *Music and Aesthetics in the Eighteenth and Early Nineteenth Centuries*, ed. Peter Le Huray and James Day (Cambridge: Cambridge University Press, 1981), 17–22.

17.   See Richard Grusin, "Premediation," *Criticism* 1 (2004): 17–39. Grusin uses the term premediation with reference to the culture industry and, within this context, specifically presents it as a colonization of the future with medial-technological modes. By contrast, I here use the term as a more open projection of medial possibilities into the future.

18.   The *Three Treatises* were widely read in the second half of the eighteenth century, a fifth edition being edited in 1794. Burke will most probably have been familiar with the work, though there are no indications for actual references. Kevin

Barry proposes a link from Burke to Harris through David Hartley, the famous author of the *Observations on Man* (1749), but it still a speculative link. Barry, *Language, Music, and the Sign*, 31.

19. Harris, *Three Treatises*, 38.

20. The most well-known eighteenth-century work on this issue is Johann Mattheson's massive *Der vollkommene Capellmeister* (1739). Johann Mattheson, *Der vollkommene Capellmeister*, ed. Friederike Ramm (Kassel: Bärenreiter, 1999); Johann Mattheson, *Der vollkommene Capellmeister: A Revised Translation with Critical Commentary*, trans. Ernest C. Harris (Ann Arbor, Mich.: UMI Research Press, 1981). Here, Mattheson famously declares that instrumental melodies can do without words but not without affections and shows how music can be developed into an independent "language" of feelings. For more on the *Affektenlehre* or doctrine of affections, see Hans Lenneberg, "Johann Mattheson on Affect and Rhetoric in Music (I)," *Journal of Music Theory* 1 (1958): 47–84; John Neubauer, *The Emancipation of Music from Language*; Don Harrán, "Toward a Rhetorical Code of Early Music Performance," *The Journal of Musicology* 1 (1997): 19–42; Francis Sparshott, "Reflections on *Affektenlehre* and Dance Theory in the Eighteenth Century," *The Journal of Aesthetics and Art Criticism* 1 (1998): 21–28; Paola-Ludovica Coriando, *Affektenlehre und Phänomenologie der Stimmungen. Wege einer Ontologie und Ethik des Emotionalen* (Frankfurt am Main: Klostermann, 2002).

21. Harris, *Three Treatises*, 37.

22. Ibid., 38.

23. James Beattie, *An Essay on Poetry and Music as They Affect the Mind* (1776), in *Essays* (New York: Garland Publishing, 1971), 465.

24. Ibid.

25. Ibid.

26. Ibid., 445.

27. Ibid., 442.

28. Ibid., 449–50.

29. Matthew Riley, "Straying from Nature: The Labyrinthine Harmonic Theory of Diderot and Bemetzrieder's *Leçons de clavecin* (1771)," *The Journal of Musicology* 1 (2002): 3–38.

30. See also Downing A. Thomas, *Music and the Origins of Language: Theories from the French Enlightenment* (Cambridge: Cambridge University Press, 1995).

31. Riley, "Straying from Nature," 4.

32. Denis Diderot, *Leçons de clavecin et principes d'harmonie en dialogues* [1771], in *Oeuvres complètes de Diderot*, ed. J. Assézat (Paris: Garnier Frères, 1876), 12:179–534.

33. Paul Michel-Guy de Chabanon, *De la musique considerée en elle-même et dans ses rapports avec la parole, les langues, la poésie et le théâtre* [1785] (Genève: Slatkine Reprints, 1969), 62. Claude Lévi-Strauss has already offered an extensive reading of Chabanon's philosophy of music and has even suggested that it foreshadows the structuralist theory of language as devised by Ferdinand de Saussure. As Lévi-Strauss quotes Chabanon: "A musical sound by itself does not carry signification. . . . Each sound is more or less empty, and has neither its own meaning or character," but will

only acquire such meaning or character in relation to other sounds. See Claude Levi-Strauss, *Look, Listen, Read*, trans. Brian C. J. Slinger (New York: Basic Books, 1997), 97.

34. Diderot suggests as much in his reworking of Burke's substitution theory in the *Salon de 1767*. Burke had turned the "deficits" of the verbal supplement into an advantage with respect to the sublime, and Diderot repeats the gesture in the *Salon*: not-showing, suspending revelation, "imperfect" mediation, the sonorous triggering of affects without the intervention of image-ideas; these qualities of "musical" mediation have here become poetic qualities that rouse or trigger the imagination. See Gita May, "Diderot and Burke: A Study in Aesthetic Affinity," *PMLA* 5 (December 1960): 527–39; and Lawrence Kerslake's chapter on Diderot in his *Essays on the Sublime*, 331–52.

35. James Beattie, "Of Imagination," in "Of Memory and Imagination," in *Dissertations Moral and Critical* [1783] (Stuttgart-Bad Cannstatt: Friedrich Frommann Verlag [Günther Holzboog], 1970), 67.

36. Beattie, "Of Imagination," 99–100.

37. Beattie, "Illustrations on Sublimity," in *Dissertations Moral and Critical*, 641.

38. Ibid., 642.

39. John Locke, *An Essay Concerning Human Understanding* [1690], ed. John W. Yolton (London: J. M. Dent & Sons, 1991), II, XVII, 98.

40. Ibid., II, XVII, 96.

41. Ibid., II, XVII, 98.

42. Thomas Twining, *Aristotle's Treatise on Poetry, Translated: with Notes on the Translation, and on the Original; and Two Dissertations, on Poetical, and Musical, Imitation* [1789] (Westmead: Gregg International Publishers Limited, 1972), 49 s ff.

43. Ibid., 104.

44. James Usher, *Clio, or a Discourse on Taste* [1769] (Bristol & Sterling: Thoemmes Press, 1998). Hereafter *CD*. All further references will be given in the text.

45. For Lacan's analysis of desire, see Jacques Lacan, *Écrits. A Selection*, trans. Bruce Fink (New York: W. W. Norton, 2004); Jacques Lacan, *The Four Fundamental Concepts of Psychoanalysis* (*The Seminar of Jacques Lacan, Book 11*), trans. Alan Sheridan, ed. Jacques-Alain Miller (New York: W. W. Norton, 1998).

46. Barry, *Language, Music, and the Sign*, 61.

47. Roland Barthes, "Listening," in *The Responsibility of Forms*, ed. Richard Howard (Berkeley: University of California Press, 1991), 245–61.

2. Sehnsucht, *Music, and the Sublime*

1. Johann Georg Sulzer, *Allgemeine Theorie der schönen Künste* [1771–1774] [1792] (Hildesheim: Georg Olms Verlagsbuchhandlung, 1967), II: 98, my translation.

2. Mark Evan Bonds, "Idealism and the Aesthetics of Instrumental Music at the Turn of the Nineteenth Century," *Journal of the American Musicological Society* 2/3 (1997): 389.

3. Daniel Chua, *Absolute Music and the Construction of Meaning* (Cambridge: Cambridge University Press, 1999), 177–83, 224–35.

4. See also Andrew Bowie, *Aesthetics and Subjectivity. From Kant to Nietzsche* (Manchester: Manchester University Press, 1993), 77–80, 176–205. All further references will be given in the text.

5. E. T. A. Hoffmann, "Ludwig van Beethoven, 5.Sinfonie," [1810] in *E. T. A. Hoffmann. Schriften zur Musik. Singspiele*, ed. Hans-Joachim Kruse and Viktor Liebrenz (Berlin: Aufbau-Verlag, 1988), 22–42; E. T. A. Hoffmann, "Review of Beethoven's Fifth Symphony," in *E. T. A. Hoffmann's Musical Writings. Kreisleriana, the Poet and the Composer, Music Criticism*, ed. David Charlton, trans. Martyn Clarke (Cambridge: Cambridge University Press, 1989), 234–251. Hereafter *BS*. All further references will be given in the text. See also E. T. A. Hoffmann, "Beethovens Instrumentalmusik," [1813] in *E. T. A. Hoffmann: Betrachtungen über Musik*, 56–65; E. T. A. Hoffmann, "Beethoven's Instrumental Music," [1813] in *E. T. A. Hoffmann and Music*, ed. and trans. Murray Schafer (Toronto: University of Toronto Press, 1975), 83–91.

6. On the aesthetic judgment, see Paul Guyer, *Kant and the Experience of Freedom* (Cambridge: Cambridge University Press, 1996); or Dieter Heinrich, *Aesthetic Judgment and the Moral Image of the World* (Stanford, Calif.: Stanford University Press, 1992). Frank Ankersmit has already pointed to a connection between *Sehnsucht* and the Kantian aesthetic judgment. See his *History and Tropology* (Berkeley: University of California Press, 1994), 198–200.

7. Johann Wolfgang von Goethe, *Die Leiden des jungen Werthers* [1774] (Stuttgart: Reklam Verlag, 1985), 31, my translation.

8. Goethe, *Die Leiden*, 12.

9. Dieter Henrich, *Aesthetic Judgment*, 51. One is reminded here of Burke's and Beattie's delight of imagination in the incomplete and undetermined (chapter 1)— the pleasure in an openness that always leaves the promise of something more.

10. Johann Wolfgang von Goethe, *Faust* [1787–1790] (Frankfurt am Main: Insel Verlag, 1974), I, ll. 15–16, my translation.

11. See Andrew Bowie, *Aesthetics and Subjectivity from Kant to Nietzsche*; Azade Seyhan, *The Critical Legacy of German Romanticism* (Berkeley: University of California Press, 1992); James H. Donelan, "Hölderlin's Music of Self-Consciousness" *Philosophy and Literature* 1 (2002): 125–42; J. M. Bernstein, *The Fate of Art: Aesthetic Alienation from Kant to Derrida and Adorno* (Cambridge: Cambridge University Press, 1991); Karl Ameriks, ed., *The Cambridge Companion to German Idealism* (Cambridge: Cambridge University Press, 2000); J. M. Bernstein, "Introduction," in *Classic and Romantic German Aesthetics*, ed. J. M. Bernstein (Cambridge: Cambridge University Press, 2003), vii–xxxiii; Simon Lumsden, "Fichte's Striving Subject," *Inquiry* 1 (2004): 123–42.

12. Quoted in Bowie, *Aesthetics and Subjectivity*, 63.

13. Friedrich Hölderlin, "Urteil und Sein," [1795] in *Friedrich Hölderlin. Werke, Briefe, Dokumente* (Munich: Winkler Verlag, 1990), 490; Friedrich Hölderlin, "Being Judgment Possible," in *Classic and Romantic German Aesthetics*, trans. Stefan

Bird-Pollan, 191. An excellent book on the fragments of Hölderlin is Dieter Henrich's *The Course of Remembrance and Other Essays on Hölderlin* (Stanford, Calif.: Stanford University Press, 1997).

14. Hölderlin, "Being Judgment Possible," 191–92.

15. Holderlin, "An Hegel," in *Friedrich Hölderlin. Werke, Briefe, Dokumente*, 718; Friedrich Hölderlin, "Letter to Hegel, 26 January 1795," in *Classic and Romantic German Aesthetics*, trans. Stefan Bird-Pollan, 189.

16. Hölderlin, "*Pyrgo* in Morea," from *Fragment von Hyperion* [1799], in *Friedrich Hölderlin. Werke, Briefe, Dokumente*, 365, my translation.

17. For helpful studies of Novalis's *Fichte Studies*, see Géza von Molnár, *Novalis' "Fichte Studies": The Foundation of His Aesthetics* (The Hague: Mouton, 1970); Manfred Frank, *Einführung in die Frühromantische Ästhetik* (Frankfurt am Main: Surhkamp, 1989); Andrew Bowie, *From Romanticism to Critical Theory* (London: Routledge, 1997); William Arctander O'Brien, *Novalis: Signs of Revolution* (Durham, N.C.: Duke University Press, 1995).

18. Novalis, *Fichte Studien* [1795–1796], in *Novalis: Schriften: Das Philosophische Werk I*, ed. Richard Samuel, Hans-Joachim Mähl, and Gerhard Schulz (Darmstadt: Wissenschaftliche Buchgesellschaft, 1981), vol. 2, sect. II, 104–296; Novalis, *Fichte Studies*, ed. and trans. Jane Kneller (Cambridge: Cambridge University Press, 2003), no. 15, 13.

19. Novalis, *Fichte Studies*, no. 44, 32.

20. Ibid., no. 566, 167, 168.

21. Ibid., 78.

22. William Fitzgerald, "The Questionability of Music," *Representations* 46 (1994): 123.

23. Jean-Paul Richter, *Hesperus, oder 45 Hunposttage. Eine Lebensbeschreibung* [1795], in *Jean Paul. Werke*, vol. 1 (Munich: Carl Hanser Verlag, 1960), chap. 19, 776, my translation.

24. Ibid., 776.

25. Wilhelm Wackenroder, "Phantasien über die Kunst," [1799] in *Tieck und Wackenroder*, ed. Joseph Kürschner (Berlin: W. Spemann Verlag, 1886), 72–73, my translation. Hereafter *PK*. All further references will be given in the text. For more on Wackenroder and music see, for instance, Kwon Chung-Sun, *Studie zur Idee des Gesamtkunstwerks in der Frühromantik: zur Utopie einer Musikanschauung von Wackenroder bis Schopenhauer* (Frankfurt am Main: Peter Lang, 2003).

26. See also Richard Littlejohns, "Iniquitous Innocence: The Ambiguity of Music in the *Phantasien über die Kunst* (1799)," in *Music and Literature in German Romanticism*, ed. Siobhán Donovan and Robin Elliott (Rochester: Camden House, 2004), 1–12.

27. Paul de Man, *Blindness and Insight: Essays in the Rhetoric of Contemporary Criticism* [1971], 2nd ed. (London: Routledge, 1983), 129.

28. Jean-Paul Richter, *Vorschule der Aesthetik* [1804], in *Jean Paul. Werke*, vol. 5 (Munich: Calr Hanser Verlag, 1963), §18, 75–81; Jean-Paul Richter, *Elementary*

Course in Aesthetics, in *Strunk's Source Readings in Music History. The Nineteenth Century*, trans. O. Strunk, ed. Ruth A. Solie (New York: W. W. Norton, 1998), 6:15.

29. Richter, *Elementary Course*, 6:16, 6:18.

30. Carl Grosse, *Über das Erhabene* [1788], ed. Carsten Zelle (St. Ingbert: Werner J. Röhrig Verlag, 1991), 41, my translation. Further references will be given in the text.

31. Ibid., 41–42.

32. James Hodkinson, "The Cosmic-Symphonic: Novalis, Music, and Universal Discourse" in *Music and Literature in German Romanticism*, 27–42, 15; Bowie, *Aesthetics and Subjectivity*, 79.

33. Bowie, *Aesthetics and Subjectivity*, 19.

34. Ulrich Schmitt, *Revolution im Konzertsaal. Zur Beethoven-Rezeption im 19. Jahrhundert* (Mainz: Schott Musikwissenschaft, 1990), 24, my translation.

35. See Hans Heinrich Eggebrecht, *Zur Geschichte der Beethoven-Rezeption: Beethoven 1970* (Mainz: Akademie der Wissenschaften, 1972); Ulrich Schmitt, *Revolution im Konzertsaal*; Scott Burnham, *Beethoven Hero* (Princeton, N.J.: Princeton University Press, 2000); K. M. Knittel, "Wagner, Deafness, and the Reception of Beethoven's Late Style," *Journal of the American Musicological Society* 1 (1998): 49–82; Wayne Senner, Robin Wallace, and William Meredith, eds., *The Contemporary German Reception of Beethoven* (Lincoln: University of Nebraska Press, 1999–2003); Maynard Solomon, *Late Beethoven: Music, Thought, Imagination* (Berkeley: University of California Press, 2003). For the reception of the Eroica, see also the following Web site: http://www.raptusassociation.org/eroicaerezeptionsgesch.html (last accessed February 8, 2008).

36. Sulzer, *Allgemeine Theorie der schönen Künste* II, 99.

37. Robert Lowth, *Lectures on the Sacred Poetry of the Hebrews* [1787] (Hildesheim: Georg Olms Verlag, 1969), I: Lect. 16, 353.

38. C. F. Michaelis, "The Beautiful and Sublime in Music," [1805] in *Music and Aesthetics*, ed. and trans. James Day and Peter Le Huray (Cambridge: Cambridge University Press, 1981), 286–90.

39. Werner Klein, "The Voice of the Hereafter: Hoffmann's Ideal of Sound and its Realization," in *Music and Literature in German Romanticism*, 147.

40. Hoffmann, "Beethoven's Instrumental Music," 83.

41. E. T. A. Hoffmann, "Ludwig van Beethoven, Coriolan-Ouvertüre," in *E. T. A. Hoffmann. Schriften zur Musik*, 94–102, 100; E. T. A. Hoffmann, "Review of Beethoven's Overture to *Coriolan*," 286–93, 292, 291, 292. For a more extensive account of the overture, see Lawrence Kramer, "The Strange Case of Beethoven's 'Coriolan': Romantic Aesthetics, Modern Subjectivity, and the Cult of Shakespeare," *The Musical Quarterly* 2 (1995): 256–80.

42. Chua, *Absolute Music and the Construction of Meaning*, 252, 253.

43. The English translation here uses "overall character" instead of "whole." I deviate from the English translation, since the *Ganze* in Hoffmann's German text does not allude to a general impression but rather an abstract idea (i.e., the whole) that cannot be grasped.

44. Again, the English translation here uses "overall pattern" rather than "whole."

45. Immanuel Kant, *Kritik der Reinen Vernunft* [1781, 1787], ed. Raymund Schmidt (Hamburg: Felix Meiner Verlag, 1990), B460, 456, my translation. On the basis of this triple distinction of faculties (intuition or *Anschauung*, imagination, and understanding), Kant presents the idea of a triple synthesis in the Transcendental Deduction of the first edition of the *Critique of Pure Reason*. As the term "synthesis" indicates, this is a combining of separate, diverse "raw materials" into a single entity, and for Kant it is the source of all cognition: a triple process of coordination (senses), association (imagination), and ultimate unification (understanding). It moves from an "I see and contain" in (strictly sensuous) apprehension, via an "I reproduce and relate" by means of the power of imagination, to a final "I recognize and identify" by means of the faculty of understanding. Roughly said, the last stage of this triple synthesis, the stage of conceptual identification, coincides with the Kantian moment of cognition.

46. Christine Pries, *Übergänge Ohne Brücke. Kants Erhabenes zwischen Kritik und Metaphysik* (Berlin: Akademie Verlag, 1995), 161, my translation.

47. Indeed, Kant stresses the subjective finality (i.e., pleasure) of the sublime feeling in view of its being rooted—just like the experience of the beautiful—in an aesthetic judgment: a judgment referring to a *specific or distinctive, harmonious mental state of a subject*; a subject that experiences its own mental faculties as being in fundamental accord with one another. The sublime may be painful for the imagination, yet it is pleasurable for the *entire* province of mind in discovering a "higher" faculty transcending sensibility.

48. Bowie, *Aesthetics and Subjectivity*, 37.

49. Peter Schnaus, *E. T. A. Hoffmann als Beethoven Rezensent der Allgemeinen Musikalische Zeitung* (München: Katzbichler, 1977), 64.

50. Theresa de Lauretis, *Alice Doesn't. Feminism, Semiotics, Cinema* (Bloomington: Indiana University Press, 1984), 125. Further references to this text will be given in parenthesis.

51. Paul Guyer, *Kant and the Experience of Freedom*, 213.

52. De Lauretis, *Alice Doesn't*, 118.

53. Ibid., 125.

54. Weiskel, *The Romantic Sublime*, 174.

55. For a critique of Kant's analytic as regards the subject's mastery over nature, see Theodor Adorno, *Aesthetische Theorie* (Frankfurt am Main: Suhrkamp, 1970); Theodor Adorno, *Aesthetic Theory* [1970], ed. Gretel Adorno and Rolf Tiedemann, trans. Robert Hullot-Kenter (London: Athlone Press, 1999), esp. 196–99, 275–76. Here, Adorno stresses that "the sublime speaks against domination" and argues that true freedom for the subject arises out of a reconciliation with nature.

3. Ruins and (Un)forgetfulness: A Genealogy of the Musically Sublime

1. Michel Foucault, "Nietzsche, la généalogie, l'histoire," [1971] in *Dits et Ecrits 1954–1988 II* (Paris: Gallimard, 1994), 136–56; Michel Foucault, "Nietzsche,

Genealogy, History," in *The Foucault Reader*, ed. Paul Rabinow (London: Penguin Books, 1984), 76–100.

2. Foucault, "Nietzsche, Genealogy, History," 81.

3. Ibid., 80.

4. Ibid., 82.

5. Gotthold Ephraim Lessing, *Laokoön: über die Grenzen der Malerie und Poesie* [1766] (Munich: Winkler, 1974), 7–166; Gotthold Ephraim Lessing, *Laocoön: On the Limits of Painting and Poetry*, in *Classic and Romantic German Aesthetics*, 25–130.

6. Jos de Mul, *Romantic Desire in (Post)modern Art and Philosophy* (Albany, N.Y.: SUNY Press, 1999), 125.

7. Richard Wagner, *Oper und Drama* (1851, 1871), in *Richard Wagner: Gesammelte Schriften und Dichtungen*, IV (Boston: Elibron Classics, Adamant Media Corporation, 2001), parts 2–3, 1–164; Richard Wagner, *Opera and Drama*, in *Richard Wagner's Prose Works*, trans. William Ashton Ellis, available online at *The Wagner Library*: http://users.belgacom.net/wagnerlibrary/prose/wlpro063.htm (last accessed February 13, 2008), part 2, 17. Further references will be given in the text.

8. Carl Dahlhaus and Mary Whittal, "What Is a Musical Drama?" *Cambridge Opera Journal* 2 (1989), 98.

9. Bryan Magee, *Wagner and Philosophy* (London: Penguin Books, 2000), 229.

10. However, Wagner's defense of a nonarchitectonic music may also have been directed against music critics and philosophers who propagated the kind of medial confusion that Schopenhauer had wished to undo.

11. Eduard Hanslick, *Vom Musikalisch-Schönen* [1854, 1894]; *On the Musically Beautiful*, trans. Geoffrey Payzant (Indianapolis, Ind.: Hackett Publishing Company, 1986), 28.

12. Curt Sachs, *Rhythm and Tempo: A Study in Music History* (New York: Columbia University Press, 1953), 13.

13. Lydia Goehr, "Wagnerian Endings: On the Curse and Promise of Purely Musical Listening. A Metaphysical Reading of *Tristan and Isolde*," in *ASCA Brief: Come to Your Senses!*, ed. Mieke Bal et al. (Amsterdam: Amsterdam School of Cultural Analysis, Theory and Interpretation, 1999), 48. For eyes turning into ears, see also Wagner's *Beethoven*, 79.

14. Hence, Schopenhauer adds, "life swings like a pendulum to and fro between pain and boredom": willing is needing and constant suffering (*WW*, I, bk. 4, §57, 312).

15. Paul Deusen, *Die Elemente der Metaphysik . . . nebst einer Vorbetrachtung über das Wesen des Idealismus* [1877] (Leipzig: F. A. Brockhaus, 1919), 157, my translation.

16. For more on Wagner's chromatic style and his conception of the (later) music drama, see Robert Bailey, *Richard Wagner: Prelude and Transfiguration from Tristan and Isolde* (New York: W. W. Norton, 1985); Dieter Borchmeyer, *Richard Wagner: Theory and Theatre*, trans. Stewart Spencer (Oxford: Clarendon Press, 1991); Robert Morgan, "Circular Form in the *Tristan* Prelude," *Journal of the American Musicological*

Society 1 (2000): 69–103, Alexander Rehding, "Liszt und die Suche nach dem 'Tris-Ztan'-Akkord" in *Acta Musicologica* 2 (2000): 185; Eric Chafe, *The Tragic and the Ecstatic. The Musical Revolution of Wagner's* Tristan and Isolde (Oxford: Oxford University Press, 2003).

17. James Levine, The MET Orchestra: Wagner: Orchestral Works (Deutsche Grammophon 1169581, 1997).

18. Hanslick, *On the Musically Beautiful*, xxiii.

19. H. F. Frost, "Some Remarks on Wagner's Music Drama 'Tristan and Isolde'" in *Proceedings of the Musical Association*, 8th sess. (1881–1882), 147–67, 150–51.

20. Ibid., 150–51.

21. Peter Rummenhöller, *Romantik in der Musik* (Kassel: Bärenreiter, 1989), 166.

22. Quoted in Christian Lipperheide, *Die Ästhetik des Erhabenen bei Friedrich Nietzsche. Die Verwindung der Metaphysik der Erhabenheit* (Würzburg: Verlag Königshausen & Neumann, 1999), 14, my translation.

23. Ibid., 14–32.

24. The sustaining of the Dionysian element is in fact not just topical with respect to music, but also with respect to the drama: only in combination with music's Dionysian power can drama become more than it can ever achieve on its own—if the Apollonian illusion relieves the excess of the Dionysian, then the latter nevertheless also infuses the former in a crucial way, expanding and enlightening it way beyond itself. Still, Nietzsche adds to this that only so much of the Dionysian can enter consciousness as the Apollonian can transfigure.

25. Jos de Mul, *Romantic Desire*, 58.

26. Bowie, *Aesthetics and Subjectivity*, 227.

27. Arthur Seidl, *Vom Musikalisch-Erhabenen. Prolegomena zur Aesthetik der Tonkunst. Inauguraldissertation der Philosophischen Fakultät der Universität Leipzig zur erlangung der Doktorwürde vorgelegt von Arthur Seidl* (Regensburg, 1887). Hereafter *ME*. All further references will be given in the text.

28. Hanslick, *Musically Beautiful*, 29.

29. See Federico Busoni's *New Esthetics of Music* [1907, 1911] in *Three Classics in the Aesthetic of Music: Monsieur Croche the Dilettante Hater, by Claude Debussy; Sketch of a New Esthetic of Music, by Ferruccio Busoni; Essays Before a Sonata, by Charles E. Ives* (New York: Dover Publications, 1962), 73–102, 78. Busoni concludes, tellingly enough: "Let us take thought, how music may be restored to its primitive, natural essence; let us free it from architectonic, acoustic and esthetic dogmas" (95).

30. Hugh Silverman has brilliantly analyzed this occurring of the instant in Lyotard. See for this especially his "Textualität der Postmoderne: Lyotard, Ereignis, Erhabene", translated by Erik Vogt. In *Textualität der Philosophie und Literatur*, Wiener Reihe Themen der Philosophie, vol. 7., edited by Ludwig Nagl & Hugh J. Silverman (Vienna and Munich: Oldenbourg, 1994), pp. 236–45; "Lyotard and the Events of the Postmodern Sublime" in *Lyotard: Philosophy, Politics, and the Sublime*, edited by Hugh J. Silverman (New York and London: Routledge, 2002), pp. 222–29.

4. Sounds Like Now: Form-Contrariness, Romanticism, and the Postmodern Sublime

1. For this "modality" of the (postmodern) sublime experience as an experience of one's own creativity, see the Dutch philosopher Renée van de Val, *Een subliem gevoel van plaats*, and her "Silent Visions: Lyotard on the Sublime," in *The Contemporary Sublime: Sensibilities of Transcendence and Shock* (Cambridge: VCH Publishers, 1995), 69–75.

2. All this echoes, however faintly, Clement Greenberg's famous reading of avant-garde paintings as flat, introverted, and self-reflexive, yet, precisely as such, musically informed: the "method" of these paintings is no longer traditionally pictorial—as embodiments of the postmodern sublime, these paintings mimic the sonic materiality of music insofar as they would contain nothing but their own, bare chromaticism. See Clement Greenberg, "Towards a Newer Laocöon," [1948] in *Art in Theory 1900–1990: An Anthology of Changing Ideas*, ed. Charles Harrison and Paul Wood (Oxford: Blackwell Publishers, 1999), 554–60.

3. See especially Lyotard's "Response to the Question: What Is Postmodernism?" [1983] in *Art in Theory 1900–1990*, 1008–15.

4. Leonard Bernstein and the Boston Symphony Orchestra, with Kenneth Riegel as Tenor: Franz Liszt, *Faust Symphonie* (Deutsche Grammophon 431 470–2, 1977).

5. Franz Liszt, *Eine Faust Symphonie* (1853) (London: Ernst Eulenberg, nr. 477), 279–304. My emphasis.

6. Quoted in Frank Hentschel, "Das 'Ewig-Weibliche'—Liszt, Mahler und das bürgerliche Frauenbild," *Archiv für Musikwissenschaft* 4 (1994): 276.

7. Lawrence Kramer, Richard Leppert, and Susan McClary have thoroughly explored the consequences of this mode of thinking (which can be easily called symptomatic of modern Western binary thought systems) with respect to music—and especially the way in which music in Western culture familiarly embodies the "positive" force of the eternal-feminine on the one hand and the "negative" force of a devilish temptress on the other: alluring and dangerous at the same time. To that extent "music" as a cultural medium already projects the paradoxical combination of fascination and fear associated with the sublime. For such representations of music, see Lawrence Kramer, *Music as Cultural Practice, 1800–1900* (Berkeley: University of California Press, 1990); and his *After the Lovedeath. Sexual Violence and the Making of Culture* (Berkeley: University of California Press, 1997); Richard Leppert, *The Sight of Sound: Music, Representation, and the History of the Body* (Berkeley: University of California Press, 1995); Susan McClary, *Feminine Endings: Music, Gender, and Sexuality* [1991] (Minneapolis: University of Minnesota Press, 2002).

8. See for this Philippe Lacoue-Labarthe, "Sublime Truth (part 1)," *Cultural Critique* 18 (1991): 5–31; "Sublime Truth (part 2)," *Cultural Critique* 20 (1991): 207–29.

9. Georg Wilhelm Friedrich Hegel, *Science of Logic*, trans. A. V. Miller (London: Allen & Unwin, 1969).

10. Paolo Zellini, *A Brief History of Infinity*, trans. Allan Lane (London: Penguin Books, 2005), 4.

11. Philosophically, the problem of this rereading of the sublime is, of course, that matter conceived of as an "in itself" cannot quite be disconnected from Kant's transcendental scheme of things: the notion of an "in itself," to think matter *as* an in itself, is already an idea of reason that cannot be made to fit the forms of sensibility (since the thing in itself always eludes the forms of time and space to which sensibility is bound). If "raw" matter replaces ideas of reason in Lyotard's writings, there is always already an overlap between the two insofar as neither fits the "forms and concepts . . . constitutive of objects" (*TI* 140).

12. Lyotard, "A Few Words to Sing," in *Music/Ideology: Resisting the Aesthetic*, ed. Adam Krims (Amsterdam: G + B Arts International), 15–36, 21.

13. For an extremely interesting study on Liszt and virtuosity, see Jim Samson, *Virtuosity and the Musical Work: The Transcendental Studies of Liszt* (Cambridge: Cambridge University Press, 2003).

14. Arnaldo Cohen: *Totentanz/Danse Macabre*, S525/R188, Franz Liszt (1811–1886): Complete Piano Music, vol. 1 (Naxos 8.553852, 1997).

15. For a helpful analysis of the terms "experimental music" and "musical experiment," see Frank X. Mauceri, "From Experimental Music to Musical Experiment," *Perspectives of New Music* 1 (1997): 187–204.

16. Martha Argerich, Frédéric Chopin: 24 Preludes/ Sonata no. 2 (Deutsche Grammophon, Universal 463 6632, 2002).

17. See, for instance, Leonard B. Meyer, *Emotion and Meaning in Music* (Chicago: University of Chicago Press, 1956), 93–97; Rose Rosengard Subotnik, "Romantic Music as Post-Kantian Critique: Classicism, Romanticism, and the Concept of the Semiotic Universe," in Kingsley Price, ed., *On Criticizing Music* (Baltimore, Md.: The Johns Hopkins University Press, 1981), 87–95; Lawrence Kramer, "Romantic Meaning in Chopin's Prelude in A Minor," *Nineteenth-Century Music* 2 (1985): 145–55; V. Kofi Agawu, "Concepts of Closure and Chopin's Opus 28," *Music Spectrum* 9 (1987): 1–17.

18. See the introduction to this book.

19. William Gardiner, *Leicester Chronicle*, September 12, 1840, in David Ian Allsobrook, *Liszt: My Traveling Circus Life* (Carbondale: Southern Illinois University Press, 1991), 79.

20. Ibid., 83.

21. For more on violence, virtuosity, and Liszt, see Dana Gooley, "Warhorses: Liszt, Weber's 'Konzertstück,' and the Cult of Napoléon," *Nineteenth-Century Music* 1 (Summer 2000). 62–88.

22. Heinrich Heine [1837], "Bürgerliche Oper," in *Zeitungsberichte über Musik und Malerei*, ed. Michael Mann (Frankfurt: Insel Verlag, 1964), 103, my translation.

23. Susan Bernstein, *Virtuosity of the Nineteenth Century: Performing Music and Language in Heine, Liszt, and Baudelaire* (Stanford, Calif.: Stanford University Press, 1998).

24. Heinrich Heine, "Musikalische Saison in Paris," [1841] in *Zeitungsberichte über Musik*, 115, my translation.

25. See Nietzsche, *The Birth of Tragedy*.

26. Heinrich Heine [1843], "Musikalische Saison in Paris. Virtuosentum," in *Zeitungsberichte*, 141–50.

27. On the rise and uses of the pianola and player piano (which can arguably be regarded as one of the first modern, technological storage devices), see Arthur Loesser, *Men, Women, and Pianos: A Social History* [1954] (New York: Dover Publications, 1990); Michael Chanan, "The Player Piano," in *Piano Roles: Three Hundred Years of Life with the Piano*, ed. James Parakilas (New Haven, Conn.: Yale University Press, 1999), 72–77.

28. Heinrich Heine, "Musikalische Saison in Paris I" [1844], in *Zeitungsberichte*, 159–68.

29. Richard Leppert, "The Concert and the Virtuoso," in *Piano Roles*, 259.

30. From a review in *Musical World* 20 (August 28, 1845), quoted in Richard Leppert, "The Concert and the Virtuoso," 260.

31. The *Totentanz* was completed for piano and orchestra in 1849, revised in 1853 and 1859, rewritten again for piano solo between 1860 and 1865, and premiered in that last year in both versions at The Hague with pianist Hans von Bülow. For the piano solo edition, see: Franz Liszt, *Totentanz* S525/R188 (Budapest: Editio Musica Budapest, 1982).

32. Adolph Kullak, *Die Ästhetik des Klavierspiels* [1860, 1876], ed. Walter Niemann, 4th ed. (Leipzig: C. F. Kahnt Nachfolger, 1905), 240.

33. John Shepherd, *Music as Social Text* (Cambridge: Polity Press, 1991), 152–73.

34. Charles Rosen, *The Romantic Generation*, 491–11. All further references will be given in the text.

35. This is already implied in the "classical" musical sublime as analyzed by Sisman and Webster, especially in view of the significance of originality (Sisman) in relation to the sublime and on unexpected combinations and contrasts (Webster)—though this is still a far cry from Liszt's uncompromising, almost abstract sound productions.

36. Heinrich Heine, "Musikalische Saison in Paris I" [1844], in *Zeitungsberichte über Musik und Malerei*, ed. Michael Mann (Frankfurt: Insel Verlag, 1964), 159–60.

37. Franz Liszt and Caroline von Sayn-Wittgenstein, "Berlioz and His 'Harold' Symphony," in *Strunk's Source Readings in Music History: The Nineteenth Century*, ed. Ruth A. Solie (New York: W. W. Norton & Co., 1998), 6:117–18.

38. Rudolf Otto, *Das Heilige: Über das Irrationale in der Idee des Göttlichen und sein Verhältnis zum Rationalen* [1917] (Munich: Verlag C. H. Beck, 1979), 54, my translation.

39. Ibid., 54.

40. Kramer, *Music as Cultural Practice*, 77.

41. Sigmund Freud, *Das Unheimlichte. Aufsätze zur Literatur* (Frankfurt: Fischer, 1963); Sigmund Freud, *The Uncanny*, trans. David McLintock (London: Penguin Books, 2003).

42. For the score, see: Frédéric Chopin, *Préludes*, op. 28, Urtext Edition (Munich: G. Henle Verlag), p. 7.

43. Kramer, *Music as Cultural Practice*, 91.

44. Michael R. Rogers, "Chopin's Prelude in A Minor, opus 28," *Nineteenth-Century Music* 3 (1981): 244–50.

45. I am here referring to the same Argerich recording of the Chopin Preludes as referred to above.

46. John Cage, "45' for a Speaker," [1954] in *Silence: Lectures and Writings by John Cage* (London: Marion Boyars, 1999), 175–76.

47. Saint Augustine, *Confessions* [ca. 397–401], trans. R. S. Pine-Coffin (Harmondsworth: Penguin Books, 1961), book XI, sect. 21, 269.

48. William Barrett, "The Flow of Time," in *The Philosophy of Time*, ed. Richard M. Gale (London: Macmillan, 1969), 369, 370.

49. Ibid., 370.

50. John Cage, "History of Experimental Music in the United States," in *Silence*, 68.

51. Quoted in Michael Nyman, *Experimental Music: Cage and Beyond* (Cambridge: Cambridge University Press, 1999), 1.

52. Cage, "45' For a Speaker," 187.

53. Ibid., 175.

54. For instance, see Stan Godlovich, *Musical Performance: A Philosophical Study* (London: Routledge, 1998).

55. Jean-François Lyotard, *Peregrinations. Law, Form, Event* (New York: Columbia University Press, 1988), 9, 20, 25.

56. Morton Feldman, "Anxiety of Art," in *The Music of Morton Feldman*, ed. Thomas Delio (New York: Excelsior Publishing, 1996), 207.

57. I have based my comments on a performance by Alan Feinberg (piano) and Michael Tilson Thomas conducting the New World Symphony Orchestra: Morton Feldman: Piano and Orchestra/Cello and Orchestra/Coptic Light (Argo [Decca] 2894485132, 1998).

58. See, for instance, Jean-François Lyotard's "Music, Mutic" and "Anima Minima," in *Postmodern Fables*, 217–34, 235–49.

59. For a detailed account on the soul as the effect of affection and the consequences for such an approach to the soul with respect to Western conceptions of musical experience, see Sander van Maas, *The Reinvention of Religious Music: Olivier Messiaen's Breakthrough Toward the Beyond* (New York: Fordham University Press, 2009).

60. John Cage, "Lecture on Something," [1959] in *Silence*, 135. These lines reappear in a slightly altered version in "45' for a Speaker," in *Silence*, 173.

61. Cage, "Lecture on Something," 131.

62. Renée van de Vall, "Silent Visions: Lyotard on the Sublime," in *The Contemporary Sublime*, 69–75.

63. Lyotard, *The Differend*, 9, nr. 12.

64. Lyotard, *Lessons on the Analytic of the Sublime*, 123. Hereafter *LA*. All further references will be given in the text.

65. Christine Pries, *Übergänge Ohne Brücke. Kants Erhabenes zwischen Kritik und Metaphysik* (Berlin: Akademie Verlag, 1995), 62.

66. However, one could also argue in reverse that the irresolvable conflict between imagination and reason covers up a harmony between them that is implicit in the subjective finality of the sublime feeling (see also chapter 2).

67. James Williams, *Lyotard and the Political* (London: Routledge, 2000), 4.

68. Ibid., 4.

69. Ibid.

5. Anxiety: The Sublime as Trauma and Repetition

1. In the early eighteenth century, John Baillie observes that though the sublime—to his mind—fills the mind "with one vast and uniform idea," affecting it "with a solemn sedateness," it is frequently mixed with the pathetic: with a violent "agitation of the passions" such as fear or anxiety. That is to say, the "grand may be so blended with the pathetic and warm" (for instance in "the description of battles" firing and heating rather than calmly elevating the mind) as "difficultly to be divided." This confusion of the sublime and pathetic makes for a "complex," not a "simple," sensation that proves to be just as "difficulty to be resolved": the "sublime dilates and elevates the soul, fear sinks and contracts it; yet both are felt upon viewing what is great and awful." It is a feeling characterized by an internal contradiction. Baillie, *Essay on the Sublime*, 32–33.

2. Theodor Adorno, *Aesthetische Theorie* (Frankfurt: Suhrkamp, 1970); Theodor Adorno, *Aesthetic Theory*, ed. Gretel Adorno and Rolf Tiedemann, trans. Robert Hullot-Kentor (London: The Athlone Press, 1999), 198.

3. Kiene Brillenburg Wurth, "The Musicality of the Past: *Sehnsucht*, Trauma, and the Sublime," *Journal of the Philosophy of History* 2 (2007): 219–47.

4. Martin Jay, *Songs of Experience: Modern American and European Variations on a Universal Theme* (Berkeley: University of California Press, 2006), 12.

5. Ibid., 11.

6. Ibid., 225.

7. Walter Benjamin, "Zum Bilde Prousts" [1929] and "Über einige Motive bei Baudelaire," [1939] in *Walter Benjamin. Medienästhetische Schriften* (Frankfurt: Suhrkamp, 2002), 9–21, 32–66; Walter Benjamin, "The Image of Proust" and "On Some Motifs in Baudelaire," in *Illuminations: Essays and Reflections* (New York: Shocken, 1969), 201–16; 155–200, 136.

8. Ibid., 340.

9. See, for instance, Jean-François Lyotard, "Emma," in *Misère de la philosophie* (Paris: Galliléé, 2000), 55–97.

10. Lyotard, *Misère de la philosophie*, 48–49.

11. See Lyotard's *The Differend*.

12. Claire Nouvet, "The Inarticulate Affect. Lyotard and Psychoanalytic Testimony," *Discourse* 25, nos. 1–2 (2003): 233.

13. Anne Tomiche, "Rephrasing the Freudian Unconscious: Lyotard's Affect-Phrase," *Diacritics* 1 (2004), 45.

14. Sigmund Freud, *Das Unbewußte* [1913], in *Sigmund Freud: Gesammelte Werke Band X* (= *Werke aus den Jahren 1913–1917*) (London: Imago, 1946), 263–303; Sigmund Freud, *The Unconscious*, in *Sigmund Freud: On Metapsychology: The Theory of Psychoanalysis*, ed. Angela Richards and Albert Dickson, trans. James Strachey (London: Penguin Books, 1991), 179–82. Freud here insists that an instinct, of which the unconscious affect is a representative, "can never become an object of consciousness—only the idea that represents the instinct can. Even in the unconscious, moreover, an instinct cannot be represented otherwise than by an idea. If the instinct did not attach itself to an idea or manifest itself as an affective state, we could know nothing about it. When we nevertheless speak of an unconscious instinctual impulse or a repressed instinctual impulse, the looseness of phraseology is a harmless one. We can only mean an instinctual impulse the ideational representative of which is unconscious."

15. Tomiche, "Rephrasing the Freudian Unconscious," 46.

16. Ibid., 47.

17. Lyotard, *Misère de la philosophie*, 68–76.

18. Quoted in Cathy Caruth, "Trauma and Experience: Introduction," in *Trauma: Explorations in Memory*, ed. Cathy Caruth (Baltimore, Md.: The Johns Hopkins University Press, 1995), 6.

19. See for instance, Paul Antze and Michael Lambek, eds., *Tense Past: Cultural Essays in Trauma and Memory* (New York: Routledge, 1996); Cathy Caruth, *Unclaimed Experience: Trauma, Narrative, and History* (Baltimore, Md.: The Johns Hopkins University Press, 1996); Sigmund Freud, *Jenseits des Lustprinzips* [1920], in *Sigmund Freud: Gesammelte Werke Dreizehnter Band* (Frankfurt: Fischer, 1967); Sigmund Freud, *Beyond the Pleasure Principle*, trans. James Strachey (New York: W. W. Norton & Company, 1961); Ruth Leys, *Trauma: A Genealogy* (Chicago: University of Chicago Press, 2000); Judith Lewis Herman, *Trauma and Recovery: From Domestic Abuse to Political Terror* (London: Pandora, 1994); Richard McNally, *Remembering Trauma* (Cambridge, Mass.: Harvard University Press, 2003).

20. Frank Ankersmit, "The Sublime Dissociation of the Past; or, How to Become What One is No Longer," *History and Theory: Studies in the Philosophy of History* 3 (2001): 301.

21. Ibid., 310.

22. Ibid.

23. Leys, *Trauma: A Genealogy*, 32. Hereafter *TG*. All further references will be given in the text.

24. Freud, *Beyond the Pleasure Principle*, 12. Hereafter *BP*. All further references will be given in the text.

25. Caruth, *Unclaimed Experience*, 5.

26. Bessel A. van der Kolk and Onno van der Hart, "The Intrusive Past: The Flexibility of Memory and the Engraving of Trauma," in *Trauma: Explorations in Memory*, 160.

27. Ibid., 163–64.

28. Quoted in McNally, *Remembering Trauma*, 179.

29. See, for instance, Bessel van der Kolk, *Traumatic Stress: The Effects of Overwhelming Experience on Mind, Body, and Society* (New York: Guildford Press, 1996).

30. Van der Kolk and Van der Hart, "The Intrusive Past," 176.

31. Leys, "Traumatic Cures," in *Tense Past*, 119.

32. Ibid.

33. Jennifer M. Bean, "Book Review: *Trauma. A Genealogy*," *Modernism/Modernity* 8, no. 3 (2001): 526.

34. See chapter 4 and Jean-François Lyotard, *Postmodern Fables*, 235–49.

35. Frank Ankersmit, "Trauma als bron van historisch besef," *Feit en Fictie* 3 (1999): 9.

36. Cf. Jean-François Lyotard, *Heidegger et "les juifs"* (Paris: Galilée, 1988); Jean-François Lyotard, *Heidegger and "The Jews,"* trans. Andreas Michel and Marc Roberts (Minneapolis: University of Minnesota Press, 1990); Saul Friedlander, *Probing the Limits of Representation: Nazism and the "Final Solution"* (Cambridge, Mass.: Harvard University Press, 1992); Dominick LaCapra, *History and Memory After Auschwitz* (Ithaca, N.Y.: Cornell University Press, 1998).

37. See, for instance, Harald Hendrix, "Renaissance Rotts of the Sublime: Ugliness, Horror, and Pleasure in Early Modern Italian Debates on Literature and Art," in *Histories of the Sublime* (Brussels: Koninklijke Vlaamsche Academie van België voor wetenschappen en kunsten, 2005), 13–22; Amy Lyford, "The Aesthetics of Dismemberment: Surrealism and the Musée du Val-de-Grâce in 1917," *Cultural Critique* 46 (2000): 45–79; Laura Wixley Brooks, "Damien Hirst and the Sensibility of Shock," *Art & Design* 1/2 (1995): 54–67; or Gene Ray's compelling exploration in the relations between the sublime, the traumatic, and the destructive, *Terror and the Sublime in Art and Critical Theory: From Auschwitz and Hiroshima to September 11* (London: Palgrave Macmillan, 2005).

38. For more on art, trauma, and experimentation, see Ernst van Alphen's excellent *Art in Mind: How Contemporary Images Shape Thought* (Chicago: The University of Chicago Press, 2005).

39. For more studies on music and trauma (of which the first and last are mostly culturally-historically minded, and the second psychologically), see Ulrike Kienzle, *Das Trauma hinter den Traum. Franz Schrekers Oper "Die Ferne Klang" und die Wiener Moderne* (Schliengen: Argus, 1998); Julie P. Sutton, ed., *Music, Music Therapy, and Trauma: International Perspectives* (London: Jessica Kingsley Publishers, 2002); Elliott Antokoletz, *Musical Symbolism in the Operas of Debussy and Bartók: Trauma, Gender, and the Unfolding of the Unconscious* (New York: Oxford University Press, 2004).

40. Rosen, *The Romantic Generation*, 151–210, 218.

41. Ibid., 210.

42. Robert Schumann, *Dichterliebe* opus 48 (1840), in *Schumann Sämtliche Lieder*, vol. 1 (London: Edition Peters, nr. 2383a), 106–40, 128–29, 138–40.

43. Anselm Gerhard has related the use of violent contrasts in so-called urban operas of the post-Revolutionary, early nineteenth century to the "shock-experience" of the city that Baudelaire was to evoke in the 1840s—and that Benjamin

would recapture in the beginning of the twentieth century. See Anselm Gerhard, *Die Verstädterung der Oper: Paris und das Musiktheater des 19. Jahrhunderts* (Stuttgart: Verlag J. B. Metzler, 1992).

44. Radu Lupu, *Schubert: Piano Sonatas/Klaviersonaten D. 959, D. 784, D. 157* (Decca: Ovation, 425 033–2, 1991). I have compared the performance of Radu Lupu with Alfred Brendel (rec. 1971, rel. 2003; Philips Duo), Maurizio Pollini (rec. 1983, rel. 2003, Deutsche Grammophon), Adnrás Schiff (rec. 1992–1993, rel. 1996; Decca), Mitsiko Uchida (rec. 1997, rel. 1998; Philips), Murray Perahia (rec. 2002, rel. 2003; Sony), and Paul Lewis (rec. 2003, rel. 2003; Harmonia Mundi).

45. For more on chromaticism as the "other" of diatonicism see Susan McClary, *Feminine Endings: Music, Gender, and Sexuality* (Minnesota: University of Minnesota Press, 1991).

46. Alfred Brendel "Schuberts letzte Sonaten," in *Musik beim Wort genommen. Über Musik, Musiker, und das Metier des Pianisten* (Munich: R. Piper, 1996), 80–153, 91.

47. Kramer, *Music as Cultural Practice*, 94.

48. William Kinderman and Harald Krebs, eds., *The Second Practice of Nineteenth-Century Tonality* (Lincoln: University of Nebraska Press, 1996).

49. Alexander Stein, "Well-Tempered Bagatelles: A Meditation on Listening in Psychoanalysis and Music," *American Imago* 4 (1999): 393.

50. For more on music, narrative, and narrativity, see Vincent Meelberg, *New Sounds, New Stories: Narrativity in Contemporary Music* (Leiden: Leiden University Press, 2006). Further references to this book will be given in parentheses in the text.

51. Ibid., 13–38.

52. Ibid., 37.

53. Scott Burnham, *Beethoven Hero* (Princeton, N.J.: Princeton University Press, 2000), 3.

54. Ibid., 161.

55. Anthony Newcomb, "Schumann and Late-Eighteenth-Century Narrative Strategies," in *Nineteenth-Century Music* 2 (1987): 169.

56. Arnold Schoenberg, "Opinion or Insight?" [1926] in *Style and Idea: Selected Writings of Arnold Schoenberg*, ed. Leonard Stein, trans. Leo Black (London: Faber and Faber, 1984), 258–64.

57. Jacques Attali, *Bruits* [1977] (Paris: Fayard, 2001); Jacques Attali, *Noise: The Political Economy of Music* [1985], trans. Brian Masumi (Minneapolis: University of Minnesota Press, 1996), 64.

58. Attali, *Noise*, 64.

59. Arnold Schoenberg, "New Music: My Music" [1930] in *Style and Idea*, 99–106.

60. Andreas Staier, *Schubert Piano Sonatas D. 958 & D. 959* (Elatus, Studio DeutschlandRadio, Cologne, 1996, 2564–60442–2).

61. Anton Ehrenzweig, *The Psycho-Analysis of Artistic Vision and Hearing* [1953] (London: Sheldon Press, 1965), 40.

62. Jacques Derrida, "Speculer—sur Freud," in *La carte postale: de Socrate à Freud et au delà* (Paris: Flammarion, 1980), 275–437; Jacques Derrida, "To Speculate—On Freud," in *The Postcard: From Socrates to Freud and Beyond*, trans. Alan Bass (Chicago: The University of Chicago Press, 1987), 257–409.

63. Ibid., 341.

64. Ibid., 397.

65. Caruth, Unclaimed Experience, 59–60.

66. Derrida, "To Speculate—On Freud," 361.

67. Ibid., 396–97.

68. Baillie, *Essay on the Sublime*, 31.

69. Wim Mertens, *American Minimal Music: La Monte Young, Terry Riley, Steve Reich, Philip Glass*, trans. J. Hautekiet (London: Kahn & Averill, 1983); Jos de Mul, *Postmodern Desire*, 129–42.

70. There has been considerable debate about the term "repetitive music." I prefer the term "repetitive music" to the term "minimal music," which is also regularly used to denominate the music I will here address. The second term, according to Michael Nyman, refers to a music that "not only cuts down the area of sound-activity to an absolute (and absolutist) minimum, but submits the scrupulously selective, mainly tonal, material to mostly repetitive, highly disciplined procedures which are focused with an extremely fine definition (though the listener's focusing is not done for him" (Michael Nyman, *Experimental Music*, 139). In imitation of Wim Mertens, however, I prefer the term "repetitive music" because not all repetitive music is by definition minimal music and because "repetitive music" emphasizes more clearly "the decisive nature of the repetition as a structural principle in contemporary American music" (*American Minimal Music*, 16). As Timothy Johnson has remarked, instead of approaching repetitive music as a style or a technique, Mertens (like Elaine Broad) represents repetitive music in terms an aesthetics—which is one more reason why Mertens' approach is appropriate in this context. See Timothy Johnson, "Minimalism: Aesthetics, Style, or Technique?" *Musical Quarterly* 4 (1994): 742–73; Jonathan W. Bernard, "The Minimalist Aesthetic in the Plastic Arts and in Music," *Perspectives of New Music* 1 (1993): 86–132; Elaine Broad, "A New X? An Examination of the Aesthetic Foundations of Early Minimalism," *Music Research Forum*, 5 (1990): 51–62.

71. Steve Reich, *Writings on Music, 1965–2000*, ed. Paul Hillier (Oxford: Oxford University Press, 2002), 20.

72. Ibid., 26.

73. Johnson, "Minimalism: Aesthetics, Style, or Technique?" 750.

74. Mertens, *American Minimal Music*, 15.

75. Ibid., 16.

76. Terry Riley, In C (Bang on a Can, Cantaloupe Music, CA21004, 2001).

77. Nyman, *Experimental Music*, 145.

Coda: The Sublime, Intermedially Speaking

1. Charles Baudelaire, "Le *Confiteor* de l'artiste," in *Le spleen de Paris: Petits poèmes en prose* [1869] (Paris: Bookking International, 1995), 14; Charles Baudelaire,

"The Artist's *Confiteor*," in *The Spleen of Paris: Small Prose Poems*, in *Baudelaire in English*, ed. Carol Clark and Robert Sykes, trans. Aleister Crowley (London: Penguin Books, 1988). Also available at http://baudelaire.litteratura.com (last accessed February 2008).

    2. Ibid., 235.

    3. Ibid., 235.

    4. Ibid.

    5. Ibid.

    6. Derrida, "To Speculate—On Freud," 290.

    7. Gilles Deleuze and Félix Guattari, *Mille Plateaux* (Paris: Les Editions de Minuit, 1980); Gilles Deleuze and Félix Guattari, *A Thousand Plateaus*, trans. Brian Massmi (New York: Continuum, 1999).

Bibliography

Addison, Joseph. *The Spectator* no. 418 [1712]. In *The Sublime: A Reader in British Eighteenth-Century Aesthetic Theory*, edited by Andrew Ashfield and Peter de Bolla, 67–68. Cambridge: Cambridge University Press, 1996.

Adorno, Theodor. *Aesthetische Theorie*. Frankfurt: Suhrkamp, 1970; *Aesthetic Theory*. Edited by Gretel Adorno and Rolf Tiedemann, translated by Robert Hullot-Kenter. London: Athlone Press, 1999.

Agawu, V. Kofi. "Concepts of Closure and Chopin's Opus 28." *Music Spectrum* 9 (1987): 1–17.

Allsobrook, David Ian. *Liszt: My Traveling Circus Life: Music in Georgian and Victorian Society*. Carbondale: Southern Illinois University Press, 1991.

Alphen, Ernst van. *Art in Mind: How Contemporary Images Shape Thought*. Chicago: The University of Chicago Press, 2005.

———. *Caught by History: Holocaust Effects in Contemporary Art, Literature, and Theory*. Stanford, Calif.: Stanford University Press, 1997.

Ameriks, Karl, ed. *The Cambridge Companion to German Idealism*. Cambridge: Cambridge University Press, 2000.

André, Yves Marie. Extracts from *L'essay sur le beau* [1741]. In *Music and Aesthetics in the Eighteenth and Early Nineteenth Centuries*, edited by Peter Le Huray and James Day, 27–35. Cambridge: Cambridge University Press, 1981.

Andrews, Malcolm. *The Search for the Picturesque: Landscape, Aesthetics, and Tourism in Britain, 1760–1800*. Aldershot: Scolar Press, 1989.

Ankersmit, F. R. *History and Tropology: The Rise and Fall of Metaphor*. Berkeley: University of California Press, 1994.

———. *Sublime Historical Experience*. Stanford, Calif.: Stanford University Press, 2005.

——— "The Sublime Dissociation of the Past; or, How to Become What One is No Longer." *History and Theory: Studies in the Philosophy of History* 3 (2001): 295–323.

———. "Trauma als bron van historisch besef." *Feit en Fictie* 3 (1999): 7–19.

Antokoletz, Elliott, and Juana Canabal Antokoletz. *Musical Symbolism in the Operas of Debussy and Bartók: Trauma, Gender, and the Unfolding of the Unconscious*. New York: Oxford University Press, 2004.

Antze, Paul, and Michael Lambek. *Tense Past: Cultural Essays in Trauma and Memory*. New York: Routledge, 1996.

Asfour, Amal, and Paul Williamson. "Splendid Impositions: Gainsborough, Berkeley, Hume." *Eighteenth-Century Studies* 4 (1998): 403–32.

Ashfield, Andrew, and Peter de Bolla. "Introduction." In *The Sublime: A Reader in British Eighteenth-Century Aesthetic Theory*, edited by Andrew Ashfield and Peter de Bolla, 1–16. Cambridge: Cambridge University Press, 1996.

Attali, Jacques. *Bruits* [1977] (Paris: Fayard, 2001).

———. *Noise: The Political Economy of Music*. Translated by Brian Masumi. Minneapolis: University of Minnesota Press, 1996.

Augustine. *Confessions* [ca. 397–401]. Translated by R. S. Pine-Coffin. Harmondsworth: Penguin, 1961.

Avison, Charles. *An Essay on Musical Expression* [1753]. In *Music and Aesthetics in the Eighteenth and Early Nineteenth Centuries*, edited by Peter Le Huray and James Day, 60–63. Cambridge: Cambridge University Press, 1981.

Bailey, Robert. *Richard Wagner: Prelude and Transfiguration from Tristan and Isolde*. New York: W. W. Norton, 1985.

Baillie, John. *An Essay on the Sublime* [1747]. Los Angeles: William Andrews Clark Memorial Library of California, 1953.

Bal, Mieke. "Narrative Inside Out: Louise Bourgeois' Spider as a Theoretical Object." *Oxford Art Journal* 2 (1999): 101–26.

———. *Quoting Caravaggio: Contemporary Art, Preposterous History*. Chicago: University of Chicago Press, 1999.

———. *Traveling Concepts in the Humanities*. Chicago: University of Chicago Press, 2002.

Barrett, William. "The Flow of Time." In *The Philosophy of Time*, edited by Richard M. Gale, 355–77. London: Macmillan, 1969.

Barry, Kevin. *Language, Music, and the Sign: A Study in Aesthetics, Poetics, and Poetic Practice from Collins to Coleridge*. Cambridge: Cambridge University Press, 1987.

Barthes, Roland. "Listening" [1976]. In *The Responsibility of Forms*, translated by Richard Howard, 245–60. Berkeley: University of California Press, 1991.

———. "The Romantic Song" [1976]. In *The Responsibility of Forms*, translated by Richard Howard, 286–92. Berkeley: University of California Press, 1991.

Battersby, Christine. "Stages on Kant's Way: Aesthetics, Morality, and the Gendered Sublime." In *Feminism and Tradition in Aesthetics*, edited by Peggy Zeglin Brand and Carolyn Korsmeyer, 88–114. Pennsylvania: Pennsylvania State University Press, 1995.

Baudelaire, Charles. "Le *Confiteor* de l'artiste." In *Le spleen de Paris: Petits poèmes en prose* [1869] (Paris: Bookking International, 1995); "The Artist's *Confiteor*." In *The Spleen of Paris: Small Prose Poems*. In *Baudelaire in English*, edited by Carol Clark and Robert Sykes. London: Penguin Books, 1988.

Beattie, James. *An Essay on Poetry and Music as They Affect the Mind* [1776]. In *Essays*, 352–580. New York: Garland Publishing, 1971.

———. "Illustrations on Sublimity." In *Dissertations Moral and Critical* [1783], 605–55. Stuttgart-Bad Cannstatt: Friedrich Frommann Verlag (Günther Holzboog), 1970.

————. "Of Memory and Imagination." In *Dissertations Moral and Critical* [1783], 72–230. Stuttgart-Bad Cannstatt: Friedrich Frommann Verlag (Günther Holzboog), 1970.

Beckley, Bill, ed. *Sticky Sublime*. New York: Allworth Press, 2001.

Bell, Claudia, and John Lyall. *The Accelerated Sublime: Landscape, Tourism, and Identity*. Westport, Conn.: Praeger Publishers, 2001.

Benjamin, Walter. "Zum Bilde Prousts" [1929] and "Über einige Motive bei Baudelaire" [1939]. In *Walter Benjamin. Medienästhetische Schriften*, 9–21, 32–66. Frankfurt: Suhrkamp, 2002; "The Image of Proust" and "On Some Motifs in Baudelaire." In *Illuminations: Essays and Reflections*, 201–216, 155–200. New York: Shocken, 1969.

Berkeley, George. "Introduction." In *Principles of Human Knowledge* [1710], 19–20. Oxford: Oxford University Press, 1996.

Bernard, Jonathan W. "The Minimalist Aesthetic in the Plastic Arts and in Music." *Perspectives of New Music* 1 (1993): 86–132.

Bernstein, J. M. *The Fate of Art: Aesthetic Alienation from Kant to Derrida and Adorno*. Cambridge: Cambridge University Press, 1991.

————. "Introduction." In *Classic and Romantic German Aesthetics*, edited by J. M. Bernstein, vii–xxxiii. Cambridge: Cambridge University Press, 2003.

Bernstein, Susan. *Virtuosity of the Nineteenth Century: Performing Music and Language in Heine, Liszt, and Baudelaire*. Stanford, Calif.: Stanford University Press, 1998.

Boileau-Despréaux, Nicolas. *Traité du sublime. Ou du Merveilleux dans le discours* [1674]. In *Boileau. Œuvres Complètes*, edited by Françoise Escal, 333–402. Paris: Éditions Gallimard, 1966.

Bonds, Mark Evan. "Idealism and the Aesthetics of Instrumental Music at the Turn of the Nineteenth Century." *Journal of the American Musicological Society* 2/3 (1997): 387–420.

Borchmeyer, Dieter. *Richard Wagner: Theory and Theatre*. Translated by Stewart Spencer. Oxford: Clarendon Press, 1991.

Bowie, Andrew. *Aesthetics and Subjectivity: From Kant to Nietzsche*. Manchester: Manchester University Press, 1993.

————. *From Romanticism to Critical Theory*. London: Routledge, 1997.

Brendel, Alfred. "Schuberts letzte Sonaten." In *Musik beim Wort genommen. Über Musik, Musiker, und das Metier des Pianisten*, 80–153. Munich: R. Piper, 1996.

Brillenburg Wurth, Kiene. "Coleridge's Kantian Appropriation of Sublime Nature in the Lake District." In *England's Green and Pleasant Land: English Culture and the Romantic Countryside*, edited by Amanda Gilroy, 19–31. Brussels: Peeters, 2004.

————. "Decorum, Duplicity, and Faith: Afterthoughts on the Sublime." In *Histories of the Sublime*, edited by Jurgen Pieters and Bart Vandenabeele, 135–46. Brussels: Akademie van Wetenschappen, 2006.

————. "The Grand Style and the Aesthetics of Terror in Eighteenth-Century Musical Performance Practices." *Dutch Journal of Music Theory* 9, no. 1 (2004): 44–55.

————. "The Musicality of the Past: *Sehnsucht,* Trauma, and the Sublime." *Journal of the Philosophy of History* 2 (2007): 219–47.

————. "Radical Indeterminacy: The Sublime Sculptures of Heringa/Van Kalsbeek." In *Controlled Accidents: The Work of Heringa/Van Kalsbeek.* Amsterdam: Idea Books, 2007.

————. "Reconsidering the Postmodern Sublime: From Kant to Lyotard, and Back to Burke." *Phrasis* 1 (2005): 63–75.

————. "Sounds Like Now: Music, Avant-Gardism, and the Post-modern Sublime." In *Music and Literary Modernism: Critical Essays and Comparative Studies,* edited by Robert McParland, 13–32. Newcastle: Cambridge Scholars Press, 2007.

Brinkmann, Reinhold. "In the Times of the 'Eroica.'" In *Beethoven and His World,* edited by Scott Burnham and Michael Steinberg, 1–26. Princeton, N.J.: Princeton University Press, 2000.

Broad, Elaine. "A New X? An Examination of the Aesthetic Foundations of Early Minimalism." *Music Research Forum* 5 (1990): 51–62.

Brown, J. A. C. *Freud and the Post-Freudians.* Harmondsworth: Penguin Books, 1961.

Burke, Edmund. *A Philosophical Enquiry Into the Origin of Our Ideas of the Sublime and Beautiful* [1759]. Edited by Adam Phillips. Oxford: Oxford University Press, 1990.

Burnet, Thomas. *The Sacred Theory of the Earth* [1690–91]. Edited by Basil Wiley. London: Centaur Press, 1965.

Burney, Charles. "Essay on Musical Criticism" [1798]. In *A General History of Music.* In *Music and Aesthetics in the Eighteenth and Early Nineteenth Centuries,* edited by Peter Le Huray and James Day, 191–96. Cambridge: Cambridge University Press, 1981.

————. *Musical Performances in Westminster-Abbey and the Pantheon in Commemoration of Händel* [1785]. Amsterdam: Frits A. Knuf, 1964.

Burnham, Scott. *Beethoven Hero.* Princeton, N.J.: Princeton University Press, 2000.

Busoni, Ferucio. *Sketches of a New Esthetics of Music* [1907, 1911]. In *Three Classics in the Aesthetic of Music: Monsieur Croche the Dilettante Hater, by Claude Debussy; Sketch of a New Esthetic of Music, by Ferruccio Busoni; Essays Before a Sonata, by Charles E. Ives,* 73–102. New York: Dover Publications, 1962.

Cage, John. "45' for a Speaker" [1954]. In *Silence: Lectures and Writings by John Cage,* 146–93. London: Marion Boyars, 1999.

————. "History of Experimental Music in the United States" [1959]. In *Silence: Lectures and Writings by John Cage,* 67–75. London: Marion Boyars, 1999.

————. "Indeterminacy" [1958]. In *Silence: Lectures and Writings by John Cage,* 35–40. London: Marion Boyars, 1999.

————. "Lecture on Something" [1959]. In *Silence: Lectures and Writings by John Cage,* 128–40. London: Marion Boyars, 1999.

Caruth, Cathy. "An Interview with Robert Jay Lifton." In *Trauma: Explorations in Memory,* edited by Cathy Caruth, 128–47. Baltimore, Md.: The Johns Hopkins University Press, 1995.

————. "Trauma and Experience: Introduction." In *Trauma: Explorations in Memory*, edited by Cathy Caruth, 3–12. Baltimore, Md.: The Johns Hopkins University Press, 1995.

————. *Unclaimed Experience: Trauma, Narrative, and History*. Baltimore, Md.: The Johns Hopkins University Press, 1996.

Caygill, Howard. *A Kant Dictionary*. Oxford: Blackwell Publishers, 1999.

Cerf de la Viéville, Jean Laurent le. *Comparison Between Italian and French Music* [1704]. In *Strunk's Source Readings in Music History: The Baroque Era*, edited by Leo Treitler and Margaret Murata, 4:171–74. New York: W. W. Norton & Company, 1998.

Chabanon, Paul Michel-Guy de. *De la musique considerée en elle-même et dans ses rapports avec la parole, les langues, la poésie et le théâtre* [1785]. Geneve: Slatkine Reprints, 1969.

Chafe, Eric. *The Tragic and the Ecstatic: The Musical Revolution of Wagner's* Tristan and Isolde. Oxford: Oxford University Press, 2003.

Chanan, Michael. "The Player Piano." In *Piano Roles: Three Hundred Years of Life with the Piano*, edited by James Parakilas, 72–77. New Haven, Conn.: Yale University Press, 1999.

Chantler, Abigail. *E. T. A. Hoffmann's Musical Aesthetics*. Aldershot: Ashgate, 2006.

Charlton, David, ed. *E. T. A. Hoffmann's Musical Writings: Kreisleriana, the Poet and the Composer, Music Criticism*. Translated by Martyn Clarke. Cambridge: Cambridge University Press, 1989.

Cheetham, Mark. *Kant, Art, and History: Moments of Discipline*. Cambridge: Cambridge University Press, 2001.

Chua, Daniel. *Absolute Music and the Construction of Meaning*. Cambridge: Cambridge University Press, 1999.

Chung-Sun, Kwon. *Studie zur Idee des Gesamtkunstwerks in der Frühromantik: zur Utopie einer Musikanschauung von Wackenroder bis Schopenhauer*. Frankfurt: Peter Lang, 2003.

Coriando, Paola-Ludovica. *Affektenlehre und Phänomenologie der Stimmungen. Wege einer Ontologie und Ethik des Emotionalen*. Frankfurt am Main: Klostermann, 2002.

Crotch, William. *Substance of Several Courses of Lectures* [1831]. In *Music and Aesthetics in the Eighteenth and Early Nineteenth Centuries*, edited by Peter Le Huray and James Day, 427–42. Cambridge: Cambridge University Press, 1981.

Crowther, Paul. *Critical Aesthetics and Postmodernism*. Oxford: Clarendon Press, 1996.

————. *The Kantian Sublime: From Morality to Art*. Oxford: Oxford University Press, 1989.

Culler, Jonathan. "The Hertzian Sublime." *MLN* 120 (2005): 969–85.

Dahlhaus, Carl. *Die Idee der absolute Musik*. Kassel: Bärenreiter, 1978.

————. *Klassische und romantische Musikästhetik*. Laaber: Laaber Verlag, 1988.

————. "Tristan und Isolde." In *Richard Wagner: Tristan und Isolde: Texte, Materialien, Kommentare*, edited by Attila Csampai and Dietmar Holland, 231–43. Reinbek bei Hamburg: Rowohlt Taschenbuch Verlag, 1983.

————, and Mary Whittal. "What Is a Musical Drama?" *Cambridge Opera Journal* 2 (1989): 95–111.

Deleuze, Gilles. *Différence et Répétition.* Paris: Presses Universitaires, 1968; *Difference and Repetition.* Translated by Paul Patton. London: The Athlone Press, 1994.

————. *La philosophie critique de Kant.* Paris: Presses Universitaires de France, 1963; *Kant's Critical Philosophy: The Doctrine of the Faculties.* Translated by Hugh Tomlinson and Barbara Habberjam. London: The Athlone Press, 1995.

Deleuze, Gilles, and Félix Guattari. *Mille Plateaux.* Paris: Les Editions de Minuit, 1980; *A Thousand Plateaus,* trans. Brian Massumi. New York: Continuum, 1999.

————. *Qu'est-ce que la philosophie?* (Paris: Les Editions de minuit, 1991); *What Is Philosophy?* Translated by Graham Burchwell and Hugh Tomlinson. London: Verso, 1994.

De Man, Paul. *Blindness and Insight: Essays in the Rhetoric of Contemporary Criticism.* 2nd ed. London: Routledge, 1986.

Dennis, John. *The Grounds of Criticism in Poetry* [1704]. In *The Critical Works of John Dennis,* edited by Edward Niles Hooker, 1:325–73. Baltimore, Md.: The Johns Hopkins Press, 1939.

————. "Nature's Extravagancies: Letter from Turin, 25 October 1688." In *Mountains: An Anthology,* edited by Anthony Kenny, 64–66. London: John Murray, 1991.

————. *Remarks on a Book Entitled, Prince Arthur* [1696]. In *The Sublime: A Reader in British Eighteenth-Century Aesthetic Theory,* edited by Andrew Ashfield and Peter de Bolla, 30–31. Cambridge: Cambridge University Press, 1996.

Denora, Tia. *Beethoven and the Construction of Genius: Musical Politics in Vienna, 1792–1803.* Berkeley: University of California Press, 1997.

Derrida, Jacques. ". . . Ce dangereux supplement . . ." In *De la grammatologie* [1967], 203–234. Paris: Éditions de Minuit, 1967; ". . . That Dangerous Supplement . . ." In *Of Grammatology,* translated by Gayatri Chakravorty Spivak, 141–64. Baltimore, Md.: The Johns Hopkins University Press, 1997.

————. "Speculer—Sur Freud." In *La carte postale: De Socrate à Freud et au de-là,* 275–437. Paris: Flammarion, 1980; "To Speculate—on Freud." In *The Postcard: From Socrates to Freud and Beyond,* translated by Allan Bass, 257–409. Chicago: University of Chicago Press, 1987.

Deusen, Paul. *Die Elemente der Metaphysik . . . nebst einer Vorbetrachtung über das Wesen des Idealismus* [1877]. Leipzig: F. A. Brockhaus, 1919.

Deutsch, Otto Erich. *Handel: A Documentary Biography.* London: Black, 1955.

Diderot, Denis. *Leçons de clavecin et principes d'harmonie en dialogues* [1771]. In *Oeuvres complètes de Diderot,* edited by J. Assézat, 12:179–534. Paris: Garnier Frères, 1876.

Donelan, James H. "Hölderlin's Music of Self-Consciousness." *Philosophy and Literature* 1 (2002): 125–42.

Donougho, Martin. "Stages of the Sublime in North America." *MLN* 5 (2000): 909–40.

Dorsch, T. S., trans. *Aristotle/Horace/Longinus: Classical Literary Criticism.* Harmondsworth: Penguin, 1965.

Downing, A. Thomas. *Music and the Origins of Language: Theories from the French Enlightenment*. Cambridge: Cambridge University Press, 1995.

Dubos, Abbé. *Réflexions critiques sur la Poësie et sur la Peinture* [1719]. Paris: École nationale supérieure des Beaux-Arts, 1993; *Critical Reflections on Poetry and Painting*. In *Music and Aesthetics in the Eighteenth and Early Nineteenth Centuries*, edited by Peter Le Huray and James Day, 17–22. Cambridge: Cambridge University Press, 1981.

Eggebrecht, Hans Heinrich. *Zur Geschichte der Beethoven-Rezeption: Beethoven 1970*. Mainz: Akademie der Wissenschaften, 1972.

Ehrenzweig, Anton. *The Hidden Order of Art* [1967]. London: Phoenix Press, 2000.

———. *The Psycho-Analysis of Artistic Vision and Hearing* [1953]. London: Sheldon Press, 1965.

Feldman, Morton. "The Anxiety of Art" [1973]. In *Art in America*. In *The Music of Morton Feldman*, edited by Thomas Delio, 205–12. New York: Excelsior Music Publishing Company, 1996.

Fend, Michael. "Die ästhetische Kategorie des Erhabenen und die Entdeckung der Alpen in der Musik." In *Schweizer Töne. Die Schweiz im Spiegel der Musik*, edited by A. Gerhard and A. Landau, 29–43. Zürich: Chronos, 2000.

———. "Literary Motifs, Musical Form, and the Quest for the 'Sublime': Cherubini's 'Eliza ou le Voyage aux glaciers du Mont St Bernard'" in *Cambridge Opera Journal* 1 (1993): 17–38.

Fenves, Peter. "Taking Stock of the Kantian Sublime." *Eighteenth-Century Studies* 1 (1994): 65–82.

Fitzgerald, William. "The Questionability of Music." *Representations* 46 (1994): 121–47.

Foucault, Michel. "Nietzsche, la généalogie, l'histoire" [1971]. In *Dits et Ecrits 1954–1988 II*, 136–56. Paris: Gallimard, 1994; "Nietzsche, Genealogy, History." In *The Foucault Reader*, edited by Paul Rabinow, 76–100. London: Penguin, 1984.

Frank, Manfred. *Einführung in die Frühromantische Ästhetik*. Frankfurt: Suhrkamp, 1989.

Freimarck, Vincent. "Introduction." In *Robert Lowth: Lectures on the Sacred Poetry of the Hebrews*, vi–xxxv. Hildesheim: Georg Olms Verlag, 1969.

Freud, Sigmund. *Jenseits des Lustprinzips* [1920]. In *Sigmund Freud: Gesammelte Werke Dreizehnter Band*. Frankfurt: Fischer, 1967; *Beyond the Pleasure Principle*. Translated by James Strachey. New York: W. W. Norton & Company, 1961.

———. *Das Unbewußte* [1913]. In *Sigmund Freud: Gesammelte Werke Band X (= Werke aus den Jahren 1913–1917)*, 263–303. London: Imago, 1946; *The Unconscious*. In *Sigmund Freud: On Metapsychology: The Theory of Psychoanalysis*, edited by Angela Richards and Albert Dickson, translated by James Strachey, 179–82. London: Penguin, 1991.

———. *Das Unheimlichte. Aufsätze zur Literatur*. Frankfurt: Fischer, 1963; *The Uncanny*, Translated by David McLintock. London: Penguin Books, 2003.

Friedlander, Saul, ed. *Probing the Limits of Representation: Nazism and the "Final Solution."* Cambridge, Mass.: Harvard University Press, 1992.

Frost, H. F. "Some Remarks on Wagner's Music Drama 'Tristan and Isolde.'" *Proceedings of the Musical Association*, 8th Sess. (1881–82): 147–67.

Gasché, Rodolphe. "The Sublime, Ontologically Speaking." *Yale French Studies* 99 (2001): 117–28.

Gay, Peter. *The Enlightenment: An Interpretation. The Science of Freedom* [1969]. New York: W. W. Norton & Company, 1977.

Gerhard, Anselm. *Die Verstädterung der Oper: Paris und das Musiktheater des 19. Jahrhunderts.* Stuttgart: Verlag J. B. Metzler, 1992.

Godlovich, Stan. *Musical Performance: A Philosophical Study.* London: Routledge, 1998.

Goehr, Lydia. "Wagnerian Endings: On the Curse and Promise of Purely Musical Listening. A Metaphysical Reading of *Tristan and Isolde.*" In *ASCA Brief: Come to Your Senses!*, edited by Mieke Bal et al., 37–60. Amsterdam: Amsterdam School of Cultural Analysis, Theory and Interpretation, 1999.

Goethe, Johann Wolfgang von. *Faust* [1787–90]. Frankfurt: Insel Verlag, 1974.

———. *Die Leiden des jungen Werthers* [1774]. Stuttgart: Phillip Reclam Jun., 1985.

Greenberg, Clement. "Towards a Newer Laocoon" [1948]. In *Art in Theory 1900–1990: An Anthology of Changing Ideas*, edited by Charles Harrison and Paul Wood, 554–60. Oxford: Blackwell Publishers, 1999.

Grosse, Carl. *Über das Erhabene* [1788]. Edited by Carsten Zelle. St. Ingbert: Werner J. Röhrig Verlag, 1990.

Grusin, Richard. "Premediation." *Criticism* 1 (2004): 17–39.

Guerlac, Suzanne. *The Impersonal Sublime: Hugo, Baudelaire, Lautréamont.* Stanford, Calif.: Stanford University Press, 1990.

Guyer, Paul. *Kant and the Experience of Freedom.* Cambridge: Cambridge University Press, 1996.

Hamashita, Masahiro. "Genealogy of the Aesthetics of the Sublime: To Addison and Shaftsbury." *KCS* 38 (1992): 105–27.

Hanslick, Eduard. *Vom Musikalisch-Schönen* [1854, 1891]. In *Hanslick: Vom Musikalisch-Schönen; Aufsätze; Musikkritiken.* Leipzig: Reclam, 1982; *On the Musically Beautiful* [1891]. Translated by Geoffrey Payzant. Indianapolis, Ind.: Hackett Publishing Company, 1983.

Hardenberg, Friedrich von [Novalis]. *Fichte Studien* [1795–96]. In *Novalis: Schriften: Das Philosophische Werk I*, edited by Richard Samuel et al., vol. 2, sect. II, 104–296. Darmstadt: Wissenschaftliche Buchgesellschaft, 1981; *Fichte Studies.* Edited and translated by Jane Kneller. Cambridge: Cambridge University Press, 2003.

Harrán, Don. "Toward a Rhetorical Code of Early Music Performance." *The Journal of Musicology* 1 (1997): 19–42.

Harris, James. *Three Treatises. The First, Concerning Art, the Second Concerning Music, Painting and Poetry, the Third Concerning Happiness* [1744]. In *Music and Aesthetics in the Eighteenth and Early Nineteenth Centuries*, edited by Peter Le Huray and James Day, 36–39. Cambridge: Cambridge University Press, 1981.

Hawkins, John. "Preliminary Discourse." In *A General History of the Science and Practice of Music* [1776]. In *Music and Aesthetics in the Eighteenth and Early Nineteenth Centuries*, edited by Peter Le Huray and James Day, 157–60. Cambridge: Cambridge University Press, 1981.

Hegel, Georg Wilhelm Friedrich. *Science of Logic*. Translated by A. V. Miller. London: Allen & Unwin, 1969.

Heine, Heinrich. "Bürgerliche Oper" [1837]. In *Zeitungsberichte über Musik und Malerei*, edited by Michael Mann, 95–107. Frankfurt: Insel Verlag, 1964.

———. "Musikalische Saison in Paris" [1841]. In *Zeitungsberichte über Musik und Malerei*, edited by Michael Mann, 113–22. Frankfurt: Insel Verlag, 1964.

———. "Musikalische Saison in Paris. Virtuosentum" [1843]. In *Zeitungsberichte über Musik und Malerei*, edited by Michael Mann, 141–50. Frankfurt: Insel Verlag, 1964.

———. "Musikalische Saison in Paris I" [1844]. In *Zeitungsberichte über Musik und Malerei*, edited by Michael Mann, 159–68. Frankfurt: Insel Verlag, 1964.

Hendrix, Harald. "Renaissance Roots of the Sublime. Ugliness, Horror, and Pleasure in Early Modern Italian Debates on Literature and Art." In *Histories of the Sublime*, edited by Jurgen Pieters and Bart Vandenabeele, 13–22. Brussels: Akademie van Wetenschappen, 2006.

Henrich, Dieter. *Aesthetic Judgment and the Moral Image of the World*. Stanford, Calif.: Stanford University Press, 1997.

———. *The Course of Remembrance and Other Essays on Hölderlin*. Stanford, Calif.: Stanford University Press, 1997.

Hentschel, Frank. "Das 'Ewig-Weibliche'—Liszt, Mahler und das bürgerliche Frauenbild." *Archiv für Musikwissenschaft* 4 (1994): 274–93.

Herman, Judith Lewis. *Trauma and Recovery: From Domestic Abuse to Political Terror*. London: Pandora, 1994.

Hertz, Neil. "The Notion of Blockage in the Literature of the Sublime." In *Romanticism*, edited by Cynthia Chase, 78–97. London: Longman, 1993.

Hess, Jonathan. *Reconstituting the Body Politic: Enlightenment, Public Culture, and the Invention of Aesthetic Autonomy*. Detroit, Mich.: Wayne State University Press, 1999.

Hirsbrunner, Theo. "Das Erhabene in Bedrich Smetanas 'Mein Vaterland.'" *Archiv für Musikwissenschaft* 1 (1984): 35–41.

Hodkinson, James. "The Cosmic-Symphonic: Novalis, Music, and Universal Discourse." In *Music and Literature in German Romanticism*, edited by Siobhán Donovan and Roboin Elliott, 27–42. Rochester, N.Y.: Camden House, 2004.

Hoeckner, Berthold. *Programming the Absolute: Nineteenth-Century German Music and the Hermeneutics of the Moment*. Princeton, N.J.: Princeton University Press, 2002.

Hoffmann, E. T. A. "Alte und Neue Kirchenmusik" [1814]. In *E. T. A. Hoffmann: Betrachtungen über Musik*, 85–103. Stuttgart: Phillip Otto Röhm Verlag, 1947.

———. "Bescheidene Bemerkung zu dem die letzte Aufführung der Oper 'Don Juan' betreffenden, in No. 142 dieser Zeitschrift enthaltenen Aufsatze" [1820].

In *E. T. A. Hoffmann. Schriften zur Musik. Singspiele*, edited by Hans-Joachim Kruse and Viktor Liebrenz, 362–64. Berlin: Aufbau-Verlag, 1988.

———. "Beethovens Instrumentalmusik" [1813]. In: *E. T. A. Hoffmann: Betrachtungen über Musik*, 56–65. Stuttgart: Phillip Otto Röhm Verlag, 1947; "Beethoven's Instrumental Music" [1813]. In *E. T. A. Hoffmann and Music*, edited and translated by Murray Schafer, 83–91. Toronto: University of Toronto Press, 1975.

———. "Ludwig van Beethoven, 5. Sinfonie" [1810]. In *E. T. A. Hoffmann. Schriften zur Musik. Singspiele*, edited by Hans-Joachim Kruse and Viktor Liebrenz, 22–42. Berlin: Aufbau-Verlag, 1988; "Review of Beethoven's Fifth Symphony." In *E. T. A. Hoffmann's Musical Writings. Kreisleriana, the Poet and the Composer, Music Criticism*, edited by David Charlton, translated by Martyn Clarke, 234–51. Cambridge: Cambridge University Press, 1989.

———. "Ludwig van Beethoven, Coriolan-Ouvertüre" [1812]. In *E. T. A. Hoffmann. Schriften zur Musik. Singspiele*, edited by Hans-Joachim Kruse and Viktor Liebrenz, 94–102. Berlin: Aufbau-Verlag, 1988.

———. "Über Kirchenmusik" [1813]. In: *E. T. A. Hoffmann: Betrachtungen über Musik*, 82–84. Stuttgart: Phillip Otto Röhm Verlag, 1947.

Hölderlin, Friedrich. "An Hegel." In *Friedrich Hölderlin. Werke, Briefe, Dokumente*, 716–718. Munich: Winkler Verlag, 1990; "Letter to Hegel, 26 January 1795." In *Classic and Romantic German Aesthetics*, edited by J. M. Bernstein, translated by Stefan Bird-Pollan, 188–90. Cambridge: Cambridge University Press, 2003.

———. "*Pyrgo* in Morea." In *Fragment von Hyperion* [1799]. In *Friedrich Hölderlin. Werke, Briefe, Dokumente*, 365. Munich: Winkler Verlag, 1990.

———. "Urteil und Sein" [1795]. In *Friedrich Hölderlin. Werke, Briefe, Dokumente*, 490. Munich: Winkler Verlag, 1990; "Being Judgment Possibility." In *Classic and Romantic German Aesthetics*, edited by J. M. Bernstein, translated by Stefan Bird-Pollan, 191. Cambridge: Cambridge University Press, 2003.

Japaridze, Tamar. *The Kantian Subject: Sensus Communis, Mimesis, Work of Mourning*. Albany, N.Y.: SUNY Press, 2000.

Jay, Martin. *Downcast Eyes: The Denigration of Vision in Twentieth-Century French Thought*. Berkeley: University of California Press, 1994.

———. *Songs of Experience. Modern American and European Variations on a Universal Theme*. Berkeley: University of California Press, 2006.

Johnson, Claudia. "'Giant Handel' and the Musical Sublime." *Eighteenth-Century Studies* 4 (1986): 515–33.

Johnson, James H. *Listening in Paris: A Cultural History*. Berkeley: University of California Press, 1995.

Johnson, Timothy. "Minimalism: Aesthetics, Style, or Technique?" *Musical Quarterly* 4 (1994): 742–73.

Kallberg, Jeffrey. *Chopin at the Boundaries: Sex, History, and Musical Genre*. Cambridge, Mass.: Harvard University Press, 1998.

Kant, Immanuel. *Anthropologie in Pragmatischer Hinsicht* [1789]. In *Vermischte Schriften von Immanuel Kant*, edited by Felix Gross, 291–537. Leipzig: IM Inselverlag, 1960.

————. *Kritik der praktischen Vernunft* [1788]. Edited by Wilhelm Weischedel. Wiesbaden: Inselverlag, 1996.

————. *Kritik der reinen Vernunft* [1781, 1787]. Edited by Raymund Schmidt. Hamburg: Felix Meiner Verlag, 1990.

————. *Kritik der Urteilskraft* [1790]. Edited by Karl Vorländer. Hamburg: Felix Meiner Verlag, 1790; "Critique of Judgment." In *Immanuel Kant: Philosophical Writings*, translated by J. M. D. Meiklejohn, edited by Ernst Behler, 129–246. New York: Continuum, 1991.

————. *Observations on the Feeling of the Beautiful and Sublime* [1764]. Translated by John T. Goldthwait. Berkeley: University of California Press, 1991.

————. "Preface to the Second Edition of the *Critique of Pure Reason*." Translated by J. M. D. Meiklejohn, edited by Ernst Behler, 3–20. New York: Continuum, 1991.

Keats, John. "To J. H. Reynolds, Esq" [1818, 1848]. In *John Keats: The Complete Poems*, 235–38. Harmondsworth: Penguin, 1986.

Kerslake, Lawrence. *Essays on the Sublime: Analyses of French Writings on the Sublime from Boileau to La Harpe*. Bern: Lang, 2000.

Kienzle, Ulrike. *Das Trauma hinter den Traum. Franz Schrekers Oper "Die Ferne Klang" und die Wiener Moderne*. Schliengen: Edition Argus, 1998.

Kindermann, William. *Beethoven*. Oxford: Oxford University Press, 1997.

Kindermann, William, and Harald Krebs, eds. *The Second Practice of Nineteenth-Century Tonality*. Lincoln: University of Nebraska Press, 1996.

Kivy, Peter. *The Possessor and the Possessed: Handel, Mozart, Beethoven, and the Idea of Musical Genius*. New Haven, Conn.: Yale University Press, 2001.

Klein, Werner. "The Voice of the Hereafter: Hoffmann's Ideal of Sound and its Realization." In *Music and Literature in German Romanticism*, edited by Siobhán Donovan and Roboin Elliott, 143–64. Rochester, N.Y.: Camden House, 2004.

Kloppenburg, C. M. *De pianosonates van Franz Schubert*. Katwijk: Panta Rhei, 1997.

Knittel, K. M. "Wagner, Deafness, and the Reception of Beethoven's Late Style." *Journal of the American Musicological Society* 1 (1998): 49–82.

Kolk, Bessel van der. *Traumatic Stress: The Effects of Overwhelming Experience on Mind, Body, and Society*. New York: Guilford Press, 1996.

Kolk, Bessel van der, and Onno van der Hart. "The Intrusive Past: The Flexibility of Memory and the Engraving of Trauma." In *Trauma: Explorations in Memory*, edited by Cathy Caruth, 158–82. Baltimore, Md.: The Johns Hopkins University Press, 1995.

Kramer, Lawrence. *Classical Music and Postmodern Knowledge*. Berkeley: University of California Press, 1995.

————. *Music as Cultural Practice, 1800–1900*. Berkeley: University of California Press, 1990.

————. *Musical Meaning: Toward a Critical History*. Berkeley: University of California Press, 2001.

————. "Romantic Meaning in Chopin's Prelude in A Minor." *Nineteenth-Century Music* 2 (1985): 145–55.

————. "The Strange Case of Beethoven's 'Coriolan': Romantic Aesthetics, Modern Subjectivity, and the Cult of Shakespeare." *The Musical Quarterly* 2 (1995): 256–80.

————. *Why Classical Music Still Matters.* Berkeley: University of California Press, 2007.

Kullak, Adolph. *Die Ästhetik des Klavierspiels* [1860, 1876]. 4th rev. ed. Edited by Walter Niemann. Leipzig: C. F. Kahnt Nachfolger, 1905.

Kunze, Stefan. *Der Kunstbegriff Richard Wagners. Voraussetzungen und Folgerungen.* Regensburg: Gustav Boss Verlag, 1983.

Lacan, Jacques. *Écrits: A Selection.* Translated by Bruce Fink. New York: W. W. Norton, 2004.

————. *The Four Fundamental Concepts of Psychoanalysis (The Seminar of Jacques Lacan, Book 11).* Translated by Alan Sheridan, edited by Jacques-Alain Miller. New York: W. W. Norton, 1998.

Lacapra, Dominick. *History and Memory After Auschwitz.* Ithaca, N.Y.: Cornell University Press, 1998.

————. "Representing the Holocaust: Reflections on the Historians' Debate." In *Probing the Limits of Representation: Nazism and the "Final Solution,"* edited by Saul Friedlander, 108–26. Cambridge, Mass.: Harvard University Press, 1992.

Lacoue-Labarthe, Philippe. *Poetry as Experience.* Translated by Andrea Tarnowski. Stanford, Calif.: Stanford University Press, 1986.

————. "Sublime Truth (part 1)." *Cultural Critique* 18 (1991): 5–31.

————. "Sublime Truth (part 2)." *Cultural Critique* 20 (1991): 207–29.

Lauretis, Theresa de. *Alice Doesn't: Feminism, Semiotics, Cinema.* Bloomington: Indiana University Press, 1984.

Lebenzstejn, Jean-Claude. *L'art de la tache: introduction à la "Nouvelle méthode" d'Alexander Cozens.* Éditions du Limon, 1990.

Leighton, Angela. *Shelley and the Sublime: An Interpretation of the Major Poems.* Cambridge: Cambridge University Press, 1984.

Lenneberg, Hans. "Johann Mattheson on Affect and Rhetoric in Music (I)." *Journal of Music Theory* 1 (1958): 47–84.

Leppert, Richard. "The Concert and the Virtuoso." In *Piano Roles: Three Hundred Years of Life with the Piano,* edited by James Parakilas, 237–81. New Haven, Conn.: Yale University Press, 1999.

Lessing, Gotthold Ephraim. *Laokoön: über die Grenzen der Malerie und Poesie* [1766]. Munich: Winkler, 1974; *Laocoön: on the Limits of Painting and Poetry.* In *Classic and Romantic German Aesthetics,* edited by J. M. Bernstein, 25–130. Cambridge: Cambridge University Press, 2003.

Lévi-Strauss, Claude. *Regarder, Ecouoter, Lire* [1966]. Paris: Plon, 1993; *Look, Listen, Read.* Translated by Brian C.J. Slinger. New York: Basic Books, 1997.

Levine, Steven Z. "Seascapes of the Sublime: Vernet, Monet, and the Oceanic Feeling." *New Literary History* 2 (1985): 377–400.

Leys, Ruth. *Trauma: A Genealogy.* Chicago: University of Chicago Press, 2000.

————. "Traumatic Cures." In *Tense Past: Cultural Essays in Trauma and Memory*, edited by Paul Antze and Michael Lambek, 103–45. New York: Routledge, 1996.

Libret, Jeffery, ed. and trans. *Of the Sublime: Presence in Question*. Albany, N.Y.: SUNY Press, 1993.

Lipperheide, Christian. *Die Ästhetik des Erhabenen bei Friedrich Nietzsche. Die Verwindung der Metaphysik der Erhabenheit*. Würzburg: Verlag Königshausen & Neumann, 1999.

Liszt, Franz, and Caroline von Sayn-Wittgenstein. "Berlioz and his 'Harold' Symphony" [1855]. In *Strunk's Source Readings in Music History: The Nineteenth Century*, edited by Ruth A. Solie, 116–32. New York: W. W. Norton & Company, 1998.

Litman, Théodore A. *Le Sublime en France (1660–1714)*. Paris: A. G. Nizet, 1971.

Littlejohns, Richard. "Iniquitous Innocence: The Ambiguity of Music in the *Phantasien über die Kunst* (1799)." In *Music and Literature in German Romanticism*, edited by Siobhán Donovan and Robin Elliott, 1–12. Rochester, N.Y.: Camden House, 2004.

Locke, John. *An Essay Concerning Human Understanding* [1690]. Edited by John W. Yolton. London: J. M. Dent & Sons, 1991.

Lockspeiser, Edward. *Music and Painting: A Study in Comparative Ideas from Turner to Schoenberg*. London: Cassell, 1973.

Lowth, Robert. *Lectures on the Sacred Poetry of the Hebrews* [1787]. 2 vols. Hildesheim: Georg Olms Verlag, 1969.

Lumsden, Simon. "Fichte's Striving Subject." *Inquiry* 1 (2004): 123–42.

Lupu, Radu. *Schubert: Piano Sonatas/Klaviersonaten D. 959, D. 784, D. 157*. Decca: Ovation, 425 033-2, 1991.

Lyotard, Jean-François. *Le Différend*. Paris: Éditions de Minuit, 1983; *The Différend: Phrases in Dispute*. Translated by George Van Den Abbeele. Minneapolis: University of Minnesota Press, 1996.

————. "Emma." In *Misère de la philosophie*, 55–97. Paris: Galliléé, 2000.

————. "A Few Words to Sing." In *Music/Ideology: Resisting the Aesthetic*, edited by Adam Krims, 15–36. Amsterdam: G + B Arts International.

————. *Heidegger et "les juifs."* Paris: Galilée, 1988; *Heidegger and "The Jews."* Translated by Andreas Michel and Marc Roberts. Minneapolis: University of Minnesota Press, 1990.

————. *L'Inhumain. Causeries sur les temps*. Paris: Galilée, 1988; *The Inhuman: Reflections on Time*. Translated by Geoffrey Bennington and Rachel Bowlby. Cambridge: Polity Press, 1991.

————. *Karel Appel: ein Farbegestus. Essays zur Kunst Karel Appels mit der Bildauswahl des Autors*. Translated by Jessica Beer. Bern: Verlag Gachnan & Springer, 1998.

————. *Leçons sur l'Analytique du sublime*. Paris: Galilée, 1991; *Lessons on the Analytic of the Sublime*. Translated by Elizabeth Rottenberg. Stanford, Calif.: Stanford University Press, 1994.

————. *Moralités Postmodernes.* Paris: Galilée, 1993; *Postmodern Fables.* Translated by Georges van den Abbeele. Minneapolis: University of Minnesota Press, 1997.

————. *Peregrinations: Law, Form, Event.* New York: Columbia University Press, 1988.

————. "Response to the Question: What Is Postmodernism?" [1983]. In *Art in Theory 1900–1990: An Anthology of Changing Ideas,* edited by Charles Harrison and Paul Wood, 1008–15. Oxford: Blackwell Publishers, 1999.

Maas, Sander van. *The Reinvention of Religious Music: Olivier Messiaen's Breakthrough Toward the Beyond.* New York: Fordham University Press, 2009.

Mach, Elyse. *Great Contemporary Pianists Speak for Themselves.* Toronto: General Publishing Company, 1980.

Magee, Bryan. *Wagner and Philosophy.* London: Penguin Books, 2000.

Makkreel, Rudolf A. *Imagination and Interpretation in Kant: The Hermeneutical Import of the* Critique of Judgment. Chicago: University of Chicago Press, 1994.

Marschall, Isabelle von. *Zwischen Skizze und Gemälde: John Robert Cozens (1752–1797) und das englische Landschaftsaquarell.* Munich: Scaneg, 2006.

Mattheson, Johann. *Der vollkommene Capellmeister* [1783]. Edited by Friederike Ramm. Kassel: Bärenreiter, 1999; *Der vollkommene Capellmeister: A Revised Translation with Critical Commentary.* Translated by Ernest C. Harris. Ann Arbor, Mich.: UMI Research Press, 1981.

Mauceri, Frank. "From Experimental Music to Musical Experiment." *Perspectives of New Music* 1 (1997): 187–204.

May, Gita. "Diderot and Burke: A Study in Aesthetic Affinity." *PMLA* 5 (1960): 527–39.

McClary, Susan. *Feminine Endings: Music, Gender, and Sexuality.* Minnesota: University of Minnesota Press, 1991.

McNally, Richard. *Remembering Trauma.* Cambridge, Mass.: Harvard University Press, 2003.

Meelberg, Vincent. *New Sounds, New Stories: Narrativity in Contemporary Music.* Leiden: Leiden University Press, 2006.

Mertens, Wim. *American Minimal Music: La Monte Young, Terry Riley, Steve Reich, Philip Glass.* Translated by J. Hautekiet. London: Kahn & Averill, 1983.

Meyer, Leonard B. *Emotion and Meaning in Music.* Chicago: University of Chicago Press, 1956.

Meyer-Baer, Kathy. *Music of the Spheres and the Dance of Death. Studies in Musical Iconology.* Princeton, N.J.: Princeton University Press, 1970.

Michaelis, C. F. "The Beautiful and Sublime in Music" [1805]. In *Music and Aesthetics in the Eighteenth and Early Nineteenth Centuries,* edited by Peter Le Huray and James Day, 286–87. Cambridge: Cambridge University Press, 1981.

Mitchell, W. J. T. *Iconology: Image, Text, Ideology.* Chicago: University of Chicago Press, 1996.

Molnár, Géza von. *Novalis' "Fichte Studies": The Foundation of His Aesthetics.* The Hague: Mouton, 1970.

Monk, Samuel Holt. *The Sublime: A Study of English Critical Theories in XVIII-Century England* [1935]. Ann Arbor: University of Michigan Press, 1960.

Morgan, Robert. "Circular Form in the *Tristan* Prelude." *Journal of the American Musicological Society* 53, no. 1 (2000): 69–103.

Morrow, Mary Sue. *German Music Criticism in the Late Eighteenth Century: Aesthetic Issues in Instrumental Music.* Princeton, N.J.: Princeton University Press, 1997.

———. "Of Unity and Passion: The Aesthetics of Concert Criticism in Early Nineteenth-Century Vienna." *Nineteenth-Century Music* 3 (1990): 193–206.

Mul, Jos de. *Romantic Desire in (Post)modern Art and Philosophy.* New York: SUNY Press, 1999.

Nattiez, Jean-Jacques. *Music and Discourse: Towards a Semiology of Music.* Translated by Carolyn Abbate. Princeton, N.J.: Princeton University Press, 1990.

Neubauer, John. *The Emancipation of Music from Language: Departure from Mimesis in Eighteenth-Century Aesthetics.* New Haven, Conn.: Yale University Press, 1986.

Newcomb, Anthony. "Schumann and Late-Eighteenth-Century Narrative Strategies." *Nineteenth-Century Music* 2 (1987): 164–74.

Newman, Barnett. "The Sublime Is Now" [1948]. In *Art in Theory 1900–1990: An Anthology of Changing Ideas*, edited by Charles Harrison and Paul Wood, 572–74. Oxford: Blackwell Publishers, 1999.

Nicolson, Marjorie Hope. *Mountain Gloom and Mountain Glory: The Development of the Aesthetics of the Infinite.* New York: W. W. Norton, 1963.

Nietzsche, Friedrich. *Die Geburt der Tragödie aus dem Geiste der Musik* [1871]. Frankfurt: Insel Verlag, 1987; *The Birth of Tragedy out of the Spirit of Music.* In *Friedrich Nietzsche: The Birth of Tragedy and Other Writings.* Edited by Raymond Geuss and Ronald Speirs. Cambridge: Cambridge University Press, 1999.

———. *Nachgelassene Fragmente 1869–1874.* Edited by Giorgio Colli and Mazzino Montinari. Munich: DTV, 1988.

———. *Nachgelassene Fragmente 1875–1879.* Edited by Giorgio Colli and Mazzino Montinari. Munich: DTV, 1988.

———. "Wagner als Gefahr" [1895]. In *Nietzsche Contra Wagner.* In *Friedrich Nietzsche. Der Fall Wagner, Götzen-dämmerung, Der Antichrist, Ecce Homo, Dionysos-Dithyramben, Nietzsche contra Wagner.* Edited by Giorgio Colli and Mazzino Montinari. Munich: DTV, 1988.

Nouvet, Claire. "The Inarticulate Affect. Lyotard and Psychoanalytic Testimony." *Discourse* 25, nos. 1–2 (2003): 231–43

Nyman, Michael. *Experimental Music: Cage and Beyond.* Cambridge: Cambridge University Press, 1999.

O'Brien, William Arctander. *Novalis: Signs of Revolution.* Durham, N.C.: Duke University Press, 1995.

Otto, Rudolf. *Das Heilige: Über das Irrationale in der Idee des Göttlichen und sein Verhältnis zum Rationalen* [1917]. Munich: Verlag C. H. Beck, 1979.

Peña Aguado, María Isabel. *Ästhetik des Erhabenen. Burke, Kant, Adorno, Lyotard.* Vienna: Passagen Verlag, 1991.

Petrarch. "The Ascent of Mont Ventoux" [1336]. In *Petrarch: Selections from the Canzoniere and Other Works*. Translated by Mark Musa. Oxford: Oxford University Press, 1985.

Pillow, Kirk. *Sublime Understanding: Aesthetic Reflection in Kant and Hegel*. Cambridge, Mass.: The MIT Press, 2000.

Pries, Christine. *Übergänge Ohne Brücke: Kants Erhabenes zwischen Kritik und Metaphysik*. Berlin: Akademie Verlag, 1995.

Priest, Stephen. *The British Empiricists: A Critical Introduction to the Leading Thinkers and Key Ideas of the British Philosophical Tradition from Hobbes to Ayer*. Harmondsworth: Penguin, 1990.

Ray, Gene. *Terror and the Sublime in Art and Critical Theory from Auschwitz and Hiroshima to September 11*. London: Palgrave Macmillan, 2005.

Rehding, Alexander. "Liszt und die Suche nach dem 'TrisZtan'-Akkord." *Acta Musicologica* 72, no. 2 (2000): 169–88.

Reich, Steve. *Writings on Music, 1965–2000*. Oxford: Oxford University Press, 2002.

Reynolds, Frances. *An Enquiry Concerning the Principles of Taste, and the Origin of Our Ideas of Beauty, &c.* [1785]. Los Angeles: The Augustan Reprint Society, William Andrews Clark Memorial Library, 1951.

Richter, Jean Paul. *Elementary Course in Aesthetics*. In *Strunk's Source Readings in Music History: The Baroque Era*, edited by Leo Treitler and Margaret Murata, translated by O. Strunk, 14–18. New York: W. W. Norton & Company, 1998.

———. *Hesperus, oder 45 Hunposttage. Eine Lebensbeschreibung* [1795]. In *Jean Paul. Werke*, vol. 1. Munich: Carl Hanser Verlag, 1960.

———. *Vorschule der Aesthetik* [1804]. In *Jean Paul. Werke*, vol. 5. Munich: Carl Hanser Verlag, 1963.

Riethmüller, Albrecht. "Aspekte des musikalisch Erhabenen im 19. Jahrhundert." *Archiv für Musikwissenschaft* 1 (1983): 38–49.

Riley, Matthew. *Musical Listening in the Eighteenth Century: Attention, Wonder, and Astonishment*. Aldershot: Ashgate, 2004.

———. "Straying from Nature: The Labyrinthine Harmonic Theory of Diderot and Bemetzrieder's *Leçons de clavecin* (1771)." *The Journal of Musicology* 1 (2002): 3–38.

Riley, Terry. *In C*. Bang on a Can, Cantaloupe Music, CA21004, 2001.

Rogers, Michael. "Chopin's Prelude in A Minor, opus 28." *Nineteenth-Century Music* 3 (1981): 244–50.

Rosen, Charles. *The Classical Style: Haydn, Mozart, Beethoven*. London: Faber and Faber, 1976.

———. *The Romantic Generation*. Cambridge, Mass.: Harvard University Press, 1995.

———. *Sonata Forms*. New York: W. W. Norton, 1988.

Rosiek, Jan. *Maintaining the Sublime: Heidegger and Adorno*. New York: P. Lang, 2000.

Roston, Murray. *Changing Perspectives in Literature and the Visual Arts: 1650–1820*. Princeton, N.J.: Princeton University Press, 1990.

Rummenhöller, Peter. *Romantik in der Musik*. Kassel: Bärenreiter, 1989.

Sachs, Curt. *Rhythm and Tempo: A Study in Music History*. New York: Columbia University Press, 1953.

Samson, Jim. *Virtuosity and the Musical Work. The Transcendental Studies of Liszt*. Cambridge: Cambridge University Press, 2003.

Schafer, R. Murray. *E. T. A. Hoffmann and Music*. Toronto: University of Toronto Press, 1975.

Schama, Simon. *Landscape and Memory*. London: HarperCollins, 1995.

Schilling, Gustav. "Erhaben" [1834–38]. In *Encyclopädie der gesammten musikalischen Wissenschaften, oder Universal Lexicon der Tonkunst*. In *Music and Aesthetics in the Eighteenth and Early Nineteenth Centuries*, edited by Peter Le Huray and James Day, 615–17. Cambridge: Cambridge University Press, 1981.

Schmitt, Ulrich. *Revolution im Konzertsaal. Zur Beethoven-Rezeption im 19. Jahrhundert*. Mainz: Schott Musikwissenschaft, 1990.

Schnaus, Peter. *E. T. A. Hoffmann als Beethoven Rezensent der Allgemeinen Musikalische Zeitung*. München: Katzbichler, 1977.

Schoenberg, Arnold. "New Music: My Music" [c. 1930]. In *Style and Idea: Selected Writings of Arnold Schoenberg*, edited by Leonard Stein and Leo Black, 99–106. London: Faber and Faber, 1984.

———. "Opinion or Insight?" [1926]. In *Style and Idea: Selected Writings of Arnold Schoenberg*, edited by Leonard Stein and Leo Black, 258–64. London: Faber and Faber, 1984.

———. "Problems of Harmony" [1934]. In *Style and Idea: Selected Writings of Arnold Schoenberg*, edited by Leonard Stein and Leo Black, 268–87. London: Faber and Faber, 1984.

Schopenhauer, Arthur. *Die Welt als Wille und Vorstellung* [1819, 1844]. Frankfurt: Suhrkamp, 1986; *The World as Will and Representation*. Translated by E. F. J. Payne. New York: Dover Publications, 1958.

Schroeder, David P. *Haydn and the Enlightenment: The Late Symphonies and Their Audience*. Oxford: Oxford University Press, 1997.

Schueller, Herbert. "'Imitation' and 'Expression' in British Music Criticism in the Eighteenth Century." *The Musical Quarterly* 4 (1948): 544–66.

———. "The Pleasures of Music: Speculation in British Music Criticism, 1750–1800." *The Journal of Aesthetics and Art Criticism* 3 (1950): 155–71.

Schumann, Robert. *Dichterliebe* opus 48 (1840) In *Schumann: Sämtliche Lieder*, vol. 1. London: Edition Peters, nr. 2383a.

———. *Gesammelte Schriften*. Edited by Martin Kreisig. Leipzig: Breitkopf & Härtel, 1914.

Seidl, Arthur. *Vom Musikalisch-Erhabenen. Prolegomena zur Aesthetik der Tonkunst. Inauguraldissertation der Philosophischen Fakultät der Universität Leipzig zur erlangung der Doktorwürde vorgelegt von Arthur Seidl*. Regensburg, 1887.

Senner, Wayne, Robin Wallace, and William Meredith, eds. *The Contemporary German Reception of Beethoven*. Lincoln: University of Nebraska Press, 1999–2003.

Seyhan, Azade. *The Critical Legacy of German Romanticism.* Berkeley: University of
California Press, 1992.

Shapiro, Alexander H. "Drama of an Infinitely Superior Nature: Handel's Early
English Oratorios and the Religious Sublime." *Music & Letters* 2 (1993): 215–45.

Shelley, Mary. "Author's Introduction." In *Frankenstein or, the Modern Prometheus*
[1817, 1831], edited by Maurice Hindle, 55–62. Harmondsworth: Penguin,
1985.

Shelley, Percy Bysshe. *A Defence of Poetry* [1821, 1840]. In *The Norton Anthology of
English Literature*, edited by M. H. Abrams et al., 6th ed., 2:753–65. New York:
W. W. Norton & Company, 1993.

Shepherd, John. *Music as Social Text.* Cambridge: Polity Press, 1991.

Shepherd, John, and Stephen Wicke. *Music and Cultural Theory.* Cambridge: Polity
Press, 1997.

Silverman, Hugh. "Textualität der Postmoderne: Lyotard, Ereignis, Erhabene",
translated by Erik Vogt. In *Textualität der Philosophie und Literatur*, Wiener Reihe
Themen der Philosophie, vol. 7., edited by Ludwig Nagl & Hugh J. Silverman
(Vienna and Munich: Oldenbourg, 1994), pp. 236–45.

———. "Lyotard and the Events of the Postmodern Sublime" in *Lyotard: Philosophy, Politics, and the Sublime*, edited by Hugh J. Silverman (New York and London: Routledge, 2002), pp. 222–29.

Sisman, Elaine Rochelle. "Haydn, Shakespeare, and the Rules of Originality." In
Haydn and His World, edited by Elaine Rochelle Sisman, 3–56. Princeton, N.J.:
Princeton University Press, 1997.

———. "Learned Style and the Rhetoric of the Sublime in the 'Jupiter' Symphony." In *Wolfgang Amadè Mozart: Essays on His Life and his Music*, edited by
Stanley Sadie, 213–38. Oxford: Clarendon Press, 1996.

———. *Mozart: The "Jupiter" Symphony No. 41 in C Major.* Cambridge: Cambridge
University Press, 1993.

Smith, Adam. *Essays on Philosophical Subjects* [1795]. In *The Sublime: A Reader in
British Eighteenth-Century Aesthetic Theory*, edited by Andrew Ashfield and Peter
de Bolla, 233–43. Cambridge: Cambridge University Press, 1996.

Solomon, Maynard. *Late Beethoven: Music, Thought, Imagination.* Berkeley: University of California Press, 2003.

Sparshott, Francis. "Reflections on Affektenlehre and Dance Theory in the Eighteenth Century." *The Journal of Aesthetics and Art Criticism* 1 (1998): 21–28.

Staier, Andreas. Schubert Piano Sonatas D. 958 & D. 959. Elatus, Studio DeutschlandRadio, Cologne, 1996, 2564–60442–2.

Stein, Alexander. "Well-Tempered Bagatelles: A Meditation on Listening in Psychoanalysis and Music." *American Imago* 4 (1999): 387–41.

Strickland, Edward, *Minimalism: Origins.* Bloomington: Indiana University Press,
1993.

Subotnik, Rose Rosengard. "Romantic Music as Post-Kantian Critique: Classicism,
Romanticism, and the Concept of the Semiotic Universe." In *On Criticizing*

Music, edited by Kingsley Price, 87–95. Baltimore, Md.: The Johns Hopkins University Press, 1981.

Sulzer, Georg. *Allgemeine Theorie der schönen Künste* [1771–74] [1792]. Hildesheim: Georg Olms Verlagsbuchhandlung, 1967.

Sutton, Julie P., ed. *Music, Music Therapy, and Trauma: International Perspectives*. London: Jessica Kingsley Publishers, 2002.

Tellegen, Toon. *Misschien wisten zij alles. Alle verhalen over de eekhoorn en andere dieren* [*Perhaps They Knew Everything: All Stories of the Squirrel and Other Animals*]. Amsterdam: Querido, 1995.

Thomas, Downing A. *Music and the Origins of Language: Theories from the French Enlightenment*. Cambridge: Cambridge University Press, 1995.

Tieck, Ludwig, and Wilhelm Heinrich Wackenroder. "Phantasien über die Kunst" [1799]. In *Tieck und Wackenroder*, edited by Joseph Kürschner, 42–98. Berlin: W. Spemann Verlag, 1886, 42–98.

Tomiche, Anne. "Rephrasing the Freudian Unconscious: Lyotard's Affect-Phrase." *Diacritics* 1 (2004): 43–63.

Twining, Thomas. *Aristotle's Treatise on Poetry, Translated, with Notes on the Translation, and on the Original; and Two Dissertations, on Poetical, and Musical, Imitation* [1789]. Westmead: Gregg International Publishers Limited, 1972.

Twitchell, James B. *Romantic Horizons: Aspects of the Sublime in English Poetry and Painting, 1770–1850*. Columbia: University of Missouri Press, 1983.

Usher, James. *Clio, or a Discourse on Taste* [1769]. Bristol: Thoemmes Press, 1998.

Vall, Renée van de. *Een subliem gevoel van plaats. Een filosofische interpretatie van het werk van Barnett Newman*. Groningen: De Historische Uitgeverij, 1994.

———. "Silent Visions. Lyotard on the Sublime." In *The Contemporary Sublime: Sensibilities of Transcendence and Shock*, 69–75. Cambridge: VCH Publishers, 1995.

Wackenroder, Wilhelm Heinrich. "Letter to Ludwig Tieck" [1792]. In *Music and Aesthetics in the Eighteenth and Early Nineteenth Centuries*, edited by Peter Le Huray and James Day, 248–50. Cambridge: Cambridge University Press, 1981.

Wagner, Richard. *Beethoven* [1870]. In *Richard Wagner: Dichtungen und Schriften: Beethoven, Späte Dramaturgische Schriften*, 9:38–109. Frankfurt: Insel Verlag, 1983; *Beethoven*. Translated by William Ashton Ellis. Available online at http://users.be lgacom.net/wagnerlibrary/prose/wlpro133.htm (last accessed September 5, 2007).

———. *Oper und Drama* [1851, 1871]. In *Richard Wagner: Gesammelte Schriften und Dichtungen*, 4:1–164. Boston: Elibron Classics, Adamant Media Corporation, 2001; *Opera and Drama*. In *Richard Wagner's Prose Works*. Translated by William Ashton Ellis. Available online at http://users.belgacom.net/wagnerlibrary/prose/wlpro063.htm (last accessed September 5, 2007).

Walker, Alan. *Franz Liszt*. 3 vols. New York: Alfred A. Knopf, 1983.

Walker, Ralph S., ed. *A Selection of Thomas Twining's Letters, 1734–1804: The Record of a Tranquil Life*. Lewiston, N.Y.: The Edwin Mellen Press, 1991.

Weber, Caroline. *Terror and Its Discontents: Suspected Words in Revolutionary France*. Minneapolis: University of Minnesota Press, 2003.

Webster, James. "Between Enlightenment and Romanticism in Music History: 'First Viennese Modernism' and the Delayed Nineteenth Century." *Nineteenth-Century Music* 2/3 (2002): 108–26.

———. "The *Creation*, Haydn's Late Vocal Music, and the Musical Sublime." In *Haydn and His World*, edited by Elaine Rochelle Sisman, 57–102. Princeton, N.J.: Princeton University Press, 1997.

———. "Haydn's Aesthetics." In *The Cambridge Companion to Haydn*, edited by Caryl L. Clark, 30–44. Cambridge: Cambridge University Press, 2005.

———. "The Sublime and the Pastoral in *The Creation* and *The Seasons*." In *The Cambridge Companion to Haydn*, edited by Caryl L. Clark, 150–63. Cambridge: Cambridge University Press, 2005.

Weiskel, Thomas. *The Romantic Sublime: Essays in the Structure and Psychology of Transcendence*. Baltimore, Md.: The Johns Hopkins University Press, 1976.

Williams, James. *Lyotard and the Political*. London: Routledge, 2000.

Wixley Brooks, Laura. "Damien Hirst and the Sensibility of Shock." *Art & Design* 1/2 (1995): 54–67.

Wordsworth, William. "Ode: Intimations of Immortality" [1807]. In *The Norton Anthology of English Literature*, edited by M. H. Abrams et al., 6th ed., 187–93. New York: W. W. Norton & Company, 1993.

Young, Edward. *Conjectures on Original Genius* [1759]. In *The Sublime: A Reader in British Eighteenth-Century Aesthetic Theory*, edited by Andrew Ashfield and Peter de Bolla, 114. Cambridge: Cambridge University Press, 1996.

Zelle, Carsten. "Nachwort." in *Carl Grosse. Über das Erhabene*, 79–85.

Zellini, Paolo. *A Brief History of Infinity*. Translated by Allan Lane. London: Penguin, 2005.

Zuckert, Rachel. "Awe or Envy: Herder contra Kant on the Sublime." *The Journal of Aesthetics and Art Criticism* 3 (2003): 217–32.